The Experiment in the History of Economics

I0885549

Throughout the evolution of economic ideas, it has often been asserted that experimentation in economics is impossible. Yet, the historical record shows that the idea of "experimentation" has, in fact, been important in the field of economics, and has been interpreted and put to use in many ways. These range from the "thought experiment", where counterfactuals are explored in the mind of the theorist, to social experiments, where alternative economic arrangements have been tried out historically, and laboratory experimentation, which is currently a burgeoning field of empirical research.

This book provides testament to the great variety of ways in which experimentation has mattered in the creation of economic knowledge. The accessible essays contained within this volume will interest all those seeking to broaden their historical understanding of the discipline and will be essential reading for students who wish to acquire a greater knowledge of how economics has grown and developed.

Philippe Fontaine is a historian of postwar social science. He has published in various journals, such as *Economics and Philosophy*, *History of Political Economy*, and *Isis*, and is co-editor with Albert Jolink of *Historical Perspectives on Macroeconomics* (Routledge, 1998). **Robert Leonard** is a historian of game theory and contemporary economics. His work has appeared in various journals in economics and in the history of science, and he is author of the forthcoming *From Red Vienna to Santa Monica: von Neumann, Morgenstern and the Creation of Game Theory, 1900–1960* (Cambridge University Press).

Routledge studies in the history of economics

1 **Economics as Literature**
Willie Henderson

2 **Socialism and Marginalism in Economics 1870–1930**
Edited by Ian Steedman

3 **Hayek's Political Economy**
The socio-economics of order
Steve Fleetwood

4 **On the Origins of Classical Economics**
Distribution and value from William Petty to Adam Smith
Tony Aspromourgos

5 **The Economics of Joan Robinson**
Edited by Maria Cristina Marcuzzo, Luigi Pasinetti and Alesandro Roncaglia

6 **The Evolutionist Economics of Léon Walras**
Albert Jolink

7 **Keynes and the 'Classics'**
A study in language, epistemology and mistaken identities
Michel Verdon

8 **The History of Game Theory, Vol. 1**
From the beginnings to 1945
Robert W. Dimand and Mary Ann Dimand

9 **The Economics of W. S. Jevons**
Sandra Peart

10 **Gandhi's Economic Thought**
Ajit K. Dasgupta

11 **Equilibrium and Economic Theory**
Edited by Giovanni Caravale

12 **Austrian Economics in Debate**
Edited by Willem Keizer, Bert Tieben and Rudy van Zijp

13 **Ancient Economic Thought**
Edited by B. B. Price

14 **The Political Economy of Social Credit and Guild Socialism**
Frances Hutchinson and Brian Burkitt

15 **Economic Careers**
Economics and economists in Britain 1930–1970
Keith Tribe

16 **Understanding 'Classical' Economics**
Studies in the long-period theory
Heinz Kurz and Neri Salvadori

17 **History of Environmental Economic Thought**
E. Kula

18 **Economic Thought in Communist and Post-Communist Europe**
Edited by Hans-Jürgen Wagener

19 **Studies in the History of French Political Economy**
From Bodin to Walras
Edited by Gilbert Faccarello

20 **The Economics of John Rae**
Edited by O. F. Hamouda, C. Lee and D. Mair

21 **Keynes and the Neoclassical Synthesis**
Einsteinian versus Newtonian macroeconomics
Teodoro Dario Togati

22 **Historical Perspectives on Macroeconomics**
Sixty years after the 'General Theory'
Edited by Philippe Fontaine and Albert Jolink

23 **The Founding of Institutional Economics**
The leisure class and sovereignty
Edited by Warren J. Samuels

24 **Evolution of Austrian Economics**
From Menger to Lachmann
Sandye Gloria

25 **Marx's Concept of Money: the God of Commodities**
Anitra Nelson

26 **The Economics of James Steuart**
Edited by Ramón Tortajada

27 **The Development of Economics in Europe since 1945**
Edited by A. W. Bob Coats

28 **The Canon in the History of Economics**
Critical essays
Edited by Michalis Psalidopoulos

29 **Money and Growth**
Selected papers of Allyn Abbott Young
Edited by Perry G. Mehrling and Roger J. Sandilands

30 **The Social Economics of Jean-Baptiste Say**
Markets and virtue
Evelyn L. Forget

31 **The Foundations of Laissez-Faire**
The economics of Pierre de Boisguilbert
Gilbert Faccarello

32 **John Ruskin's Political Economy**
Willie Henderson

33 **Contributions to the History of Economic Thought**
Essays in honour of R. D. C. Black
Edited by Antoin E. Murphy and Renee Prendergast

34 **Towards an Unknown Marx**
A commentary on the manuscripts of 1861–63
Enrique Dussel

35 **Economics and Interdisciplinary Exchange**
Edited by Guido Erreygers

36 **Economics as the Art of Thought**
Essays in memory of G. L. S. Shackle
Edited by Stephen F. Frowen and Peter Earl

37 **The Decline of Ricardian Economics**
Politics and economics in post-Ricardian theory
Susan Pashkoff

38 **Piero Sraffa**
His life, thought and cultural heritage
Alessandro Roncaglia

39 **Equilibrium and Disequilibrium in Economic Theory**
The Marshall–Walras divide
Michel de Vroey

40 **The German Historical School**
The historical and ethical approach to economics
Edited by Yuichi Shionoya

41 **Reflections on the Classical Canon in Economics**
Essays in honor of Samuel Hollander
Edited by Sandra Peart and Evelyn Forget

42 **Piero Sraffa's Political Economy**
A centenary estimate
Edited by Terenzio Cozzi and Roberto Marchionatti

43 **The Contribution of Joseph Schumpeter to Economics**
Economic development and institutional change
Richard Arena and Cecile Dangel

44 **On the Development of Long-run Neo-Classical Theory**
Tom Kompas

45 **F. A. Hayek as a Political Economist**
Economic analysis and values
Edited by Jack Birner, Pierre Garrouste and Thierry Aimar

46 **Pareto, Economics and Society**
The mechanical analogy
Michael McLure

47 **The Cambridge Controversies in Capital Theory**
A study in the logic of theory development
Jack Birner

48 **Economics Broadly Considered**
Essays in honor of Warren J. Samuels
Edited by Steven G. Medema, Jeff Biddle and John B. Davis

49 **Physicians and Political Economy**
Six studies of the work of doctor-economists
Edited by Peter Groenewegen

50 **The Spread of Political Economy and the Professionalisation of Economists**
Economic societies in Europe, America and Japan in the nineteenth century
Massimo Augello and Marco Guidi

51 **Historians of Economics and Economic Thought**
The construction of disciplinary memory
Steven G. Medema and Warren J. Samuels

52 **Competing Economic Theories**
Essays in memory of Giovanni Caravale
Sergio Nisticò and Domenico Tosato

53 **Economic Thought and Policy in Less Developed Europe**
The nineteenth century
Edited by Michalis Psalidopoulos and Maria-Eugenia Almedia Mata

54 **Family Fictions and Family Facts**
Harriet Martineau, Adolphe Quetelet and the population question in England 1798–1859
Brian Cooper

55 **Eighteenth-Century Economics**
Peter Groenewegen

56 **The Rise of Political Economy in the Scottish Enlightenment**
Edited by Tatsuya Sakamoto and Hideo Tanaka

57 **Classics and Moderns in Economics Volume I**
Essays on nineteenth- and twentieth-century economic thought
Peter Groenewegen

58 **Classics and Moderns in Economics Volume II**
Essays on nineteenth- and twentieth-century economic thought
Peter Groenewegen

59 **Marshall's Evolutionary Economics**
Tiziano Raffaelli

60 **Money, Time and Rationality in Max Weber**
Austrian connections
Stephen D. Parsons

61 **Classical Macroeconomics**
Some modern variations and distortions
James C. W. Ahiakpor

62 **The Historical School of Economics in England and Japan**
Tamotsu Nishizawa

63 **Classical Economics and Modern Theory**
Studies in long-period analysis
Heinz D. Kurz and Neri Salvadori

64 **A Bibliography of Female Economic Thought to 1940**
Kirsten K. Madden, Janet A. Sietz and Michele Pujol

65 **Economics, Economists and Expectations**
From microfoundations to macroeconomics
Warren Young, Robert Leeson and William Darity Jnr

66 **The Political Economy of Public Finance in Britain, 1767–1873**
Takuo Dome

67 **Essays in the History of Economics**
Warren J. Samuels, Willie Henderson, Kirk D. Johnson and Marianne Johnson

68 **History and Political Economy**
Essays in honour of P. D. Groenewegen
Edited by Tony Aspromourgos and John Lodewijks

69 **The Tradition of Free Trade**
Lars Magnusson

70 **Evolution of the Market Process**
Austrian and Swedish economics
Edited by Michel Bellet, Sandye Gloria-Palermo and Abdallah Zouache

71 **Consumption as an Investment**
The fear of goods from Hesiod to Adam Smith
Cosimo Perrotta

72 **Jean-Baptiste Say and the Classical Canon in Economics**
The British connection in French classicism
Samuel Hollander

73 **Knut Wicksell on Poverty**
No place is too exalted
Knut Wicksell

74 **Economists in Cambridge**
A study through their correspondence 1907–1946
Edited by M. C. Marcuzzo and A. Rosselli

75 **The Experiment in the History of Economics**
Edited by Philippe Fontaine and Robert Leonard

76 **At the Origins of Mathematical Economics**
The economics of A. N. Isnard (1748–1803)
Richard van den Berg

The Experiment in the History of Economics

Edited by Philippe Fontaine and Robert Leonard

Routledge
Taylor & Francis Group
LONDON AND NEW YORK

First published 2005
by Routledge

Published 2017 by Routledge
2 Park Square, Milton Park, Abingdon, Oxon OX14 4RN
711 Third Avenue, New York, NY 10017, USA

Routledge is an imprint of the Taylor & Francis Group, an informa business

Copyright © 2005 Philippe Fontaine and Robert Leonard for selection and editorial matter; individual chapters, the contributors

Typeset in Times by Wearset Ltd, Boldon, Tyne and Wear

The Open Access version of this book, available at www.tandfebooks.com, has been made available under a Creative Commons Attribution-Non Commercial-No Derivatives 4.0 license.

British Library Cataloguing in Publication Data
A catalogue record for this book is available from the British Library

Library of Congress Cataloging in Publication Data
A catalog record for this book has been requested

ISBN 9780415344296
ISBN 9780415649230 (pbk)

Contents

Notes on contributors x
Acknowledgements xiii

Introduction 1
ROBERT LEONARD AND PHILIPPE FONTAINE

1 **Experimental economic games: the early years** 5
ROBERT W. DIMAND

2 **The Allais Paradox and its immediate consequences for expected utility theory** 25
SOPHIE JALLAIS AND PIERRE-CHARLES PRADIER

3 **Experimentation, general equilibrium and games** 50
S. ABU TURAB RIZVI

4 **Thought- and performed experiments in Hayek and Morgenstern** 71
ALESSANDRO INNOCENTI AND CARLO ZAPPIA

5 **Social comptabilism and pure credit systems: Solvay and Wicksell on monetary reform** 98
MAURO BOIANOVSKY AND GUIDO ERREYGERS

6 **The vanity of rigour in economics: theoretical models and Galilean experiments** 135
NANCY CARTWRIGHT

Index 154

Contributors

Mauro Boianovsky is Associate Professor of Economics at the Universidade de Brasilia. He received the History of Economics Society's Best Article Award for 1998, as well the Haralambos Simeonidis Award given by ANPEC (Brazilian Economic Association) for the best article published by a Brazilian economist in 1996 and 1998. His research interests are in the history of macroeconomics and business-cycle theory, especially in the twentieth century. He is the editor of the second set of the collection *Business Cycle Theory – Selected Texts, 1860–1939* (vols V–VIII) (Pickering and Chatto, 2004). His articles have appeared in *History of Political Economy*, *European Journal of the History of Economic Thought*, *Cambridge Journal of Economics*, *American Journal of Economics and Sociology*, *Journal of the History of Economic Thought*, and a number of edited volumes. He is currently working on the history of disequilibrium macroeconomics (especially Don Patinkin's contributions) and on controversies in business-cycle theory in the 1930s.

Nancy Cartwright is the Chair of the Centre for Philosophy of Natural and Social Science, and Professor of Philosophy at the Department of Philosophy, Logic and Scientific Method at the London School of Economics. She is also Professor of Philosophy at the University of California, San Diego. Her principal interests are philosophy and history of science (especially physics and economics), causal inference and objectivity in science. Her publications include *How the Laws of Physics Lie* (Clarendon Press, 1983), *Nature's Capacities and their Measurement* (Clarendon Press, 1989), *Otto Neurath: Philosophy between Science and Politics* (co-author) (Cambridge University Press, 1996), *The Dappled World: A Study of the Boundaries of Science* (Cambridge University Press, 1999), and *Hunting Causes and Using Them* (Cambridge University Press, forthcoming).

Robert W. Dimand is Professor of Economics, holding a Chancellor's Chair for Research Excellence, at Brock University, St. Catharines, Ontario, Canada. His research interests are in the history of game theory, the early history of macroeconomics, and the history of women in economics. He is the author of *The Origins of the Keynesian Revolution* (Edward Elgar and Stanford University Press, 1988) and (with M. A. Dimand) *A History of Game Theory*, Vol. 1 (Routledge, 1996), and edited *The Foundations of Game Theory* (3 vols, Edward Elgar, 1997, with M. A. Dimand), *The Origins of Macroeconomics* (10 vols, Routledge, 2002), and *The Status of Women in Classical Economic Thought* (Edward Elgar, 2003, with Chris Nyland). His articles have appeared in *American Economic Review (Papers and Proceedings)*, *British Journal for the History of Science*, *Economic Journal*, *Journal of Economic Perspectives*, and *Journal of Money, Credit, and Banking*. He is currently working on the second volume of *A History of Game Theory*.

Guido Erreygers is Professor of Economics at the Faculty of Applied Economics of the University of Antwerp. His current research interests include the history of economic thought in Belgium, linear-production theory, basic income and basic capital, and natural-resource economics. He has edited *Economics and Interdisciplinary Exchange* (Routledge, 2001) and co-edited, with Toon Vandevelde, *Is Inheritance Legitimate?* (Springer, 1997). His articles have appeared in *Cambridge Journal of Economics*, *European Journal of the History of Economic Thought*, *History of Political Economy*, *Journal of Economics*, *Journal of Political Philosophy*, and *Metroeconomica*.

Philippe Fontaine is professor of Economics at the École normale supérieure de Cachan and Ludwig M. Lachmann Fellow at the London School of Economics and Political Science. He received the History of Economics Society's Best Article Award for 2002. His research interests are in the history of recent social science, notably altruism and empathy theory. He is the co-editor (with Albert Jolink) of *Historical Perspectives on Macroeconomics: 60 Years after the 'General Theory'* (Routledge, 1998). His articles have appeared in *Canadian Journal of Economics*, *Economics and Philosophy*, *European Journal of the History of Economic Thought*, *History of Political Economy*, and *Isis*. He is currently working on John Harsanyi's game theory and bargaining theory, and Kenneth Boulding's effort to integrate the social sciences.

Alessandro Innocenti obtained his PhD in History of Economic Thought from the University of Firenze. He is now Associate Professor of Economics at the University of Siena where he teaches microeconomics and game theory. His main research interests cover the introduction of game theory into economics and the history of experimental economics. He is the author of many articles published in academic journals, including a paper on Morgenstern's contribution to game theory in the *Journal of the History of Economic Thought*.

Sophie Jallais is Assistant Professor of Economics at the Université Panthéon-Sorbonne. Her work has appeared in various journals in the history of economics. She is author of *Mathématiques des modèles dynamiques pour économistes* (La Découverte, 2001) and is currently working on a book on the neutrality of economic science.

Robert Leonard is Professor of Economics at the Université du Québec à Montréal. He works on the history of game theory and related subjects and is author of *From Red Vienna to Santa Monica: von Neumann, Morgenstern and the Creation of Theory, 1900–1960* (Cambridge University Press, forthcoming). He was recently editor of a mini-symposium on the subject of visual representation in economics in *European Journal of the History of Economic Thought*. Other contributions have appeared in *Journal of Economic Literature*, *Economic Journal*, *History of Political Economy,* and *Isis*.

Pierre-Charles Pradier is Assistant Professor of Economics at the Université Panthéon-Sorbonne. His research interests are in the history of decision theory and finance. His research has been published in *Revue économique*, *Revue de synthèse*, and *Œconomia.*

S. Abu Turab Rizvi is Associate Professor of Economics at the University of Vermont. His research, concerning microeconomics and its history, has been published in *Cambridge Journal of Economics*, *History of Political Economy*, *Journal of the Experimental Analysis of Behavior*, and other outlets. He studies the adequacy of general equilibrium theory and alternatives to it, such as game theory and experimental economics. Another aspect of his research focuses on choice and preferences in economics. His work examines normative economics as well: he is currently working on a book project, *Poverty, Work and Freedom: Political Economy and the Moral Order* (Cambridge University Press, forthcoming, with David P. Levine).

Carlo Zappia is Associate Professor of Economics at the University of Siena (Italy), where he teaches microeconomics and history of economics. His main research interests cover the development of Austrian economics in the 1930s, with particular reference to the work of F. A. Hayek, and the history of decision theory after Savage. His articles have appeared in *European Journal of the History of Economic Thought*, *Journal of the History of Economic Thought*, *Revue d'économie politique*, *Rivista italiana degli economisti*, and a number of edited volumes.

Acknowledgements

Several individuals and organisations are to be thanked for their contributions to the production of this volume. For the conference on which it is based, the Fifth Annual European Conference on the History of Economics (22–24 April 1999), we thank the host institution, the École normale supérieure de Cachan; the principal sponsor, the French Ministère de l'éducation nationale, de la recherche et de la technologie; and fellow organisers, José Luís Cardoso, Guido Erreygers, Albert Jolink and Michalis Psalidopoulos. The quality of those papers selected for publication was assured by both the authors and a number of referees, who must, alas, remain nameless: we are grateful to them all.

Philippe Fontaine and Robert Leonard

Introduction

Robert Leonard and Philippe Fontaine

> Experiment (*ekspe•riment*), 3. An action or operation undertaken in order to discover something unknown, to test a hypothesis, or establish or illustrate some known truth.
>
> *Oxford English Dictionary*

It was with a generous definition of both "action" and "operation" implicitly in mind that, in April 1999, a number of people gathered at Cachan, near Paris, to discuss what it means when we speak of an "experiment" in economics. The term was to be understood broadly, embracing not only the examination, in deliberately contrived situations, of how human subjects make economic choices, but other, less obvious, forms of action or operation, designed to establish economic truths.

The impetus for the meeting stemmed from what might be described as a certain cognitive dissonance surrounding the concept of experimentation in the economics field. On the one hand, there was the long resistance throughout the history of the discipline to the idea that economics can lend itself to experimentation. Going back at least as far as J. S. Mill and continuing until very recently, it was widely held that economics was not an experimental discipline: "Economics . . . cannot perform the controlled experiments of chemists or biologists because [it] cannot easily control other important factors. Like astronomers or meteorologists, [economists] generally must be content largely to observe" (Samuelson and Nordhaus, 1985, p. 8). On the other hand, it was a fact that, once one began to think about it, the concept of an "experiment" has been persistently present, in various guises, throughout the history of the field. Most obvious was the rapid rise of the new area of behavioural economics, to which experimentation is central. Indeed, just as this volume was being prepared for press, that area received "official" recognition in the form of the attribution of the Bank of Sweden Nobel Memorial Prize in October 2002 to Daniel Kahneman and Vernon Smith. As if in direct contradiction of the Samuelson and Nordhaus view, the Swedish Academy, in awarding the prize, wrote that "laboratory results ... can crucially inform the development of economic theory ... [just as] laboratory results concerning small-scale phenomena in physics (such as those pertaining to elementary particles and thermodynamics) can crucially inform the development of theoretical physics" (Royal Swedish Academy of Sciences, 2002, p. 3). Once the definition was extended beyond this experimentation of the laboratory kind, there were many other kinds of action that could be regarded as "experimental" in some sense. Most obvious were experiments in economic policy, where conclusions are drawn, "knowledge" is created, from a kind of experiment that has little to do with laboratory procedure; or "thought" experiments, where it is the disciplined imagination that might be said to be the source of knowledge; or the exploration of different scenarios through the use of comparative statics or computerised simulation with theoretical and quantitative models. Indeed, it quickly became obvious that, in economics, it was not at all clear what the term "experiment" really meant.

The selected essays in this volume approach the topic from several angles, forming an interrelated and coherent set of reflections on the various meanings that may be attached to "experimentation" in economics. Three of them deal with the emergence of the field of experimental economics and, as such, are particularly timely. Robert Dimand examines the roots of experimental gaming in the activities of the RAND Corporation in the postwar US, and claims that it was the development of game theory and the openness of game theorists to cross-disciplinary collaboration that created the path by which laboratory experimentation entered economics. However, by the time the latter was well established, he suggests, the experimenters and game theorists had become quite separated from each other. Another account, which deals, in part, with the same period, is Sophie Jallais and Pierre-Charles Pradier's examination of the so-called Allais Paradox. Drawing on interviews with some of the participants in the French decision-theory community of the 1950s, and examining the interactions between Allais and Savage, Jallais and Pradier provide a detailed reconstruction of the process by which a casual lunchtime puzzle posed by Allais came to be regarded as experimental validation of a "Paradox". Moving from microscopic detail to overarching historical thesis, Abu Turab Rizvi offers an answer to a question implicitly raised in the Dimand essay, namely, why, if it began in the early 1950s, did economic experimentation not become an activity acceptable within the disciplinary mainstream until some thirty years later? Rizvi's explanation is that it was not until the demise of general equilibrium theory, the dominant analytical framework for an entire generation from the 1950s, that experimentation became acceptable. With the emphasis in general equilibrium theorising being placed on logical coherence rather than on empirical plausibility, this formalist orientation made little room for experimental investigation of any kind. Not until the dominance of that programme was challenged, says Rizvi, with the announcement of a series of theoretical results concerning stability in the 1980s, would there result a breach of sorts, into which stepped the game theoretic and experimental approaches that figure prominently today.

As we move through the other contributions, the "actions" and "operations" considered grow in range. Although, as Viennese economists in the 1930s, neither Oskar Morgenstern nor Friedrich Hayek placed emphasis on the experimental investigation in the sense considered above, in their theorising, both of them engaged freely in what may be regarded as "thought experiments". Alessandro Innocenti and Carlo Zappia, in their essay, examine how such "mental chains of deductions and conjectures" were used by these Austrians in order to reach theoretical conclusions about the meaning of economic foresight and the possibility of equilibrium. Starting from a shared intellectual background, Hayek and Morgenstern developed quite differently, with the former remaining faithful to the "thought experiment" idea in his campaign against scientism in social science, while the latter moved away from that to embrace the use of computation as an experimental method.

If part of the Austrian anti-socialist tradition involved imagining alternative economic possibilities – only to then disregard them as infeasible – something similar underlined the work of Belgian industrialist Ernest Solvay and Swedish economist Knut Wicksell, discussed here by Mauro Boianovsky and Guido Erreygers. Both Solvay and Wicksell were involved, separately, in proposing non-monetary economies, systems that relied, in the case of Solvay, on an elaborate "comptabilist" system of accounts, or, in Wicksell's case, on pure credit. Boianovsky and Erreygers show how the scientist Solvay's system was part of his broader "social energetics" interpretation of the social order – a view that drew the explicit criticism of Hayek – while Wicksell's proposal for a credit system was related to his belief in the possibilities of using economic policy as a form of experimentation.

The final essay, by philosopher Nancy Cartwright, offers a stringent critique of the use of analogue economies, that is, models that purport to represent the economic system in question, be it micro- or macro- in a highly reduced, stylised form. The manipulation of such models for the purpose of drawing conclusions about the world, which is a prevalent kind of "experimentation", is claimed by Cartwright to be unreliable. This is not because the models are built using assumptions that are unrealistic *per se*, but using ones that are non-Galilean, i.e. that enter the functioning of the model, not as "harmless" background assumptions, but in a crucial way, concretely affecting the conclusions reached. The apparent rigour of the formal apparatus thus becomes spurious, with the model, even though perhaps very elaborate, lacking "bite" on the empirical phenomenon it is supposed to capture.

References

Royal Swedish Academy of Sciences (2002), "Foundations of Behavioral and Experimental Economics: Daniel Kahneman and Vernon Smith", advance information on the Prize in Economic Sciences 2002, www.kva.se.

Samuelson, Paul and William Nordhaus (1985), *Economics*, McGraw-Hill.

1 Experimental economic games

The early years

Robert W. Dimand

1.1 Introduction

This essay, an offshoot of research for Volume II of *A History of Game Theory*, will examine the encounters of game theory and experimentation in the two decades following the Second World War, and the adoption of experimental games as a characteristic feature of game theory in contrast to the much more limited use of experimentation by economists uninfluenced by game theory. The theory of games of strategy has followed a distinctive path in attempting to confront its abstract theory of conflict and cooperation with evidence about economic and social behavior. In the first twenty years after von Neumann and Morgenstern's *Theory of Games and Economic Behavior* (1944), game theorists began, at first tentatively and then on a large scale, to conduct strategic games as controlled experiments. In contrast, another new sub-discipline, macroeconomics, devoted its efforts to regression analysis of large, simultaneous equations models during the same years: Cowles monographs edited or co-edited by Tjalling Koopmans developed econometric theory for the estimation and identification of simultaneous equations models, while Lawrence Klein and his associates constructed models growing beyond the Brookings and Wharton models to CANDIDE (the Canadian Interdepartmental Econometric Model) with more than two thousand equations and finally Project LINK, which connects such models of 79 countries or groups of countries. Demand studies in microeconomics also focussed on econometrics applied to non-experimental data. Just as survey data has been so little used in economics that the advocacy by Blinder (1990) of "Learning by Asking Those Who Are Doing" struck its audience as quite daring, experiments played little role in economics apart from game theory. This was in sharp contrast to psychology: it is noteworthy that just as the use of survey data in economics was sustained in the 1950s by George Katona, who was cross-appointed in psychology and economics at the University of Michigan, the psychologist Sidney Siegel played a crucial role in promoting experimental games in economics. Some attempts had been made by psychologists (notably L. L. Thurstone 1931; cf. Mosteller and Nogee 1951) to measure preferences experimentally, but, in an influential paper, W. Allen Wallis and Milton Friedman (1942) denied that such experiments had any value for economics. Thirty experiments in strategic interaction were published by the time of the first survey of experimental gaming by Anatol Rapoport and Carol Orwant (1962). The subsequent growth of the literature was signaled by the introduction of an experimental gaming section edited by Rapoport in the *Journal of Conflict Resolution* in 1965, and Andrew Colman (1982, 12) reports estimates of over a thousand experimental gaming studies published by 1972, and some 1500 by the early 1980s. Kagel and Roth's *Handbook of Experimental Economics* needed more than 700 pages to survey its subject in 1995 (including experiments in economics not limited to studies of strategic interaction). A specialized journal, *Experimental Economics*, began publication in June 1998; a majority of the articles in its inaugural issue were game-theoretic. A four-paper *Economic Journal* symposium on experimental economics (Loomes 1999) was the subject of an article in *The Economist* (May 8, 1999).

Experimental gaming in economics and the social sciences could draw on a long heritage of war gaming (see Young 1952 for a survey and Riley and Young 1957 for a 94-page annotated bibliography extending back to the *Kriegsspiel* of 1824). Some of these war games incorporated randomization of outcomes, although not of strategies. In the Japanese naval war game in May 1942 on board the battleship *Yamato*, flagship of the Combined Fleet, before the Battle of Midway, the umpire rolled dice to determine the result of an air strike from Midway against the Japanese aircraft carriers, and declared nine hits, sinking two carriers. The admiral presiding over the game ordered the dice turned over to predict a more favorable outcome, a decision that "arbitrarily resulted in *Kaga*'s still being sunk but *Akagi* only slightly damaged. To [the umpire's] surprise, even this revised ruling was subsequently cancelled and *Kaga* reappeared as a participant in the next part of the game. . . . The verdicts of the umpires regarding the results of air fighting were similarly juggled, always in favor of the Japanese forces" (Fuchida and Okumiya 1955, quoted by Allen 1987, 122). The actual outcome of the battle could not be similarly amended.

1.2 Chamberlin

Experimental gaming first appeared in the economics literature with Edward Chamberlin's 1948 account of his classroom supply and demand experiments at Harvard. These experiments were designed to support Chamberlin's theory of monopolistic competition (1933) by demonstrating that experimental results did not resemble perfect competition, with the implication that trading in actual markets without possibility of recontracting non-equilibrium trades would not lead to the perfectly and purely competitive equilibrium. It was thus an outlier in the literature since, unlike the Santa Monica conference discussed in the next section, its inspiration predated von Neumann and Morgenstern (1944). Chamberlin claimed both pedagogic and scientific results from his experiments. Each player dealt in one unit of the commodity traded, and received a card marked with the letter B or S (for buyer or seller) and an even number from 18 to 104, indicating that player's Marshallian demand price or supply price (reservation price), as the case might be. The players circulated in a room and, if they negotiated a trade, handed in their cards to Chamberlin along with the price they had reached, but these prices were not announced during the trading. Supply and demand schedules were constructed from the reservation prices. Chamberlin reported conducting the experiment 46 times, with the actual volume of trades higher than the equilibrium volume 42 times and the same four times, but never lower: with trades occurring at actual prices higher or lower than the competitive equilibrium, buyers and sellers who would choose not to transact at the equilibrium price were able to trade. Chamberlin (1948, 102) found that

> My own skepticism as to why actual prices should in any literal sense tend toward equilibrium during the course of a market has been increased not so much by the actual data of the experiment before us – which are certainly open to limitations – as by the failure, upon reflection stimulated by the problem, to find any reason why it should be so. It would appear that, in asserting such a tendency, economists may have been led unconsciously to share their unique knowledge of the equilibrium point with their theoretical creatures, the buyers and sellers, who, of course, in real life have no knowledge of it whatsoever.

He viewed actual markets as a series of bilateral monopolies separated in time, and concluded that

> If it seems that strange results have been here derived by subjecting market schedules to arbitrary manipulations, it is replied that the "manipulations" are intended to be realistic and not arbitrary. Perhaps it is the perfect market which is "strange"; at any rate, the nature of the discrepancies between it and reality deserve study.

The eminent experimental economist Vernon Smith (1992, 242) reports that when he took part in Chamberlin's experimental game in the first meeting of Chamberlin's course, when Smith was a beginning Harvard graduate student in 1952, the students viewed the experiment as an unimportant parlor game: they received no payment to motivate them to take the game seriously, and Chamberlin was too obviously seeking a result supporting his own theory. Smith (1962) conducted 11 experiments (beginning in January 1956) that differed from Chamberlin's experiment game in involving cash rewards and a sequence of trading "days." Contrary to

Smith's expectations and to Chamberlin's results, these repeated experimental games tended to converge quickly to the competitive equilibrium. When I started graduate school at Yale in 1978, a Chamberlin-type experimental market game with a single trading period and no cash payments was played at the first meeting of the microeconomics class, without getting close to the competitive equilibrium price.

Chamberlin confronted theory with experimental evidence, but the participants in his experimental market game felt that his mind was already made up about the result. Generations of Harvard graduate students played Chamberlin's imperfect competition game, but of them all only Vernon Smith went on in experimental economics, and he found that Chamberlin's results were very sensitive to the absence of repeated play and monetary motivation.

1.3 The Santa Monica conference

Research in the area of experimental games on a large scale began in the summer of 1952, when the Ford Foundation sponsored an eight-week interdisciplinary seminar on "The Design of Experiments in Decision Processes," held in Santa Monica, California, to be convenient for participants from RAND (the Research and Development Corporation, whose only client was the US Air Force), but also including leading figures from elsewhere (several of them also RAND consultants), notably from two key centers of game theory in the 1950s, Princeton and the University of Michigan, and from the Cowles Commission in Chicago (including John von Neumann, Oskar Morgenstern, John Nash, Lloyd Shapley, and Martin Shubik from Princeton, Gérard Debreu, Tjalling Koopmans, Jacob Marschak, and Herbert Simon from Cowles, and Howard Raiffa from Michigan). The proposal for the seminar originated at the University of Michigan, where a game-theory seminar was jointly sponsored by Robert Thrall, an algebraist (and a contributor, with Michigan graduate students Howard Raiffa and Gerald L. Thompson, to the second volume of *Contributions to the Theory of Games*), and Clyde Coombs, a social psychologist. In addition to RAND and Ford Foundation, the US Office of Naval Research sponsored several participants, Oskar Morgenstern being a founding editor of ONR's *Naval Research Logistics Quarterly*. Although 27 of the 37 listed participants were sponsored at least partially by RAND or ONR (that is, by the US Air Force or Navy), Vernon Smith (1992, 260n) notes that

> none of the papers presented and none of those published in Thrall, Coombs, and Davis (1954) dealt, or was concerned, with military applications of game theory or decision theory. In this case military support appears to have been for basic research unconnected with military applications.

(Others at RAND, notably Thomas Schelling, did examine nuclear strategy in informal game-theoretic terms, and there were applications of formal game theory to military tactics at RAND.)

Only five of the 19 papers in the resulting volume on *Decision Processes* (Thrall *et al.* 1954) reported experimental results. "Some Experimental n-Person Games" by G. K. Kalisch, John W. Milnor, John F. Nash, and E. D. Nering (1954) is of particular interest, both for its influence in stimulating later experimental work (e.g. by Reinhard Selten; cf. Luce 1959) and for its place in Nash's body of work on game theory. Nash and others at Princeton were interested in playable games (such as "So Long Sucker") but this exercise in experimental gaming was exceptional. The authors noted that "The field of n-person games has had very little empirical investigation; for this reason, and because of the relatively undeveloped status of the theory, the authors feel that the use of the experimental approach is strongly indicated" (1954, 302; see also Innocenti and Zappia, and Rizvi in this volume).

Kalisch, Milnor, Nash, and Nering played six constant-sum, cooperative games with side payments: four were four-person games played eight times each, the others a five-person game played three times and a seven-person game played twice. Players were rotated to discourage permanent coalitions. They found what they considered "a reasonably good fit between the observed data and the Shapley value" but found that results differed between games that were strategically equivalent and that symmetries between games were not well reflected in observed outcomes. They also played a three-person cooperative game with no side payments, and attempted to ascertain the workability of a negotiation model, defined as "a non-cooperative game based on a strictly formalized negotiation procedure applied to a cooperative game" (1954, 316), the solution to which could be considered as a possible solution to the underlying cooperative game. This last effort represents a tentative but striking move toward attempting implementation of what has come to be called "the Nash program" of constructing non-cooperative bargaining models to test the axioms of the Nash bargaining solution (Nash 1953). Nash did not follow up this beginning, due to his absorption in problems of pure mathematics and then to his illness and intermittent institutionalization. The most important direct impact of this paper was an inspiration to Reinhard Selten (see the interview with Selten reported by Vernon Smith 1992, 258).

The psychologist William Estes (1954) reported an experiment (similar to that of Humphreys 1939) in which subjects predicted on each trial which of two or more events would occur, and were rewarded with some probability if they were right. Estes found that the subjects adaptively converged to a "probability matching" strategy (guessing each outcome with the same probability with which it was observed to occur), rather than always predicting the most-frequent outcome, the strategy that would maximize the probability of predicting correctly. Several game theorists at the Santa

Monica seminar objected that the subjects were behaving irrationally. Merrill Flood (1954b, 288) rejected this attribution of irrationality on two grounds: "there is a reasonable payoff matrix that would rationalize the reported behavior" and "The von Neumann–Morgenstern game theory is inapplicable in this situation unless the organism can assume safely that the experimental stimulus is generated by a stationary stochastic stimulus." The second point turned out not to make a difference in later experiments by Sidney Siegel and others in which the constancy of probabilities was explained to the subjects (Smith 1992, 262–263). The first point proved much more significant, and was taken up by Herbert Simon (1956) and Sidney Siegel (1959). Simon (1956, 271) argued that

> Perhaps the most useful lesson to be learned ... is the necessity for careful distinction between subjective rationality (i.e. behavior that is rational, given the perceptual and evaluational premises of the subject), and objective rationality (behavior that is rational as viewed by the experimenter).

In addition to Merrill Flood's two chapters on learning in games (1954a, 1954b), his 1958 article "Some Experimental Games" on a prisoner's dilemma game (in which jointly dominating strategies are not Pareto efficient, and the Pareto-efficient outcome is not a Nash equilibrium) repeated a hundred times was a condensation of a 1952 RAND memorandum, written before his 1953 departure from RAND to Columbia University (and from there to the University of Michigan). (Prisoner's dilemma is called "Hangman's Paradox" in a footnote in Flood (1958), quoting a letter from Nash.) The appendix to Flood (1958) amusingly records the running comments of the two players during the frustrating repetitions of prisoner's dilemma.

The prestige of the seminar participants and of the sponsoring institutions of the Santa Monica seminar gave some impetus to an approach outside conventional economic and social-science methodology, but Vernon Smith (1992, 261) judges that "quantitatively, its success in stimulating experiment must be judged more modest than in furthering theory. The seminar's integrating theme was not experimental design, but the use of mathematics in the social sciences" (cf. Roth 1993). Thrall *et al.* (1954) passes unmentioned even in Andrew Colman's critical survey of *Game Theory and Experimental Games* (1982).

Game theory at RAND had already suffered a blow when intolerance of homosexuality led to the dismissal of J. C. C. McKinsey, whose *Introduction to the Theory of Games* (1952) was published as a RAND study: "McKinsey committed suicide in 1953 within two years of being fired by RAND" (Nasar 1998, 188). John Nash's 1954 arrest for indecent exposure led RAND to withdraw his security clearance and cancel his consulting contract (Nasar 1998, Chapter 25). Von Neumann gave up his RAND consultancy the same year upon being named to the Atomic Energy Commission. Beyond these individual departures, there was a general fading of interest in game theory at RAND in the late 1950s, as RAND perceived that its support had contributed more to pure research than to military strategy. Thomas Schelling (1960) noted that "Whenever we speak of deterrence, atomic blackmail, the balance of terror ... we are evidently deep in game theory, yet formal game theory has contributed little to the clarification of these ideas."

1.4 Siegel and Fouraker at Penn State

The most substantial body of early experimental work in strategic games and decision theory resulted from the collaboration at Pennsylvania State University of the psychologist Sidney Siegel and the economist Lawrence Fouraker, a flourishing interdisciplinary research program ended by Siegel's death of a heart attack in November 1961 at what Vernon Smith (1992, 247) terms "the beginning of a brilliant career. I am convinced that his death impeded substantially the subsequent development of experimental economics, which did not really take off until the late 1970s." Siegel came from a discipline in which experimentation was an accepted procedure, and was co-author of a volume on *Decision Making: An Experimental Approach* (Davis *et al.* 1957). Some of his experimental work (Siegel and Goldstein 1959 and Siegel *et al.* 1964, the latter published after his death) examined non-optimal strategic choice under risk, inspired by the light-guessing experiment of Humphreys (1939), which was considered a classic in the literature of experimental psychology (see Colman 1982, 21–22). Seated in front of two light bulbs, subjects are asked to predict which one will be lit next. The bulbs are lit randomly, according to probabilities set in advance. Subjects usually begin distributing their predictions evenly between the two choices, but after one or two hundred repetitions, converge to matching the distribution of their predictions to the pre-set probabilities – even though the strategy that would maximize the probability of a correct prediction would be to always predict the most frequently illuminated bulb. Siegel was also influenced by the contributions of Flood and especially of Estes to Thrall *et al.* (1954) (see Siegel 1959).

Martin Shubik (in an interview reported by Vernon Smith 1992, 250) gives a remarkable account of meeting Siegel around a campfire in Tuolomne Meadows in Yosemite National Park in 1955 or 1956:

> [Martin] Beckman and I (instead of singing "Clementine") were discussing utility theory – when a shadowy figure near us started to eavesdrop and then could not contain himself and joined in the conversation. From there I learned about Siegel's two-light experiments with rewards – as I knew [William] Estes's learning theory I was immediately fascinated. I immediately said to Sid that Mayberry,

> Nash, and I [1953] had written an article on duopoly (Cournot and Cooperative) and did he think that this might be worthwhile. He said yes, but that an economist at Penn State – Larry Fouraker – had already talked with him about bilateral monopoly and that he was committed to finish that work before looking at duopoly.

Lawrence Fouraker (1957) critiqued the assumption of complete information in the bilateral monopoly analysis of William Fellner (1947, 1949; see Dimand and Dimand 1996, Chapter 4, for the earlier history of bilateral monopoly theory). Instead, Fouraker proposed assuming that the bargainers knew only their own functions, with a seller knowing the cost conditions but not the revenue function, and the buyer knowing the revenue relations but not the cost function. According to a letter from Fouraker to Vernon Smith in 1990 (Smith 1992, 250n), Fouraker's "interest in the experimental testing of economic theory started with a master's candidate, Dave DiFedo, who wanted to test my bilateral monopoly model against Fellner's. I knew of Siegel's experiments on choice theory and suggested we talk with him." David D. DiFebo was among the five research assistants credited in the resulting book, *Bargaining and Group Decision Making* (Siegel and Fouraker 1960). Fouraker was a rising young star of Penn State's Economics Department: while the first article by him listed in the American Economic Association *Index of Economic Journals* was in 1955, his 1957 article on Fellner was already his eighth.

Siegel and Fouraker (1960, vi–vii) noted that:

> reliance on the usual sources of economic data has not provided observations suitable for disposing of alternative hypotheses emerging from economic theories of bilateral monopoly behavior. We have turned to the methods of experimental social psychology to create a context within which data relevant to hypotheses from bilateral monopoly theory could be collected.

They emphasized that:

> In the past, psychologists and economists have worked together most commonly on applied topics, such as marketing. Our research, in contrast, is concerned with fundamental topics in economic and psychological theory, and we have not given special attention to possible applications of our work. . . . Since the problem of choices among alternatives is fundamental in all the social sciences, the study of decision-making processes is of central interest to these sciences. The theory of games and decision-making theory may well provide the base for a unified conceptual structure for the social sciences (cf. Shubik, 1959, and Luce and Raiffa, 1957).
>
> (Siegel and Fouraker 1960, vi, 2)

The award of the Monograph Prize of the American Academy of Arts and Sciences in social sciences for 1959 confirmed that others shared this view of the significance of Siegel and Fouraker (1960) as an interdisciplinary methodological innovation dealing with fundamental issues of theory.

Siegel and Fouraker (1960, 17–23) recruited 116 Penn State students (58 bargaining pairs), all but one male, from an undergraduate principles section and through the campus student employment service:

> the subjects obtained through the student employment service were ostensibly hired to perform routine clerical work for wages of $1.00 an hour, a procedure that was used in an attempt to recruit subjects having a relatively high utility for the amounts of money used in the experiments.

The bargaining pairs communicated only through an intermediary, and did not know the identity of their bargaining rivals. They were given iso-profit tables for combinations of price and quantity, and were paid in cash when agreement was reached, but did not know the payoff of their bargaining rivals. Participants took part only in one bargaining session, and were asked not to discuss the experiment with anyone. Siegel and Fouraker (1960, 41) found a tendency for bargainers to maximize joint payoff by negotiating Pareto-optimal contracts, and that this tendency was strengthened by increasing the amount of relevant information and the difference in payoff between Pareto-optimal and near-optimal contracts. Further experiment with 11 bargaining pairs of Penn State undergraduates indicated that increasing the amount of relevant information available to the bargainers tended to produce a more equal division of the joint payoff: "bargainers with complete information have more realistic expectations with respect to their own profit than less informed bargainers, and are under a sort of moralistic pressure for a fifty-fifty split of the joint payoff" (Siegel and Fouraker 1960, 70).

At the end of their book on bilateral monopoly, Siegel and Fouraker identified duopoly as a promising field for experimental games, and this was the subject of their second joint book, *Bargaining Behavior* (Fouraker and Siegel 1963; cf. Dimand and Dimand 1996, Chapters 2 and 3, for earlier strategic analysis of duopoly and oligopoly). The 1963 book included a bilateral bargaining game, in which the seller first chose the price and the buyer then chose the quantity, and duopoly and triopoly experiments, in which the sellers chose quantities and demand was then simulated. Much of this work was circulated in 1961, before Siegel's death, as four research reports issued by the Psychology Department at Penn State: "Bargaining Behavior I" by Fouraker, Siegel, and a Penn State graduate student, Donald Harnett; "Bargaining Behavior II" by Fouraker and Siegel; "Bargaining, Information, and the Use of Threat" by Siegel and Harnett; and "Oligopoly Bargaining: The Quantity Adjuster Models" by Fouraker, Shubik, and Siegel. Martin Shubik, a Princeton-trained game theorist, was an adjunct research professor at Penn State from 1959 to 1961 while working for General Electric (overlapping with a visiting appointment at Yale for the 1960–61 academic year). While Siegel had been listed as first author, out of alphabetical order, on the 1960 book, the authors were listed alphabetically on the book that Fouraker produced after Siegel's death. In both the 1960 and 1963 volumes, the full instructions and data given to the participants were included.

Sidney Siegel's untimely death ended a promising interdisciplinary venture in experimental gaming. Fouraker completed and published their second book, and a volume on *Choice, Strategy, and Utility* (Sidney Siegel, Alberta Siegel, and J. M. Andrews 1964) appeared, but Penn State ceased to be a center of such research. Shubik was not affiliated with Penn State after 1961. He moved from General Electric to IBM in 1961, and then took a permanent appointment at Yale in 1963. Jessie Bernard, a Penn State sociologist introduced to game theory by Sidney Siegel, had acclaimed game theory as the basis for a modern sociology of conflict, but later moved away from game theory (see Dimand 2000). The influence of Siegel and Fouraker was felt elsewhere, notably by Vernon Smith, who was inspired by meeting Siegel in Stanford in the autumn of 1961 to read all his books and articles, and by James Friedman, who was a Yale graduate student when Tjalling Koopmans lent him the "Bargaining Behavior I and II" working papers (Smith 1992, 247, 256). Siegel's extensive contacts outside his own discipline might well have furthered the spread of experimental economic gaming had he lived longer: for instance, the opening footnote of Siegel (1959) credits consultations with John C. Harsanyi and the information theorist Claude Shannon, and "many discussions with Robert M. Solow", while Solow, Shubik, Fellner, George J. Stigler, and the statistician John W. Tukey were thanked for "helpful and incisive comments and suggestions" by Siegel and Fouraker (1960, viii).

1.5 Rapoport at Ann Arbor

Anatol Rapoport, a mathematical biologist then at the University of Michigan (now in peace science at the University of Toronto), was another pioneer in experimental games in the 1950s and 1960s. He was particularly active in experiments related to prisoner's dilemma, which were the subject of a comprehensive monograph by Rapoport and Chammah with Orwant (1965), and together with Carol Orwant, Rapoport surveyed the existing literature on experimental games (Rapoport and Orwant 1962). Rapoport's approach to games was deeply influenced by the work between the World Wars of the pacifist Lewis Fry Richardson (see Boulding 1962, Chapter 2, and Dimand and Dimand 1996, Chapter 6), who also influenced Kenneth Boulding, who was closely associated with Rapoport in founding the *Journal of Conflict Resolution* in 1957 and the University of Michigan's

Center for Research in Conflict Resolution in 1959. Rapoport saw in games such as prisoner's dilemma and chicken analogies (at a very abstract level) to the problems of avoiding nuclear war between the United States and the Soviet Union. Allowing communication in prisoner's dilemma failed to eliminate the Pareto-inefficient outcome if the players were unable to make binding commitments. Repetition, however often, also failed to remove the problem in theory if the number of repetitions was finite, since there would be an incentive to defect from the cooperative result on the last play, and therefore (anticipating that result on the last play) on the penultimate play, and so on. Nonetheless, Rapoport's experiments indicated more cooperation in finitely-repeated prisoner's dilemma games than the theory would predict.

Robert Axelrod, in *The Evolution of Cooperation* (1984), conducted an experiment in the finitely-repeated prisoner's dilemma, in which expert game theorists wrote computer programs that were matched against each other in a tournament, with the game ending at each stage with a small, fixed probability. The players thus would not lack understanding of the game, and were amply motivated by the prospect of glory. The most successful program, a "tit for tat" program rewarding cooperative choices by the other player and punishing defections, was written by Anatol Rapoport.

1.6 *Journal of Conflict Resolution*

Related to Rapoport's work, another strand in the literature of experimental gaming was motivated by disarmament concerns about nuclear deterrence and arms races, and appeared primarily in the *Journal of Conflict Resolution*, of which Rapoport was an editor. Scodel *et al.* (1959) and Minas *et al.* (1960) reported experiments with two-person, non-zero-sum games, including the game that A. W. Tucker named prisoner's dilemma, but which they called G-type games. They argued (Scodel *et al.* 1959, 118) that

> The mathematical origin and normative emphasis of game theory have inevitably led to a general neglect of psychological and sociological variables that must be assesses in order to assign utilities to outcomes. In our games, for example, the necessity to avoid an ego-deflating experience that could result from attempted collaboration that is not reciprocated could very well account for the prevalence of red plays [non-cooperation]. In G games this need to maintain self-esteem so dominates the monetary values in the matrix that subjectively players are not really in a dilemma.

In the second part of the article (Minas *et al.* 1960, 197), the authors found such Pareto-inefficient outcomes even in H-type games, in which non-cooperation was not a dominant strategy: "The most plausible account we can give of our results is that subjects tend to perceive the game as primarily a competitive one." Thomas Schelling (1961) also reported experimental results, and advocated the use of non-zero-sum gaming in the study of international relations and as a didactic tool.

1.7 Experimental games in business and economics

Experimental business gaming (Bellman *et al.* 1957; Ricciardi 1957; Hoggatt 1959) was used as a tool in management education, and influenced economists interested in experimental games such as Shubik and Selten. Linking several centers of game theory and experimental economics, Martin Shubik, part of the game-theory community at Princeton in the early 1950s, collaborated with Fouraker and Siegel on a working paper on oligopoly bargaining that became part of Fouraker and Siegel (1963). Shubik then played a crucial role at Yale (as a visiting professor in 1960–61, and permanently since 1963), both through his own experimental work (e.g. Shubik 1962) and through stimulating the work of Yale graduate students (Dolbear 1963; J. Friedman 1963, 1967). Shubik (1962, 229) drew on the work of Flood and Siegel on game learning (learning about the rules when the players are not fully informed initially), and argued that experimental games

> appear to provide a promising tool to help separate out variables in the study of bargaining, threats and other aspects of competition and cooperation. In particular the relationship among theories of games, learning and gaming need further clarification. Many of the proponents and opponents of games and of gaming have failed to appreciate the need for extreme care in interpreting and relating the axioms behind the various theories of games to the experimental conditions.

In addition to work that he published at the time (such as Shubik 1962), Shubik also constructed a computerized oligopoly game for his 1960 Yale seminar on oligopoly theory, but published the game only twenty years later in a book with Richard Levitan (Shubik and Levitan 1980). Despite the publication lag, Shubik's oligopoly game followed directly from his theoretical book on *Strategy and Market Structure* (1959), based on his Princeton thesis, and his collaboration with Siegel and Fouraker.

James Friedman was one of the three students in Shubik's oligopoly-theory seminar in 1960, and he wrote his doctoral dissertation on "Individual Behavior in Oligopolistic Markets: An Experimental Study" (1963). Friedman noted in the summary to his thesis that "These experiments build on earlier work, primarily that of Lawrence Fouraker and the late Sidney Siegel," and he thanked Shubik "for his encouragement and for initially arousing my interest in this area." William Fellner chaired Friedman's dissertation committee (which also included John W. Hooper and John F. Muth, of rational expectations) and that of F. Trenery Dolbear, Jr., who wrote on "Individual Choice Under Uncertainty – An Experimental Study" (1963). (Dolbear's committee also included James Tobin and Edmund Phelps, and Dolbear thanked Friedman and Muth for comments.) Dolbear moved into other areas of economics, but James Friedman remained active in game theory and oligopoly, and continued to contribute to experimental games, for instance Friedman (1967) and a paper in one of Sauermann's conference volumes (Friedman 1972).

Vernon Smith (1962, 1965) also began to publish in experimental economics at that time, and has gone on to become the leading researcher in the field (see also Stone 1958). Smith's strong interest in experimental economics was stimulated by taking part in Chamberlin's classroom game and by meeting Sidney Siegel shortly before Siegel's death. Smith (1992) supplemented his fascinating participant-memoir of early experimental economics with interviews with Martin Shubik, Herbert Simon, James Friedman, and Reinhard Selten.

1.8 Early experimental gaming beyond North America

At the very end of the 1950s and in the 1960s, experimental games in economics began to spread beyond the United States to Japan and Germany. (A number of early game theorists, notably Mayberry, Shubik, Tucker, and Vickrey, were born in Canada, but their work was done in the United States.) Minoru Sakaguchi (1960), reporting on two pairs of subjects in simple, two-person saddle-point, strictly competitive games, found that in each pair one player approached the minimax strategy after fifty or sixty repetitions while the other did not. This did not, however, demonstrate any irrationality on the part of the players who did not adopt a minimax strategy. As long as one subject played minimax, the other would get the same payoff with any strategy. Sakaguchi also reported forty trials of a three-player, non-zero-sum, non-negotiable game, in which the players tended to start near the Nash equilibrium point but move toward a co-operative solution. Five years earlier, Sakaguchi had published in the same journal on minimax tests of hypotheses (statistical decision theory). Martin Shubik (interviewed by Vernon Smith 1992, 251) recalls that, while he was at Yale as a visiting professor, "On 5 October 1960, I talked with Masuo Toda of Tokyo on his 3 × 3 matrix game results."

The first paper by the future Nobel laureate Reinhard Selten was an oligopoly experiment that he conducted with his economics teacher at Frankfurt, Heinz Sauermann (Sauermann and Selten 1959), a paper that was translated into English the following year in a yearbook co-edited by Rapoport. Their experiment was a multi-period Cournot oligopoly model played by volunteer Frankfurt undergraduates. A mathematics student, Selten also took psychology courses in which he took part in experiments.

Influenced by Kalisch *et al.* (1954) and by Ricciardi (1957), the American Management Association's booklet on its computerized business game (Sauermann and Selten also cited Chamberlin 1948), Selten persuaded his teacher Sauermann of the promise of experimental work in economics (interview with Selten in Smith 1992, 258–259). Sauermann went on to edit three conference volumes on experimental economics in 1967, 1970, and 1972, with Selten contributing to the first two and James Friedman (1972) to the third. Sauermann also edited a volume of experimental studies of *Coalition Forming Behaviour* (1978). Appropriately, Selten contributed to the inaugural issue of *Experimental Economics* in 1998. Only the very beginnings of experimental economic gaming in Germany and Japan occurred in the period covered by the present essay, but they foreshadowed substantial later activity, most notably at Selten's Bonn research laboratory.

1.9 Conclusion

This essay has examined the development of experimental gaming in economics from its origins as an approach completely outside mainstream economic methodology (although more compatible with accepted methodology in psychology) up to a point where, although still far from being generally accepted in the discipline of economics, it could be the subject of doctoral dissertations in economics at a major graduate school (James Friedman at Yale) and articles in one of the leading mainstream economics journals (Smith 1962, 1965 in the *Journal of Political Economy*) and had begun to spread beyond its country of origin (Sauermann and Selten 1959; Sakaguchi 1960). Experimental gaming in economics suffered some significant setbacks in its early years, especially the early death of Sidney Siegel in 1961 and the departure from RAND of key participants such as Flood and Nash by the time that Thrall *et al.* (1954) appeared in print, so that volume marked the end rather than the beginning of such work at RAND. Nonetheless, important advances were made in this period in how to conduct experimental games: the importance of meaningful remuneration, completeness or incompleteness of information, possibility of communication, the potentially differing results of one-shot and repeated games, recognition of subjective rationality.

Contrary to the methodology that was generally accepted in economics, game theory became in this period a field that looked to controlled experiments for empirical testing of its theories. Although econometrics was spreading across fields of economics, attempts to apply game theory in the era 1945–60 were attempts to use game theory in applied fields (see Dimand 2000), not empirical applications to data sets. It was through experimentation that theories of strategic interaction encountered evidence. Interest in game theory crossed disciplinary boundaries, and served to bring game theorists in economics and in applied mathematics into close contact with researchers from such fields as psychology and biology, for whom experimentation was a matter of course. Clyde Coombs, one of the organizers of the University of Michigan game-theory seminar and of the Santa Monica conference, and an editor of Thrall *et al.* (1954), was a psychologist, as was William Estes, a key participant in the Santa Monica conference. Experimental gaming at Penn State resulted from the collaboration of the economist Lawrence Fouraker with the psychologist Sidney Siegel. Anatol Rapoport was a mathematical biologist at the University of Michigan and a founder of the *Journal of Conflict Resolution*, which took a cross-disciplinary approach to peace and conflict studies, with a strong emphasis on game theory. The distinctive path of game theory within economics, making use of experimental gaming when other sub-disciplines of economics typically eschewed experimentation, reflected the exceptional degree to which economists interested in game theory interacted and collaborated with researchers from other disciplines in the period studied in this essay. This began with John von Neumann's and Oskar Morgenstern's *Theory of Games and Economic Behavior* (1944), which, despite the adjective "economic" in the title, offered its approach to a wide range of social sciences and applied mathematics, and was the result of collaboration between a non-economist (from mathematics, physics, and computing) and an economist, both of whom attended the Santa Monica conference. The game-theory community inspired by their work included such economists as Martin Shubik (Morgenstern's assistant and doctoral student) but was by no means limited to economists. Other areas of economics had far less contact with disciplines in which experimentation was traditional. While Shubik, Rapoport, Siegel and Fouraker, and the contributors to Thrall *et al.* (1954), explicitly drew inspiration from von Neumann and Morgenstern's game theory, Chamberlin (1948) stands as an exception, an exercise in experimental economic gaming rooted in Chamberlin's earlier work on monopolistic competition. However, Chamberlin (1948) had little influence, except on Vernon Smith, and even Smith did not at first appreciate the significance of what Chamberlin had attempted (Smith 1992, 242).

Some of the results, notably the very first economic experimental game used by Chamberlin in 1948 to deny that markets converge to the competitive equilibrium price, were found to be too hasty. The experimental, strictly competitive games surveyed by Colman (1982, 76–82) are characterized by him as "confusing and confused" with "wild departures from minimax observed in the subjects' strategy choices." Some of these observations resulted because any strategy is optimal against a minimax player, and because a non-minimax optimal strategy can be found to exploit an opponent's observed, persistent choice of a particular non-minimax strategy. Even allowing for these factors, these experimental results provide a challenge to game theory, just as experimentation outside strategic games has produced the Allais and Ellsberg paradoxes as challenges to accepted utility theory.

Colman (1982, 82–83) also notes that

> Over the years, a growing chorus of commentators has expressed misgivings about the ecological validity of experimental games . . . the extent to which the results of an experiment can be generalised to non-experimental, naturally occurring situations. . . . One cannot help being struck, however, by the paucity of "new research tasks" that have sprung from concern with the ecological validity of experimental games. In particular, few attempts have been made to compare behaviour in abstract experimental games with behaviour in more life-like strategic interactions.

For instance, Rapoport (1970) argues that abstract laboratory games are interesting enough in themselves to warrant study, and warns against generalizing their results to the real world. In addition, Colman's 1982 book was motivated by his complaint that, with increasing specialization and intellectual division of labor in a growing subject, "Game theorists, in general, remain largely oblivious of the empirical studies that have been inspired by the theory, and experimental investigators have tended to assume that the nuts and bolts of the theory do not concern them." This increasing specialization, and its consequences in the form of diminished communication between game theorists and experimental gamers, is ironic, since the emergence of experimental economic games as a distinctive feature of game theory within economics in the 1950s reflected the cross-disciplinary intellectual interaction of economists and such non-economists as psychologists and biologists involved in game theory. These two criticisms, insufficient comparison of the results of experimental games with empirical evidence and inadequate communication between theorists and experimenters, can be viewed as setting an agenda for further work, and one can observe promising indications of such work, for instance in *Experimental Economics*.

References

Allen, Thomas B. *War Games*. New York, Berkley Books, 1987.

Axelrod, Robert. *The Evolution of Cooperation*. New York, Basic Books, 1984.

Bellman, Richard, Charles E. Clark, Donald G. Malcolm, Clifford J. Craft, and Franc M. Ricciardi. "On the Construction of a Multi-stage, Multi-person Business Game." *Journal of the Operations Research Society of America* 5 (1957), 469–503.

Blinder, Alan S. "Learning by Asking Those Who Are Doing." *Eastern Economic Journal* 16 (1990), 297–306.

Boulding, Kenneth. *Conflict and Defense: A General Theory*. New York, Harper & Brothers for the University of Michigan Center for Research in Conflict Resolution, 1962.

Chamberlin, Edward H. *Theory of Monopolistic Competition*. Cambridge, MA, Harvard University Press, 1933.

Chamberlin, Edward H. "An Experimental Imperfect Market." *Journal of Political Economy* 56 (1948), 95–108, as reprinted in Dimand and Dimand (1997), III, 177–190 (also in Chamberlin 1957).

Chamberlin, Edward H. *Toward a More General Theory of Value*. Cambridge, MA, Harvard University Press, 1957.

Colman, Andrew M. *Game Theory and Experimental Games: The Study of Strategic Interaction*. Oxford, Pergamon Press, 1982.

Davis, D., P. Suppes, and Sidney Siegel. *Decision Making: An Experimental Approach*. Stanford, CA, Stanford University Press, 1957.

Dimand, Mary Ann, and Robert W. Dimand. *A History of Game Theory*, Vol. I: *From the Beginnings to 1945*. London and New York, Routledge, 1996.

Dimand, Mary Ann, and Robert W. Dimand (eds.). *The Foundations of Game Theory*, 3 vols. Cheltenham, UK, and Lyme, NH, Edward Elgar Publishing, 1997.

Dimand, Robert W. "Strategic Games from Theory to Application," in *Toward a History of Applied Economics*, annual supplement to Vol. 32 of *History of Political Economy*, Roger Backhouse and Jeff Biddle (eds), 2000.

Dolbear, F. Trenery. "Individual Choice: An Experimental Study." *Yale Economic Essays* 3 (1963), 419–470.

The Economist. "Economics Focus: News from the Lab." May 8, 1999, 84.

Estes, William K. "Individual Behavior in Uncertain Situations: An Interpretation in Terms of Statistical Association Theory." In Thrall *et al.* (1954), 127–137.

Fellner, William. "Prices and Wages under Bilateral Monopoly." *Quarterly Journal of Economics* 61 (1947), 503–532.

Fellner, William. *Competition Among the Few*. New York, Knopf, 1949.

Flood, Merrill M. "Game-Learning Theory and Some Decision-Making Experiments." In Thrall *et al.* (1954), 139–158. [1954a]

Flood, Merrill M. "Environmental Non-Stationarity in a Sequential Decision-Making Experiment." In Thrall *et al.* (1954), 287–299. [1954b]

Flood, Merrill M. "Some Experimental Games." *Management Science* 5 (1958), 5–26, as reprinted in Dimand and Dimand (1997), III, 200–221.

Fouraker, Lawrence E. "Professor Fellner's Bilateral Monopoly Theory." *Southern Economic Journal* 24 (1957), 182–189.

Fouraker, Lawrence E., and Sidney Siegel. *Bargaining Behavior*. New York: McGraw-Hill, 1963.

Friedman, James W. "Individual Behavior in Oligopolistic Markets." *Yale Economic Essays* 3 (1963), 359–417.

Friedman, James W. "An Experimental Study of Cooperative Duopoly." *Econometrica* 35 (1967), 379–397.

Friedman, James W. "On the Structure of Oligopoly Models with Differential Products." In Hans Sauermann (ed.), *Beitrage zur Experimentellen Wirtschaftsforschung III*, Tubingen, J. C. B. Mohr (Paul Siebeck), 1972, 28–63.

Fuchida, Mitsuo, and Masatake Okumiya. *Midway*. Annapolis, MD, Naval Institute Press, 1955.

Hoggatt, Austin C. "An Experimental Business Game." *Behavioral Science* 4 (1959), 192–203.

Humphreys, L. G. "Acquisition and Extinction of Verbal Expectations in a Situation Analogous to Conditioning." *Journal of Experimental Psychology* 25 (1939), 294–301.

Kagel, John H., and Alvin E. Roth (eds). *The Handbook of Experimental Economics*. Princeton, NJ, Princeton University Press, 1995.

Kalisch, G. K., John W. Milnor, John F. Nash, Jr., and E. D. Nering. "Some Experimental N-Person Games." In Thrall *et al.* (1954), 301–327, as reprinted in Dimand and Dimand (1997), II, 77–103.

Loomes, Graham (ed.). "Feature: Experimental Economics." *Economic Journal* 109 (1999), F1–F45.

Luce, R. Duncan. "A Note on the Article 'Some Experimental N-Person Games.'" *Contributions to the Theory of Games* 4 (1959) (Princeton University Press), 279–285.

Luce, R. Duncan, and Howard Raiffa. *Games and Decisions*. New York, John Wiley & Son, 1957.

Mayberry, John P., John F. Nash, Jr., and Martin Shubik. "A Comparison of Treatments of a Duopoly Situation." *Econometrica* 21 (1953), 141–154, as reprinted in Dimand and Dimand (1997), II, 48–61.

McKinsey, John C. *Introduction to the Theory of Games*. New York, McGraw-Hill, 1952.

Minas, J. Sayer, Alvin Scodel, David Marlowe, and Harve Rawson. "Some Descriptive Aspects of Two-Person Non-Zero-Sum Games." *Journal of Conflict Resolution* 4 (June 1960), 193–197, as reprinted in Dimand and Dimand (1997), III, 239–243.

Mosteller, Frederick, and Philip Nogee. "An Experimental Measurement of Utility." *Journal of Political Economy* 59 (1951), 371–404.

Nasar, Sylvia. *A Beautiful Mind*. New York, Simon & Schuster, 1998.

Nash, John F., Jr. "The Bargaining Problem." *Econometrica* 18 (1950), 155–162, reprinted in Dimand and Dimand 1997, II, 3–10.

Nash, John F., Jr. "Two-Person Cooperative Games." *Econometrica* 21 (1953), 128–140, reprinted in Dimand and Dimand 1997, II, 35–47.

Rapoport, Anatol. "Conflict Resolution in the Light of Game Theory and Beyond." In P. Swingle (ed.), *The Structure of Conflict*. New York, Academic Press, 1970, 1–42.

Rapoport, Anatol, and Carol Orwant. "Experimental Games: A Review." *Behavioral Science* 7 (1962), 1–37, as reprinted in Dimand and Dimand (1997), III, 244–280.

Rapoport, Anatol, and A. M. Chammah, with Carol J. Orwant. *Prisoner's Dilemma: A Study in Conflict and Cooperation*. Ann Arbor, University of Michigan Press, 1965.

Ricciardi, F. M. *Top Managerial Decision Simulation: The AMA Approach*. New York, American Management Association, 1957.

Riley, V., and J. Young. *Bibliography on War Gaming*. Chevy Chase, MD, Operations Research Office, Johns Hopkins University, 1957.

Roth, Alvin E. "On the Early History of Experimental Economics." *Journal of the History of Economic Thought* 15 (1993), 184–209.

Sakaguchi, Minoru. "Reports on Experimental Games." *Statistical Applied Research, Japanese Union of Science Engineers* 7 (1960), 156–165.

Sauermann, Heinz (ed.). (1967–72) *Beitrage zur experimentellen Wirtschaftsforschung* (*Contributions to Experimental Economics*), 3 vols. Tubingen, J. C. B. Mohr (Paul Siebeck), 1967–72.

Sauermann, Heinz (ed.). *Coalition Forming Behaviour*. Tubingen, J. C. B. Mohr (Paul Siebeck), 1978.

Sauermann, Heinz, and Reinhard Selten (1959), "Ein Oligopolexperiment," *Zeitschrift fuer die gesamte Staatswissenschaft* (1959), as trans. "An Experiment in Oligopoly," in *General Systems Yearbook of the Society for General Systems Research* 5 (1960), 85–114.

Schelling, Thomas C. *The Strategy of Conflict*. Cambridge, MA, Harvard University Press, 1960.

Schelling, Thomas C. "Experimental Games and Bargaining Theory." *World Politics* 14 (1961), 47–68.

Scodel, Alvin, J. Sayer Minas, Philburn Ratoosh, and Milton Lipetz. "Some Descriptive Aspects of Two-Person Non-Zero-Sum Games I." *Journal of Conflict Resolution* 3 (1959), 114–119, as reprinted in Dimand and Dimand (1997), III, 233–238.

Shubik, Martin. *Strategy and Market Structure*. New York, John Wiley & Son, 1959.

Shubik, Martin. "Some Experimental Non-Zero-Sum Games With Lack of Information About the Rules." *Management Science* 8 (1962), 215–234.

Shubik, Martin, and Richard Levitan. *Market Structure and Behavior*. Cambridge, MA, Harvard University Press, 1980.

Siegel, Sidney. "Theoretical Models of Choice and Strategy Behavior: Stable State Behavior in the Two-Choice Uncertain Outcome Situation." *Psychometrika* 24 (1959), 303–316, as reprinted in Dimand and Dimand 1997, III, 492–505.

Siegel, Sidney, and Lawrence E. Fouraker. *Bargaining and Group Decision Making*. New York, McGraw-Hill, 1960.

Siegel, Sidney, and D. A. Goldstein. "Decision-Making Behavior in a Two-Choice Uncertain Outcome Situation." *Journal of Experimental Psychology* 57 (1959), 37–42.

Siegel, Sidney, Alberta E. Siegel, and J. M. Andrews (1964) *Choice, Strategy, and Utility*. New York, McGraw-Hill, 1964.

Simon, Herbert A. "A Comparison of Game Theory and Learning Theory." *Psychometrika* 21 (1956), 267–272, as reprinted in Dimand and Dimand 1997, III, 486–491.

Smith, Vernon L. "An Experimental Study of Competitive Market Behavior." *Journal of Political Economy* 70 (1962), 111–137.

Smith, Vernon L. "Experimental Auction Games and the Walrasian Hypothesis." *Journal of Political Economy* 73 (1965), 387–393.

Smith, Vernon L. "Game Theory and Experimental Economics: Beginnings and Early Influences." In E. Roy Weintraub (ed.), *Toward a History of Game Theory*, annual supplement to *History of Political Economy* 24 (1992), Durham, NC, Duke University Press, 241–282.

Stone, Jeremy J. "An Experiment in Bargaining Games." *Econometrica* 26 (1958), 286–296, as reprinted in Dimand and Dimand (1997), III, 222–232.

Thrall, R. M., C. H. Coombs, and R. L. Davis (eds). *Decision Processes*. New York, John Wiley, 1954.

Thurstone, L. L. "The Indifference Function." *Journal of Social Psychology* 2 (1931), 139–167.

Von Neumann, John, and Oskar Morgenstern. *Theory of Games and Economic Behavior*. Princeton, Princeton University Press, 1944.

Wallis, W. Allen, and Milton Friedman. "The Empirical Derivation of Indifference Functions." In O. Lange, F. McIntyre and T. O. Yntema (eds), *Studies in Math-*

ematical Economics and Econometrics in Memory of Henry Schultz. Chicago, University of Chicago Press, 1942.

Young, J. *A Survey of Historical Developments in War Games*. Washington, DC: Office of the Chief of Military History, MS P- 094, 1952, reissued as Staff Paper ORO-SP-98, Operations Research Office, Johns Hopkins University, March 1959.

2 The Allais Paradox and its immediate consequences for expected utility theory

Sophie Jallais and Pierre-Charles Pradier

2.1 Introduction

The Allais Paradox, which nobody knew of 30 years ago, has become a cornerstone of both decision theory and experimental economics. Moreover, it earned its inventor the Nobel Prize and a degree of fame much greater than that afforded by his theoretical work. To the extent that it lay at the heart of the experiment initiated during the 1952 Paris Conference, the Allais Paradox can be said to have grounded modern decision theory in experimental practice, and may be acknowledged as marking the birth of a discipline. Before 1952, decision theory (from Pascal to Ramsey) implied an *a priori* approach, and was thus part of mathematics; it might even have been confused with probability theory.[1] After Allais' experiment, it was no longer possible to think entirely *a priori*, without regard for experimental feedback. The new field of study attracted many new people. From the 1970s onwards, countless papers were devoted to testing expected utility theory (hereafter EUT). Alternative decision theories were developed, numerous journals were founded to support the effort, and myriad researchers joined the quest for a decision theory that was descriptively adequate – and, as Kahneman, Slovic and Tversky would have added, *normatively unassailable*.

This account of the historical significance of the Allais Paradox may seem somewhat exaggerated insofar as it neglects the role of, among others, American psychologists, such as Edwards, Coombs and Nogee (along with Mosteller who was a statistician).[2] Nonetheless, the fact remains that Allais was one of the first to do something. The question is thus: what did he really do in 1952? In 1979, Allais edited *Expected Utility Hypotheses and the Allais Paradox*, an entire book dedicated to the 1952 experiment and its consequences. However, upon reading this book, one is struck by the fact that the schedule of events is somewhat blurred. In order to shed some light on the matter, therefore, we met with some of the participants of the conference. Notwithstanding the fact that these participants mistrusted their memories of events occurring over 50 years ago, their testimonies constitute precious evidence. We also benefited from the papers collected by Georges Guilbaud during these years.[3] We thus had the opportunity to trace the development of Allais' thought from the very first drafts of 1950 to the last 1955 paper. It appeared to us that this context greatly helped in understanding the process which led Allais to oppose EUT the way he did. This story is at the heart of the essay (section 2.3). We try, in particular, to distinguish between the *Paradox* and the *1952 experiment*.

It would have been tempting to review the consequences of the Paradox, but this would have led us far from our subject, for most of the consequences of Allais' work in decision theory followed *Expected Utility Hypotheses and the Allais Paradox* (1979). They involved replications of the original experiment, with some follow-ups adding different evidence, and were thus probably very indirect consequences of the original 1952 experiment. In our historical account of the Allais experiment of 1952, therefore, we focus on its immediate consequences. These constitute the main subject of section 2.4.

In particular, we consider a luncheon with Allais and Savage, where the American was confronted with a bitter discovery. It seems that the immediate impact of the Allais Paradox was felt by Savage, in relation to the interpretation of his own theory, and resulted in his moving from a positive interpretation of EUT to a "normative" one. The meaning of this adjective will be made more precise in the following, as it is related to Allais' exposition of his paradox. This will allow us to discuss the meanings of these adjectives in decision theory, as well as the location of the frontier between their relative fields. We hope that this work will help the reader to deal with "the subtlety and complexity of the normative/descriptive interface",[4] emphasized by Slovic in relation to rationality. We begin in section 2.2 with the interpretation of the theory before Allais entered the scene.

2.2 Interpretations of EUT by American authors before 1952

In 1952, as today, EUT stated that choice among risky prospects can be represented as a comparison between the mean utility of each prospect.[5] Given a utility function $u(.)$ (defined up to a linear transformation) the value index of any[6] lottery $f=(p_1, f_1, \ldots, p_i, f_i, \ldots, p_n, f_n)$ (giving prize f_i with probability p_i) is thus:

$$\mathrm{EU}(f)=\sum_{i=1}^{n} p_i . u(W+f_i),$$

where W stands for the initial wealth of the decision-maker to which the random variable f is added. This being a generalization of a formula by Daniel Bernoulli (which appeared in Bernoulli 1731 with a log function in place of $u(.)$), Allais has called it "the neo-Bernoullian formulation" of EUT (Allais 1952d: 78).

It should be noted that, in contrast to Bernoulli's theory, EUT is an axiomatized construction. In 1952, there existed several axiom sets imposing restrictions on preferences, each of which could lead to the same decision functional (see, for example, von Neumann and Morgenstern 1944; Friedman and Savage 1948; Marschak 1950; Friedman and Savage 1952). It is not our task here to review these axiomatizations, as this has been done elsewhere (see, for example, McClennen 1990; Fishburn and Wakker 1995). In particular, we shall set aside the rather "technical" axioms (such as continuity), to stress the importance of only the so-called "independence" condition. This axiom is somewhat tricky. Missing in von Neumann and Morgenstern's original work, many times reformulated (cf., for instance, the *sure-thing principle* of Savage 1954), it has most recently been examined by Fishburn and Wakker 1995.[7] The reason why we mention this crucial axiom is that it implies linearity in probability of the preference functional, a restriction that was attacked by later critics.

Before the 1952 Paris Conference, several interpretations of EUT were maintained in the United States. For example, Marschak (1951) interpreted it as a prescriptive theory, that is, a theory that tells individuals how they ought to behave. For his part, Samuelson writes that "the new significance of the Bernoulli theory to me is of an aesthetic and semantic character" (Samuelson 1952a, p. 128, p. 130). But most of the prominent American contributors to decision theory (Friedman, Morgenstern, von Neumann, Savage, etc.) presented EUT as a positive theory, that is, a conjecture about actual behaviour.

The first to present EUT as positive were von Neumann and Morgenstern, who revived this field of study. More precisely, these authors claimed an empirical content for the concept of utility they used through an analogy with physics and the subsequent possibility of this concept's being invalidated by empirical evidence[8, 9]:

> It is sometimes claimed in economic literature that discussions of the notions of utility and preferences are altogether unnecessary, since these are purely verbal definitions with no empirical observable consequences, i.e., entirely tautological. It does not seem to us that these notions are qualitatively inferior to certain well established and indispensable notions in physics, like force, mass, charge, etc. That is, while they are in their immediate form merely definitions, they become subject to empirical control through the theories which are built upon them – and in no other way. Thus the notion of utility is raised above the status of a tautology by such economic theories as make use of it and the result of which can be compared with experience or at least with common sense.
>
> (von Neumann and Morgenstern 1944, pp. 8–9)

It would seem then that the von Neumann and Morgenstern utility theory (as presented in Chapter I of the *Theory of Games and Economic Behavior*) can be interpreted as a conjecture about actual or observable choice involving risk.[10]

Friedman and Savage were more explicit, and prolific, on the subject. In their 1948 and 1952 papers, they assert that EUT allows for the rationalization (Friedman and Savage 1948, p. 279, p. 282, p. 287), explanation (p. 279), description (p. 297) and even prediction (Friedman and Savage 1952, pp. 464–465) of actual choices among alternatives involving risk. The only "decisive test" of the theory's validity, they argue, is comparison of its consequences or predictions with observation: "It should be accepted ... if it leads to 'correct' predictions usually or more frequently than any equally useful alternative; it should be rejected if its predictions are generally contradicted by observation" (Friedman and Savage 1952, p. 473).

This methodological stance comes from both Friedman's flirtation with falsificationism in the early 1950s and Friedman and Savage's overconfidence in their "promising conjecture" (Friedman and Savage 1952, p. 466).[11] Such confidence was partly derived from direct evidence or "direct survival of 'critical' experiments" (Friedman and Savage 1952, p. 466).[12] But, such tests being rare, confidence derives mostly from what the authors call "indirect evidence" (Friedman and Savage 1952, p. 466). The idea is that the axioms (or postulates) are "convincing", and so, according to Friedman and Savage, EUT will in general fail to be refuted by experiment. For instance, after a thorough exposition of their third postulate, the so-called "independence axiom", Friedman and Savage conclude:

> We anticipate that if the reader considers the principle ..., he will concede that the principle is not one he would deliberately violate. This in turn *we consider to be some reason for supposing that people do actually tend to avoid flagrant violation of the principle.*
>
> (1952, p. 469; emphasis added)

2.3 The 1952 Paris conference and the Allais experiment

2.3.1 Allais and the "French marginalist school" in the 1950s[13]

In the usual accounts of the Paris 1952 conference, it seems that Allais stood alone against what he called the *American school.*[14] However, it would be easy to cite several less well-known names to show that Allais was neither the only Frenchman to pay attention to EUT, nor the only one to interpret this theory in a prescriptive sense, nor the only one to think of alternative theories, nor the only one to design counterexamples.

First of all, EUT was important to French economists before 1950. According to the evidence collected by Guilbaud, who attended the seminars of Allais, Darmois and Roy (the only three research seminars in mathematical economics in France by this time), no less than 16 sessions of research seminars were devoted to the discussion of EUT between 1949 and 1952.[15] It seems that the interest in decision theory emanated mainly from Pierre Massé's trailblazing work in the early 1940s. As chief engineer in an electricity company, Massé (1898–1987) designed decision rules for both water reserves management and investment selection (see, for example, Massé 1944, 1946 and 1964). It is well known among the French that Massé independently discovered the "principle of optimality" of dynamic programming, or "principle of Pontryagin" (see Dreze 1964, p. 5 or Boiteux 1993, p. 95). When *Electricité de France* (EDF) was created in 1946, Massé was appointed engineering director and shortly thereafter, president.[16] Later (in 1958), he became the charismatic head of the French planning authority (*Commissaire Général du Plan*). Massé was thus at the heart and soul of both the French planning system *and* the research community in mathematical economics.[17] It must be emphasized here that the Plan had a didactical role as it was directed towards not only macroeconomic equilibrium but also the modernization of management. Decision theory was part of this effort to modernize France. Henceforth, the story of decision theory expresses a typically French trait: the economists were high-ranking civil servants who considered it their duty to enlighten the masses of less-educated economic practitioners.[18] The ideas developed in research seminars were broadcast by the planning authority (Carré *et al.* 1973, p. 246) and by the CNRS (the 1954 papers by Guilbaud and Massé resulted from public lectures published in a single CNRS volume). We shall now introduce the other French authors who (together with Massé and Allais) contributed to the development of decision theory, and try to characterize their attitude toward EUT.

By the time of the Paris conference, French authors were divided among two groups: the engineer-economists around Allais, and the mathematicians with the *Institut de Statistique de l'Université de Paris* (ISUP). Among the former, Massé's research was quickly backed by Allais and his students at the *Ecole Nationale Supérieure des Mines de Paris* (ENSMP), among whom were Marcel Boiteux (1922–), Gerard Debreu (1920–2004), Edmond Malinvaud (1923–) and Jacques Lesourne (1928–). Some high-ranking civil servants also attended the Allais research seminar.[19] On the other hand, Georges Darmois (1888–1960), director of the ISUP, attracted Georges Guilbaud (1912–) and Georges Morlat (1926–), together with Jean Ville (1910–1989) and Germain Kreweras (1916–1998), whose names are well-known among mathematicians. Guilbaud played a central role in the diffusion of applied mathematics, especially operations research.[20] Moreover, he was the instigator of the 1952 Paris conference. As for Morlat, although he is relatively unknown in the academic world, because he never appeared in any organization chart, in the 1960s, he became both the informal head of economic research with EDF and successor to

Darmois at the Sorbonne. It should be emphasized that these subpopulations of French decision theorists were somewhat intermingled: Guilbaud attended both the Allais and the Darmois seminars,[21] Allais was involved in the creation of the SOFRO, and Massé himself hired Morlat, an ISUP old boy, at the EDF, and so on.

Why then distinguish between engineer-economists and mathematicians, if both of them were so interested in decision theory as to organize a meeting on the subject? To put it simply, there was a real divergence as regards EUT. The mathematicians of the ISUP were in favour of it (with some provisos), while the engineers around Allais were opposed to it,[22] and there is much evidence of criticism of EUT in Allais' seminar. Allais himself presented a paper at the Paris conference (Allais 1952a, which became with some *addenda* the *Econometrica* paper) which summarized the work done in seminar. At the very same conference, Massé and Morlat (1952) put forward an axiomatization of choice which seemed to be a synthesis of Massé's 1944 and 1953 (written in 1951) works. These theories of choice shared their basic postulates (consistency of choice, "absolute preference" which amounted to first-degree stochastic dominance), and both criticized EUT for the too-strong "independence" assumption. These "French" theories of choice accounted for behaviour that contradicted EUT.[23]

It must be made clear that even the French supporters of EUT (to whom we may add de Finetti) agreed *only* on a *prescriptive* interpretation of EUT, which, they thought, lacked empirical support.[24] Much evidence is given in the seminars held before the 1952 conference, which was organized jointly by Allais and Guilbaud. The only role of decision theory was to choose decision rules for the managers of the public sector.[25] Therefore, it seems clear that Allais shared with his fellow French mathematical economists an interpretation of decision theory in general that was not positive.[26]

Another feature of the French attitude towards EUT is expressed in *counterexamples*: pairs of choices designed to ensure that a decision-maker will violate EUT. While what is now called *the Allais Paradox*, to be reviewed below, is probably the best known of such counterexamples, Allais was not alone in this regard. Savage claimed that "Another interesting example was presented *somewhat earlier* by Georges Morlat" (Savage 1954, p. 101).[27] According to Guilbaud,[28] a key witness of the conference, designing such counterexamples was a common occupation among the French during the Paris conference (and this may be further evidence of intense preparation in the many seminar sessions devoted to EUT), although there is no other example besides that given by Savage and MacCrimmon.

If most French decision theorists shared Allais' interpretation of decision theory, and some of them his dissatisfaction with EUT and taste for counterexamples, what then distinguished Allais? One might be tempted to think of Allais' theoretical works, but this would take us away from decision theory. From the end of the 1940s, Allais showed a peculiar interest in the empirical testing of theory. In his 1949 "paper" (which is, in fact, a middle-sized book) on the management of state-run coal mines, Allais offered an appendix dealing with the "objective criterion for efficient management" (Allais 1949–1953, pp. 107–112, our translation). Allais sought to infer from existing statistics a test of whether every civil servant was an efficient manager.[29] What is interesting in the test is not its object (which did not involve uncertainty) but the construction of the sample population: *only trained decision-makers* were surveyed, not ordinary people as had been done before (such as in Mosteller-Nogee 1951). That the survey showed inefficiency of the French civil servants is of no importance for our purpose, but the idea of *experimenting among a selected population* was a key feature, because it eventually brought Allais the fame his masterworks did not give him.[30]

2.3.2 The Allais experiment: the Allais Paradox and the questionnaire

What the literature commonly considers as Allais' *first* contribution to decision theory, although we have seen it was backed and anticipated by others, is the "Allais Paradox". This well-known pair of choices:

1° Do you prefer situation A to B?

Situation A
- certainty of receiving 100 million

Situation B
- a 10 per cent chance of winning 500 million
- an 89 per cent chance of winning 100 million
- a 1 per cent chance of winning nothing

2° Do you prefer C to D?

Situation C
- an 11 per cent chance of winning 100 million
- an 89 per cent chance of winning nothing

Situation D
- a 10 per cent chance of winning 500 million
- a 90 per cent chance of winning nothing

induces approximately 45 per cent of the respondents to violate EUT.[31] This 45 per cent rate seems stable and the original Allais results have been replicated by (among others) MacCrimmon 1968, Slovic and Tversky 1974 and MacCrimmon and Larsson 1975 (Allais 1979, pp. 636–637, n. 15). As we present it, the counterexample in itself is not really new, but the idea of submitting *the economists* to such questions in a matter of inquiry was

Allais' specific idea. The question is when and how Allais set his experiment up.

The Allais Paradox appears in print in Allais (1953, p. 527) with this introductory note:

> A first draft of this paper has been given in a more general study called "theoretical notes on future uncertainty and risk" which was presented at the European Econometric Congress in September 1951. A second draft was presented as a communication at the International Colloquium on risk which happened in Paris in 1952.
>
> (Allais 1953, p. 503, n. 1)[32]

This excerpt suggests that the Paradox was presented in public twice before its publication: once at Louvain in September 1951 and a second time in Paris in May 1952. The subsequent literature suggests that this presentation took place during the second of these conferences (see, e.g., Munier 1984 or Camerer 1995). As we shall see, these authors do not give an entirely exact account of the Allais experiment, not because the Paradox had been presented before but because, on the contrary, it seems that it was not presented to the general public at all at either of these conferences, but only to Savage, during a lunch-break at the second conference. This allows us to make a distinction between the Allais Paradox itself and the related experiments, and to give a clear historical account of the latter.

It must first be pointed out that what we currently call the Allais Paradox appeared for the first time in papers written *after* the conference and published in 1953.[33] It is not mentioned in any of the hectographed notes in the Guilbaud papers prior to this date. And there is no mention of it either in Allais' interventions at the conference (Allais 1952a, 1952b) nor in any of the records of the public discussions which took place (CNRS 1953). Boiteux, who was present at both conferences, and participated with a paper of his own, tells us that he only came across the Paradox later on, more precisely when he received a questionnaire from Allais.[34] All this suggests that the Paradox had not been presented to the public at the Louvain conference either, a point stressed by Malinvaud.[35] We were unable to find the paper referred to by Allais as "Notes théoriques sur l'incertitude de l'avenir et le risque". Allais' contribution is the only one reported neither by an abstract nor by the records of a discussion in "Report of the Louvain Meeting" which appeared in *Econometrica* in 1952. It is difficult then to state categorically that the Paradox was not presented to the public at this meeting. Let us point out, nevertheless (and this concurs with what Boiteux and Malinvaud say), that what is presented as the partial English translation of this text (in Allais and Hagen 1979) does not contain the Paradox. If the famous Paradox is not mentioned in the abstract published in this work dedicated to *Expected Utility Theory and the Allais Paradox*, it is probable that one cannot find it in the rest of the "Notes".

Even if no evidence of the Allais Paradox is to be found in Allais' published work before late 1952, one can nevertheless guess that the Paradox was ready by the time of the conference. However, one must read between the lines to find evidence of this. First, Allais states: "I had Savage respond over lunch to a list of some 20 questions. His answer to each was incompatible with the basic axioms of the theory" (Allais 1979, p. 533).[36] Then, Savage acknowledged that he was faced with the Paradox during a lunch – presumably the same.[37] All of this suggests that Allais presented his Paradox *while* the Paris conference was taking place (that is, before Allais 1952c or 1952d), but to Savage *alone*, and not during one of the public sessions.

This point was never made clear, and many of those who attended the conference often confuse the schedule of the conference itself with the subsequent work immediately undertaken by Allais.

After the conference and the lunchtime "trap", Allais decided to extend the testing of conformity to EUT. As he could not proceed from existing data, he designed a questionnaire which was to become famous. This questionnaire seems to have been ready by June 1952 (Allais 1979, p. 557, n. 17), and sent during the summer to the respondents, among whom there were many participants of the Paris conference (Allais 1955, p. 54).[38] Only a small sample was processed by the time of Allais 1952c, and no more until Allais 1974.[39] From the final processing of the questionnaire, Allais concluded that "no subject acts according to the neo-Bernoullian principle in respect to all the series of questions" (Allais 1979, p. 452).

Actually, Arrow, Baumol, Friedman, Marschak and Savage successfully passed the questionnaire (Allais 1979, p. 560, n. 48), some of them because "they determined their answers using the neo-Bernoullian formulation", according to a utility function they chose *a priori*.[40] Morgenstern and Samuelson did not answer the questionnaire (Allais and Hagen 1979, p. 685). Among leading members of the so-called *American school*, only Malinvaud, de Finetti and Shackle fell into the trap![41] However, they were not trapped by the Allais Paradox (Allais 1979, p. 636, n. 15), but by questions involving the calculation of certainty equivalents (Allais 1979, p. 588, n. 258; see also pp. 628–631).

Thus, the "1952 experiment" can be summed up as a personal defeat for the lone (and late) Leonard Jimmie Savage during a luncheon (many authors thus criticized the questionable nature of this experiment: see, e.g., Allais 1979, pp. 541–543 for references, and see also Rizvi in this volume for a general criticism of experiments); the other Americans were not trapped by the later questionnaire.

2.4 The normative retreat

After 1952, EUT was progressively presented by everyone who remained involved with this subject matter as a prescriptive theory, though the positive interpretation did not completely disappear. More precisely, amongst those who presented the theory as a positive one, before the Paris conference, von Neumann and Friedman remained silent on the subject, while Savage and Morgenstern changed their way of introducing the theory.[42] We will focus our attention on Savage, for he immediately reacted to Allais' criticism, during his stay in Paris, and then in *The Foundations of Statistics* (1954). Furthermore, since Morgenstern did not publish on this subject until the 1970s (Morgenstern 1972[43] and 1974), it is difficult to think of his later papers as being stimulated by the Allais Paradox, even if, as we shall see, they show noticeable similarities to Savage's writings.

2.4.1 The Allais Paradox and the fading out of the Savagian positive interpretation of EUT

After 1954, Savage no longer held that his theory was scientific because of its refutability, nor did he still believe that the theory was able to withstand empirical testing. Two years after the Paris meeting with Allais, Savage no longer presented EUT as "the promising conjecture" that would probably "fail to be contradicted" (Friedman and Savage 1952, p. 466). As a positive theory, it had been refuted by his own responses to Allais' questions; as a positive theory, it could now at best be a "crude and shallow" one (Savage 1954, p. 20), a theory that "makes factual predictions many of which can easily be observed to be false" (Savage 1954, p. 97).

Thus, from the beginning of his *Foundations of Statistics*, Savage does not present his postulates as ones relevant for actual behaviour but rather as "postulates for rational behavior": "I am, he states, about to build up a highly idealized theory of the behavior of a 'rational' person with respect to decision" (p. 7). Savage does not make any ambiguous statements: rational behaviour cannot be considered as a good approximation of actual behaviour of individuals in choosing among alternatives involving uncertainty. The aim of the theory is no longer to explain actual decisions but rather to guide them: his postulates are presented as rational "maxims of behavior" (p. 7). For Savage, the theory is now unambiguously prescriptive. Henceforth, Savage offers two possible interpretations for his postulates, a positive – or "empirical" – one, and another he calls "normative":

> Two very different sorts of interpretations can be made of P1 and the other postulates to be adduced later. First, P1 can be regarded as a prediction about the behavior of people, or animals, in decision situations. Second, it can be regarded as a logic-like criterion of consis-

> tency in decision situations. *For us, the second interpretation is the only one of direct relevance*, but it may be fruitful to discuss both, calling the first **empirical** and the second **normative**.
>
> (Savage 1954, p. 19, emphasis added)[44]

Eighty pages later, he again brings up the same idea and alludes to his change of mind. He does not clearly mention his own previous opinion, but cites von Neumann and Morgenstern 1944: "One idea *now* held by me that I think von Neumann and Morgenstern do not explicitly support, and that so far as I know they might not wish to have attributed to them, is the normative interpretation of the theory" (Savage 1954, p. 97, emphasis added). But since Savage doesn't clearly admit it himself, why do we suppose that it was the Allais Paradox that forced him to change his mind? First of all, *The Foundations of Statistics* was not written in a couple of weeks: Samuelson refers to its imminent publication as early as 1952, in a paper written right after the Paris colloquium.[45] Secondly, Savage's last paper with Friedman, in which he speaks of his theory as positive, was written just before the Paris meeting, which shows that Savage had not yet changed his mind. One can, of course, argue that the epistemology in the 1952 paper was Friedman's only (the same statements were to be found again a year later in his *Essays in Positive Economics*). But Marschak recalls an interesting anecdote that confirms that, at the beginning of the Paris meeting, Savage still thought of the theory as (mainly) positive:

> On a May day in 1952, between sessions of the International Colloquium on Risk, Professor Allais drove his luncheon guests to the Racing Club de France on the outskirts of Paris. The guests – Ragnar Frisch, L. J. Savage and myself – alighted from his car. Maurice Allais maneuvered to park it, got out, and began to cross the road hurriedly, causing the driver of an oncoming car to brake sharply. Allais just avoided being hit. Instantly, Savage snapped his fingers and exclaimed, "Bob Thrall should be there!" For our host's actions contradicted the lexicographical preference ordering that Professor Thrall had defended in the morning session and that would, of course, rank "surviving but letting one's guests wait one more minute" ahead of the smallest chance of being run over.
>
> Savage was thus arguing from observed behavior. Yet his *Foundations of Statistics* published two years later profess to be mainly normative, prescriptive – not descriptive.
>
> (Marschak 1979, p. 163)

Our conclusion is that Savage changed his mind sometime between his lunch with Allais and the completion of the manuscript of *The Foundations of Statistics*.

What then, if not the Allais Paradox, could have triggered this change?

Is it not precisely the beginning of this move that Allais reports 27 years later in the following passage?

> During the 1952 Paris Colloquium, I had Savage respond over lunch to a list of some 20 questions. His answers to each was incompatible with the basic axioms of his own theory. He was immediately troubled, and asked for time to think. A week later he told me that his reactions during our lunch conversation had indeed run counter to his own axioms, but that after further reflection, he had concluded that his responses, contrary to his axioms, were explained by the fact that he had behaved irrationally.
>
> (Allais 1979, p. 533)[46]

One can read these sentences as an early enunciation of the Savagian interpretation of EUT as a *theory of rational behaviour*, but the specific meaning Savage gave to this expression partly results from the framework where Allais inserted his Paradox, when he offered it to a public readership for the first time (in Allais 1952d and in 1953).[47] It is thus necessary to recall this framework of Allais (1952d, 1953) in order to, firstly, understand why Savage could not be satisfied – and he was not – with presenting his theory only as a theory of rational behaviour, and, secondly, explain what Savage meant by "normative".

2.4.2 The Allais Paradox: an experimental refutation of a theory of rational behaviour

The Allais Paradox as presented, for instance, in Allais 1952d (or in 1953) is in fact (and somewhat surprisingly) *a test of* EUT as a maxim for rational behaviour. More precisely, it is a part of a more general "criticism of the neo-Bernoullian formulation EUT as a behavioural rule for a *rational* man" (Allais 1952d, p. 74, emphasis added). Let us here recall this criticism.

In order to cast doubt on "the validity of the neo-Bernoullian formulation for a rational man" (Allais 1952d, p. 76), Allais first calls on the neo-Bernoullians to show in which way their theory stands for rational behaviour. From his point of view, it is not satisfying to define rationality in terms of obedience of the neo-Bernoullian axiomatics, for this leads to circular reasoning. The theory is a maxim for rational conduct *because* rational conduct is defined as conduct in agreement with the theory. As he puts it :

> The neo-Bernoullian formulation is in fact rigorously equivalent to anyone of these systems of axioms, the systems of axioms or postulates from which the neo-Bernoullian formulation is derived, and there is *no interest at all* in discussing the view that a rational man

> should behave according to the neo-Bernoullian formulation when rationality is itself defined in terms of obedience to one of the systems of axioms from which that principle is deduced. This is a tautological position, and therefore useless scientifically.
>
> (Allais 1952d, p. 78)

In order to contend that EUT is a theory of rational behaviour, one must have a definition of rationality independent of the theory itself.

Allais then proposes two definitions of rationality – an "abstract definition of rationality" and an "experimental definition of rationality" – against which EUT will be gauged (Allais 1952d), and which will be used to deny that EUT is a theory of rational behaviour.

According to Allais' first definition, rationality is synonymous with consistency; mutual consistency of ends, on the one hand, and consistency of ends and means, on the other (Allais 1952d, p. 78).[48] Allais uses this definition to show that some choices can be simultaneously rational and incompatible with EUT ("rationality in no way implies the neo-Bernoullian formulation", Allais 1952d, p. 82). For the neo-Bernoullian theory is more restrictive than the conditions one could abstractly assign to rational behaviour. In particular, Savage's independence axiom does not allow certain choices that could nevertheless be deemed rational according to Allais' abstract definition.[49] Hence one can not think of this theory as a theory of rational behaviour. Allais understands that this refutation may seem insufficient, that one may not want to rely on such an abstract definition of rationality (in Allais 1952d, p. 79, § 53). So he designates another type of refutation using what he calls "an experimental definition of rationality".

According to this definition, the individuals "*whom one has reason in other respects to believe act rationally*" (Allais 1952d, p. 79) or, in other words, "who are commonly considered as rational" (Allais 1952d, p. 80) are said to behave rationally. Starting with this definition, Allais uses his paradox as a way of confounding allegedly "rational" individuals (such as Savage), or more precisely of inducing them to make choices that are clearly incompatible with EUT (see, for example, Allais 1952d, pp. 86–95). Let us see how Allais himself introduces his Paradox:

> Under Savage's fifth axiom, the order of preference of two random prospects ... having a part in common is left unchanged by any displacement of this part. This can be called the independence principle...
>
> It is easy to build up many examples in which the answer given by reputedly rational people would run counter to Savage's fundamental axiom. One need only, as a general rule, choose extreme cases in which the advantages (or drawbacks) of complementarity[50] may be particularly strong. This is particularly true of the choice between

> certain and uncertain gains whose value is high with comparison with the player's fortune. It is easy here to show the considerable psychological importance attaching to the advantage of certainty as such.
>
> (Allais 1952d, p. 88)

From all this, Allais concludes: "What one finds, however, is that the pattern for most highly prudent persons ... who are considered generally as rational, is the pairing A>B and C<D. This contradicts Savage's independence axiom" (Allais 1952d, p. 89).

It must be emphasized that the refutation at hand is not really backed by an experimental definition; rather, it seems grounded on reasoning of the following kind:

1 Some "*facts indicated by experience*" (Allais 1952d, p. 86) show that some individuals "who are commonly considered as rational" do not conform to EUT prescription; it is the case of those who make the "Allaisian" choice of A and D (see note 31).
2 There is no reason to think that these individuals acted irrationally in this special case, because, on the one hand, no satisfactory abstract definition of rationality allows us to do so, and, on the other hand, these individuals have some good reasons to act as they did: "*nobody could say that persons acting this way are behaving irrationally* because they attach a high value to certainty, but, where the outcome is far from certain, weigh psychological values by their probabilities. If somebody does wish to argue the contrary, it would be quite fascinating to hear his grounds!" (Allais 1952d, p. 92).
3 Thus one cannot think of EUT as a theory of rational behaviour.

From here on, if Savage were to bring back the subject, arguing his first choice was irrational, he would be obliged to explain why he acted irrationally.

Hence, the Allais Paradox, as well as the reasoning it stems from, was given a particular role by Allais: it was intended to drive the EUT supporters either to give a new definition of rationality, different from the three ones we have already recalled, or to lay down their weapons and acknowledge defeat.

2.4.3 The "more subtle" Savagian "normativity"

By 1954, Savage had become fully acquainted with Allais' argument.[51] He fully understood Allais' criticism of the neo-Bernoullian theory, not only as a positive theory, but also as a theory for rational behaviour (see Savage 1954, pp. 101–102).

Thus, when Savage came to the question of what he calls the "normative" status of the theory, he seemed on the verge of giving an abstract definition (Savage 1954, p. 19), but he didn't follow this line of reasoning. For he knew that there is a gap between logic and preferences. He knew this "important sense in which preferences", even preferences of "rational" individuals like him, who had chosen gambles A and D, "cannot be in error" (Savage 1954, p. 103). But he knew too, having read Allais, that if he was to find any experimental definition of rationality, he would have to find one different from that of Allais, "a more subtle sense" (Savage 1954, p. 103) in which preferences could be "in error".

This "more subtle sense" was suggested to him by his own experience. For if he fell into Allais' trap, he also acknowledged his error. Modern utility theory is therefore "normative", not because it describes the behaviour of rational individuals, but because, *when individuals act so as to violate it, if the theory is thoroughly explained to them, they acknowledge their error.* Thus, taking the example of the Allais Paradox, Savage (1954, p. 103) presents a way of looking at the two situations that anyone should accept:

> One way in which Gambles A–D could be realized is by a lottery with a hundred numbered tickets and with prizes according to the schedule shown in Table 1.

Table 1 Prizes in units of $100,000 in a lottery realizing gambles 1–4

	Ticket number		
	1	*2–11*	*12–100*
Situation 1	5	5	5
{Gamble 1, Gamble 2	0	25	5
Situation 2	5	5	0
{Gamble 3, Gamble 4	0	25	0

> Now, if one of the tickets numbered from 12 through 100 is drawn, it will not matter, in either situation, which gamble I choose. I therefore focus on the possibility that one of the tickets numbered 1–11 will be drawn, in which case Situations 1 and 2 are exactly parallel. The subsidiary decision depends in both situations on whether I would sell have an outright gift of $500,000 for a 10-to-1 chance to win $2,500,000 – a conclusion that I think a claim to universality, or objectivity.
> (a) If I prefer the gift of $1,000,000. I should choose Gamble 1 over Gamble 2 and Gamble 3 over Gamble 4.
> (b) If I prefer to gamble for $5,000,000, I should choose Gamble 2 over Gamble 1 and Gamble 4 over Gamble 3.

The theory is then "normative", according to Savage, as long as it is "convincing". We are driven back to the "convincing" theory which seemingly appeared in Friedman and Savage 1952. It must be emphasized that the argument at hand is different: *now, the convincing character of the theory no longer derives from Savage's confidence in a positive theory, it allows rather claiming the relevance of the "normative" interpretation of the theory*, i.e. to suggest it would convince anybody whom it is suitably explained to.

The same point of view was endorsed twenty years later by Morgenstern (in Morgenstern 1972 and 1974). According to him: "That theory, as formulated by the von Neumann and Morgenstern's axioms, is normative in the sense that the theory is 'absolutely convincing' which implies that men will act accordingly. If they deviate from the theory, an explanation of theory and of their deviation will cause them to readjust their behavior" (Morgenstern 1974, p. 180).[52] But Morgenstern's change of mind is not as radical as Savage's. For, even if his vindication of the positive dimension of von Neumann and Morgenstern's 1944 utility theory is no longer absolute, Morgenstern reasserts that this theory "is a concrete theory, even amenable to experiment" (1972, p. 700, n. 2).[53]

2.5 Conclusion

The Allais Paradox can be summed up in three steps and two interpretations:

- A lunch with Savage (during the conference). During this lunch, Allais asked Savage 20 questions including the Paradox, which then appeared to Savage as a refutation of EUT as a theory of actual behaviour.
- The publication of Allais 1952d and 1953, where Allais' argumentation, in which the Paradox played a key role, appeared as a logical and experimental critique of EUT presented as a theory of rational behaviour.
- The experiment itself, that is to say the conception, mailing and processing of a questionnaire featuring no less than 400 questions (and including the Paradox). The whole process lasted from June 1952 to December 1975 (Allais 1979, p. 453).

Eventually, the main, if not the only, impact of the Allais Paradox on EUT immediately after 1952 was on Savage's interpretation of the theory. More precisely, it seems that, after the Paris conference, Savage's change in opinion was concerned more with people than with EUT. For Savage, EUT was as convincing in 1954 as in 1952. In 1954, though, it had become necessary to first explain the theory in order to ensure that people would act accordingly. In 1952, people acted accordingly by themselves, that is, without previous explanation. The Savagian interpretation of EUT was consequently modified: EUT was no longer presented as a positive theory but as a "normative" one. As a matter of fact, the interpretation of EUT found in *The Foundations of Statistics* – and later in Morgenstern 1974 – suggests that the theory is less normative than prescriptive. More precisely, it is a theory of rational conduct, where the adjective "rational" is given a very peculiar meaning. After Allais 1953 (or 1952d), Savage gave what we can call an "experimental" definition of rationality (which obviously differs from that of Allais): individuals to whom it is thoroughly explained will act in accordance to EUT. As a consequence, the theory we find in Savage 1954 (and in Morgenstern 1974) is, contrary to *usual* normative theories, refutable by experiment.[54] Savage himself suggests the adequate procedure: "If after thorough deliberation, anyone maintains a pair of distinct preferences that are in conflict with the sure thing principle, he must abandon, or modify, the principle; for that kind of discrepancy seems intolerable in a normative theory" (Savage 1954, p. 102).[55] Unfortunately, the results of an experiment constructed by Slovic and Tversky in the early 1970s show that the explanations of "Dr S." are less convincing than the ones of "Dr A." (Slovic and Tversky 1974). What a beautiful illustration of the efficiency of the plan set up by Allais to trap the neo-Bernoullian!

Acknowledgements

We are indebted to Philippe Fontaine and Robert Leonard for their patience, work and support throughout the revision process. We are grateful to the ECHE organizers, Marcello Basili, Francesco Guala, Philippe Mongin, David Teira-Serrano, Francisco Vergara and two anonymous referees for their comments and advice. Special mention must be made of Marc Barbut, Marcel Boiteux, Gérard Debreu, Ward Edwards, Georges Guilbaud, Jacques Lesourne, Edmond Malinvaud, Georges Morlat and Paul Slovic, whose patience in answering our questions greatly helped our evocation of these moments. We would also like to thank Rachel Holley for her precious help. Any remaining errors are ours only.

Notes

1 One could also cite Pascal, Daniel Bernoulli, D'alembert, Condorcet, Laplace, Cournot, Bertrand, Borel and others.

2 The role of the psychologists in the early development of experimental economic games is emphasized by the Dimand essay in this volume.

3 From 1947 to 1953, Guilbaud regularly attended not only Allais' seminar at the Institut Poincaré but also Roy's and Darmois' seminars. EUT and game theory were regularly discussed since 1948, when he presented von Neumann and Morgenstern's *Theory of Games and Economic Behavior* at Allais' seminar.

4 P. Slovic, personal communication (1999).

5 Following a plausible and common interpretation of Knight, decision theorists generally use the word "risk" to describe a situation in which objective probabilities are known, and the word "uncertainty" when no objective probabilities are known, in which case it becomes necessary to adopt "subjective"

probabilities (however, see Fontaine 1999 and Pradier and Teira-Serrano 2000 for important qualifications of this interpretation of Knight). This distinction is quite important because axiomatization of uncertain decision leads to axiomatization of the formation of subjective probabilities: this amounts to adding axioms to the case where probabilities are given (see, for example, Arrow's 1965 two-step axiomatization).

6 Reference is given only to discrete lotteries, as mathematical generality is not needed.

7 Von Neumann and Morgenstern's set of axioms appeared in the second edition of their 1944 book. This presentation was puzzling for many authors (see, e.g., Samuelson 1952a, p. 129 of English translation) who alleged the existence of a "zeroth axiom". In fact, there was no zeroth axiom in von Neumann and Morgenstern's work, rather a mathematical oddity that Marschak pointed out as early as 1950, writing that von Neumann and Morgenstern's theorem is stated "in terms of entities not susceptible to ordinary arithmetical operations" (Marschak 1950, p. 136). Fishburn and Wakker 1995 made clear that a problem arises because von Neumann and Morgenstern considered the space of equivalence-classes of lotteries, where all subsequent authors considered the space of lotteries. This peculiar feature of the von Neumann and Morgenstern theory turns out to be so tricky that many authors felt by 1950 the need for new, more explicit, axiom sets.

8 The von Neumann and Morgenstern's axiom set was, of course, first needed on mathematical grounds: "A choice of axioms is not a purely objective task. It is usually expected to achieve some definite aim – some specific theorem or theorems are to be derivable from the axioms – and to this extent the problem is exact and objective." Von Neumann was probably responsible for this formal stance (see Leonard 1995). Nevertheless, these theorems were also intended to represent risky behaviour as we argue.

9 According to the Innocenti and Zappia essay in this volume, von Neumann and Morgenstern 1944 is a turning point in Morgenstern's epistemological stance toward experimentation.

10 It is a fact that the von Neumann and Morgenstern theory explicitly neglects some "psychological influences on choice" (as Allais put it), such as the pleasure of gambling. However, this point can not be turned into an objection to a descriptive interpretation of the von Neumann and Morgenstern theory, for no positive theory gives an exhaustive description of reality. As Nagel puts it: "no finitely long statement can possibly formulate the totality of traits embodied in any concretely existing thing" (1963, p. 214). The von Neumann and Morgenstern attitude in this respect is shared by all alternative positive theories, including that of Allais: the Frenchman suggested neglecting these "psychological influences" "in a first approximation" (1952d [1979], p. 57), allowing for them "at a later stage by making appropriate adjustment" (1952d [1979], p. 47).

11 Although the first point would require further historical-methodological discussion, we will not develop it further (there is some evidence in the Rizvi essay in this volume). We emphasize the other point because, as we shall see later, the nature of Friedman and Savage's confidence (i.e. the interpretation of the "indirect evidence") is what changed after the Allais Paradox.

12 For instance, from "the willingness of persons of all income classes to buy insurance" or from "the willingness of individuals to purchase lottery tickets, or engage in similar forms of gambling" (Friedman and Savage 1948, p. 285, p. 286). Similarly "Some recent experiments by Mosteller and Nogee add to the direct observational evidence and fail to contradict the hypothesis" (Friedman and Savage 1952, p. 466). It should be emphasized that Mosteller and Nogee

made real, controlled experiments, thus providing far more sophisticated evidence than Friedman and Savage's appeal to common-sense observation.

13 The expression "French marginalist school" appears in Dreze 1964 to describe the French mathematical economists. Unless otherwise indicated, the material from this and the following sections is based both on the interviews we had with the witnesses of the 1952 conference, Marcel Boiteux, Georges Guilbaud, Jacques Lesourne, Edmond Malinvaud and Georges Morlat, and on the Guilbaud Papers.

14 This expression is Allais' own invention; Guilbaud (1999, personal communication) and Malinvaud (2000, personal communication) denied any substance to it. As we shall see later, Allais included in his *American school* many European authors such as de Finetti, Guilbaud, Malinvaud, and others born European (Marschak, Morgenstern, von Neumann). Therefore, this expression is only to be used with extreme care.

15 For instance, the 1948 Friedman and Savage paper was discussed in 1949, and Friedman was invited to present it in 1950. The title of the latter communication appears in the Guilbaud Papers as "Friedmann [sic], de Chicago: 'La mesure de l'utilité et les choix comportant un risque'".

16 Massé has thus many connections with Robert Gibrat, who had important statistical interests (see Sutton 1997) and attended the Paris conference.

17 Unfortunately, little of this history has been written. The French Plan is usually introduced as a macroeconomic practice, with little theory associated with it (Dreze 1964); moreover, historians are generally fascinated by macroeconomic aspects of the Plan, overlooking the role of microeconomic theorizing (Lordon 1997).

18 This perspective differs completely from the Planning, Programming and Budgeting Systems (PPBS) which tried to implement corporate-management rules at state level. By the 1950s, state management in France was considered more efficient, mainly because of the use of economic calculus in the tradition of Dupuit, Cournot, etc. One can assess the whole production of these economists by looking at the references in Appendix XI of Allais 1949–1953. Allais wrote here that "...in the field of theoretical studies applied to the management of public utilities, France is now much ahead" (n. 10, p. 118, our translation).

19 According to one directory in the Guilbaud papers, Massé and Desrousseaux (director of mining and steel industry with the ministry of industry) attended the seminar in 1948–49. Dreze thus emphasizes the peculiar nature of the French economists: "Members of the French Marginalist School did and do belong to the staffs of the engineering schools or statistics departments, to the research as well as the executive divisions of the nationalized industries, or to the administration, but not to the staffs of economics departments or economic research institutes" (1964, p. 6). It is worth noting that of these high-ranking civil servants, Hutter (chief engineer with the French railroad company) and Lavaill attended the Paris conference.

20 In 1956, he was the founder of the *Société Française de Recherche Opérationnelle*, SOFRO, and of the *Bureau Universitaire de Recherche Opérationnelle* with the ISUP.

21 To which Dreze 1964 refers as "Guilbaud's".

22 There is an important exception to this statement: Malinvaud quickly (i.e. before the Paris conference) acknowledged EUT. The case of Morlat is more complex: by 1952, he was on Allais and Massé's side (Massé-Morlat 1952), but he "changed sides" shortly thereafter (Morlat 1957) to join his fellow mathematicians at the ISUP.

23 Thus, Friedman attacked these theories for not being amenable to refutation; see Allais 1955, § 44, p. 24.

24 Guilbaud (1999, personal communication) confirmed this interpretation. As an example of statements from the period: "However, some psychological tests, some market observations and personal experience seemed to poorly match the absolutely general value of the theory as descriptive theory, of course" (Massé and Morlat in CNRS 1953, p. 163, our translation; see also Massé 1953). Guilbaud (1954, p. Guilbaud/I-1, written in 1951) added: "The aim of what we call 'theory of games', after Borel and von Neumann, is to prescribe rules for human action" (our translation).

25 See for instance Allais 1949, Hutter 1950, Boiteux 1956 or Boiteux 1948, Lesourne 1958, Morlat-Bessière 1971, which are directly connected with risky decision (and were, with the exception of some applied papers in Morlat-Bessière with no theoretical aim, at least partially written in 1952).

26 The title of Allais 1955, calling for a "positive theory" may seem to contradict this statement, and the epistemological stance of Allais may thus seem puzzling. In fact, the 1955 paper must be read carefully, keeping in mind the general epistemological stance of the French engineer-economists devoted to designing management rules (i.e. prescriptive theory). Actually, the "positive theory" of the 1955 paper begins with the consistency assumption (§ 2, p. 10) which is not perfectly *descriptive* (see, for example, Rizvi in this volume), and in what follows, Allais consistently holds a distinction between "real" and "rational" people (see, e.g., § 47, p. 26, § 51, p. 31, § 53, p. 32, § 60, p. 37). One may be surprised by the anti-refutationist declaration of Allais (§ 44, p. 24) which clearly indicates that the theory is not positive in the *ordinary* sense of this adjective. The confusion arises from the ambivalent expression "rational man" – one can be rational according to Allais or according to Savage – which is central to Allais argumentation; see section 2.4.

27 MacCrimmon also noticed the contribution of Morlat and gave a more precise reference (MacCrimmon 1968, p. 23), although there is a misprint in his reference ("pp. 156–67" instead of "156–7").

28 Guilbaud, G.-T., personal communication, 1999.

29 The fact that Allais relied on *existing* statistics may be put forward as a proof that Allais was thinking of *observation* rather than *experimentation*. In fact, Allais designed a test and it is pure luck that he found existing statistics matching the data he needed.

30 About his sample, Allais wrote: "Taking into account the scientific quality of the very great majority of those consulted ... the results are certainly of the *highest* scientific interest" (1979, p. 632).

31 The "Allaisian" choice of A and D contradicts EUT, since (by linearity in probability):

$$A > B \Leftrightarrow U(100) > 0{,}1U(500) + 0{,}89U(100) \Leftrightarrow 0{,}11U(100) > 0{,}1U(500) \Leftrightarrow C > D.$$

32 It must be emphasized that we have found no use of the expression "Allais Paradox" before Allais 1979. Allais himself started to refer to "the so-called Allais Paradox", though it was thus called only by him. In particular, MacCrimmon (1968, p. 9) wrote "the type of this problem has been suggested by Allais", Slovic and Tversky (1974, p. 36) refer to "counterexamples" that "have been proposed by Allais and Ellsberg". Then, the expression "common consequence effect" is sometimes used (after MacCrimmon and Larsson 1975). Finally, under the heading "Allais Paradox" of the indexes in Allais and Hagen 1979 references are only given to Allais' contributions. That is to say, neither Morgenstern 1974 nor MacCrimmon and Larsson 1975 used this expression. It is very surprising that, in November 1999, Guilbaud had never heard of the "Allais Paradox"!

33 Namely Allais 1952c (which contained the questionnaire) and Allais 1952d

which is an annex to the conference volume that was added *later*. See, e.g., Darmois 1952, p. 13:

> Furthermore, even if the work sessions reasonably filled every day, lunches and dinner were also a place for discussion, but the secretaries could not record these events. Mr Allais, using all these observations and suggestions, has done considerable work which, *while not presented at the Conference*, can be thought of as a consequence and addendum. One may find this work of Mr Allais as an appendix to this book.
>
> (our translation, emphasis added)

34 M. Boiteux, personal communication (2000).
35 E. Malinvaud, personal communication (2000).
36 Allais quotes the same text various times. This passage can also be found in Allais (1957, p. 386).
37 Savage gives an account of the lunch discussion in 1954, pp. 102–103, from which it turns out that he made the "Allaisian choice" (A and D), thus contradicting EUT.
38 This questionnaire was composed of 400 questions overall, among which are the questions of the Allais Paradox, and was published in Allais 1952c and Allais 1979.
39 Allais (1979, p. 557, n. 22) recalls that one of his friends said "you kept these results secret for twenty five years!"
40 (Allais 1979, p. 560, n. 48). Apparently, Arrow and Baumol passed the test without choosing an *a priori* utility function. Allais does not go into the details.
41 It must be remembered that the Keynesian Shackle was a declared opponent of the EUT (Shackle 1949a, 1949b).
42 Von Neumann's silence can be explained by the fact that the mathematician, who was at any rate not an economist, was no longer *directly* involved with the subject after 1947: after the second edition of the *Theory of Games and Economic Behavior*, von Neumann did not write any further economics papers – with the exception of a one-and-a-half page communication in 1956, and some very technical contributions to game theory that can be regarded as pure maths (such as, for instance, the editing of *Contributions to the Theory of Games*); see von Neumann 1957. Moreover, EUT, which seemed a minor feature of the *Theory of Games* (so that the derivation of representation theorem from the axioms was not given in the first edition), always remained a minor issue for von Neumann.
43 About the same time as *The Foundations of Statistics* was re-issued by Dover.
44 "P1 The relation $\leq$ is a simple ordering among acts" (Savage 1954, p. 18).
45 (Samuelson 1952b, p. 138). There is also an allusion to the book in Samuelson's paper at the Paris conference; see, e.g., English translation, p. 139, n. 2.
46 One must take notice that Allais' aim is different from ours, because Allais tried to show that Savage "defined rationality by his axioms, and he judged his answers irrational because they infringed the axioms!" (Allais 1979, p. 533).
47 Allais 1952d and 1953b are roughly similar papers; they were both published in 1953, although Allais claimed to have written 1952d in late 1952 (after the conference, to be published in the proceedings).
48 Essentially, Allais' definition of rationality coincides with standard consumer theory *under certainty*. The only new axiom Allais adopts in the case of uncertainty is what he calls "l'axiome de préférence absolue de Massé et Morlat", which is a restatement of First-degree Stochastic Dominance (Allais 1952d[1979], p. 39).
49 Of course, Savage 1954 is known for *the sure-thing principle*; but by the time of

the Paris conference, the "independence axiom" was a more common denomination; see Fishburn and Wakker 1995.

50 Allais interprets the choice of gamble A against gamble B (in his Paradox) as a consequence of "complementarity in the vicinity of certainty": the supplemental 1 per cent chance to win in gamble A leads to a certain gain. In the other pair of gamble, this supplemental 1 per cent, as it does not bear certainty, does not exhibit this complementarity effect. That is why A is often preferred to B while C is not preferred to D.

51 Allais (1953) is obviously the only of Allais references in Savage (1954).

52 The EUT (as formulated by the von Neuman and Morgenstern axioms) tells the individual "how he ought to behave", writes Morgenstern (1972, p. 711).

53 Morgenstern acknowledges now that the theory is only "an approximation to an undoubtedly much richer and far more complicated reality than that which the theory describes in a simple manner" (1974, p. 178). In particular, the domain of the theory is restricted because of phenomena that are somewhat similar to the Allais Paradox:

> one should now point out that the domain of our axioms on utility theory is also restricted.... For example, the probabilities used must be within certain plausible ranges and not go to 0.01 or even less to 0.001, then to be compared to other equally tiny numbers such as 0.02, etc. Rather, one imagines that a normal individual would have some intuition of what 50:50 or 25:75 means, etc. ... Beside this difficulty of exposing individuals to almost unrecognizably small probabilities, there is added another one. And it is difficult to say which is more formidable: that is, the matter of the objects which are being offered: Millions, even ten of millions of Norwegian crowns, French francs, or even dollars.

But, according to Morgenstern, these restrictions are of trifling significance.

54 Since normative theories (according to John Neville Keynes) concern, not what is, but what ought to be according to a given ideal – "The object ... of a normative science [is] the determination of ideals" (Keynes 1890 [1917], p. 35) – they are, contrary to positive ones, immune to experimental testing.

55 Notice that a similar test had been suggested *earlier* in (Strotz 1953, p. 393), quoted in (Allais 1979, p. 515).

References

Allais, M. 1949–1953. La gestion des houillères nationalisées et la théorie économique. Second edition: Paris, Imprimerie Nationale, 1953.

Allais, M. 1952a. Généralisation des théories de l'équilibre économique et du rendement social au cas du risque. In CNRS 1953.

Allais, M. 1952b. Fondements d'une théorie positive des choix comportant un risque. In CNRS 1953.

Allais, M. 1952c. La Psychologie de l'homme rationnel devant le risque: la théorie et l'expérience. *Journal de la société de statistique de Paris*, Jan. 1953: 47–72.

Allais, M. 1952d. Fondements d'une théorie positive des choix comportant un risque et critique des postulats et axiomes de l'école américaine. In CNRS 1953. Quoted from English translation in Allais and Hagen 1979.

Allais, M. 1953. Le Comportement de l'homme rationnel devant le risque: critique des postulats et axiomes de l'école américaine. *Econometrica*, XXI: 503–546.

Allais, M. 1955. Fondements d'une théorie positive des choix comportant un risque et critique des postulats et axiomes de l'école américaine. *Annales des Mines*, pp. 4–55.

Allais, M. 1957. Sur la théorie des choix aléatoires. *Revue d'économie politique*, LXXI 3: 381–390.

Allais, M. 1974. La Psychologie de l'homme rationnel devant le risque – la théorie et l'expérience – résultats du sondage de 1952. Note 3064 du Centre d'Analyse Economique. 6 mai 1974.

Allais, M. 1979. The so-called Allais Paradox and rational decisions under uncertainty. In Allais and Hagen 1979.

Allais, M., and O. Hagen. 1979. *Expected utility hypothesis and the Allais Paradox*. Dordrecht-Boston: Reidel.

Arrow, K. J. 1965. Exposition of the theory of choice under uncertainty. In *Aspects of the theory of risk bearing*. Helsinki: Yrjö Jahnssonis Säätio.

Bernoulli, D. 1731. Specimen theoriae novae de mensura sortis. Reed. In *Die Werke von Daniel Bernoulli*. t. II. Basel: Birkäuser Verlag. English translation 1954. Exposition of a new theory on the measurement of risk. *Econometrica*, XXI: 223 sqq.

Boiteux, M. 1948 [1951]. Tarification des demandes aléatoires. *Cahiers du Séminaire d'Econométrie*, 1 (from a 1948 working paper found in the Guilbaud papers).

Boiteux, M. 1956. Sur la gestion des monopoles publics astreints à l'équilibre budgétaire. *Econometrica*, XXIV, 1, 22–40.

Boiteux, M. 1993. *Haute tension*. Paris, Odile Jacob.

Camerer, C. 1995. Individual decision making. In *The Handbook of Experimental Economics*, edited by J. H. Kagel and A. E. Roth. Princeton, NJ: Princeton University Press.

Carré J.-J., Dubois, P. and Malinvaud, E. 1973. *Abrégé de la croissance française*. Paris: Le seuil.

CNRS. 1953. *Colloque "Econométrie"*. Paris 12–17 mai 1952. Paris: CNRS.

Darmois, G. 1952. Introduction. In CNRS 1953.

Dreze, J. 1964. Some postwar contributions of French economists to theory and public policy. *American Economic Review*, LIV 4: 1–64.

Fishburn, P. C. and Wakker, P. P. 1995. The invention of the independence condition. *Management Science*, XLI: 1130–1144.

Fontaine, P. 1999. Classical political economy between two fires: Jean-Baptiste Say and Frank H. Knight on the enterprise economy. *History of Political Economy*, XXXI 1: 1–28.

Friedman, M. and Savage, L. J. 1948. The utility analysis of choice involving risk. *Journal of Political Economy*, LVI 4: 279–304.

Friedman, M. and Savage, L. J. 1952. The expected-utility hypothesis and the measurability of utility. *Journal of Political Economy*, LX 6: 463–474.

Guilbaud, G.-T. 1954. Leçons sur les éléments principaux de la théorie mathématique des jeux. In CNRS. *Stratégies et décisions économiques, études théoriques et applications aux entreprises*. pp. Guilbaud/I-1-Guilbaud/V-15.

Hutter, R. 1950. *La théorie économique et la gestion commerciale des chemins de fer*. Paris: Dunod.

Keynes, J. N. 1890. *The Scope and Method of Political Economy*. London: Macmillan, fourth edition, 1917.

Leonard, R. 1995. From parlor games to social science: von Neumann, Morgenstern, and the creation of game theory 1928–1944. *Journal of Economic Literature*, XXXIII, 730–761.

Lesourne, J. 1958. *Technique économique et gestion industrielle*. Paris: Dunod.

Lordon, F. 1997. Le désir de "faire science". *Actes de la recherche en sciences sociales*, 119: 27–35.

MacCrimmon, K. R. 1968. Descriptive and normative implications of the decision-theory postulates. In *Risk and Uncertainty*, edited by K. Borch and J. Mossin. New York: St Martin's Press.

MacCrimmon, K. R. and Larsson, S. 1975. Utility theory: axioms versus "paradoxes". In Allais and Hagen 1979.

Marschak, J. 1950. Rational behavior, uncertain prospects, and measurable utility. *Econometrica*, XVIII: 111–141.

Marschak, J. 1951. Why "should" statisticians and businessmen maximize "moral Expectation"? In J. Neyman, ed., *Proceedings of the Second Berkeley Symposium on Mathematical Statistics and Probability*. Berkeley, CA: University of California Pres, 493–506.

Marschak, J. 1979. Utilities, psychological values, and the training of decision makers. In Allais and Hagen 1979, 163–174.

Massé, P. 1944. Applications des probabilités en chaîne à l'hydrologie statistique et au jeu des réservoirs. *Journal de la Société de Statistique de Paris*, LXXXV: 204–219.

Massé, P. 1946. *Les réserves et la régulation de l'avenir*. Paris: Hermann.

Massé, P. 1950 [1953]. Réflexion sur les comportements rationnels en économie aléatoire. *Cahiers du séminaire d'économétrie*, 2: 11–59 (from a 1950 working paper found in the Guilbaud papers).

Massé, P. 1964. Le choix des investissements – Critères et méthodes. 2nd edn. Paris: Dunod.

Massé, P. and Morlat, G. 1952. Sur le classement économique des perspectives aléatoires. In CNRS 1953.

McClennen, E. F. 1990. *Rationality and Dynamic Choice: Foundational Explorations*. Cambridge: Cambridge University Press.

Morlat, G. 1957. Sur la théorie des choix aléatoires – critique des idées de Maurice Allais. *Revue d'Economie Politique*, LXVII: 378–380.

Morlat, G. and Bessière, F. 1971. *Vingt-cinq ans d'économie électrique*. Paris: Dunod.

Morgenstern, O. 1972. Descriptive, predictive and normative theory. *Kyklos*, IV: 699–714.

Morgenstern, O. 1974. Some reflections on utility. In Allais and Hagen 1979.

Mosteller, F. and Nogee, P. 1951. An experimental measurement of utility. *Journal of Political Economy*, LIX: 371–404.

Munier, B. R. 1984. Quelques critiques de la rationalité économique dans l'incertain. *Revue économique*, XXXV: 65–86.

Nagel, E. 1963. Assumptions in economic theory. *The American Economic Review*, 53(2): 211–219.

Pradier, P. C. and Teira-Serrano, D. 2000. Frank H. Knight. Le risque comme critique de l'économie politique. *Revue de Synthèse*, 4th series, 1–2, 79–116.

Samuelson, P. A. 1950. Probability and the attempt to measure utility. *The Economic Review* (*Keizai Kenkyu*), 167–173. Reed. In Stiglitz 1966.

Samuelson, P. A. 1952a. Utilité, préférence et probabilité. In CNRS 1953. English translation. In Stiglitz 1966.

Samuelson, P. A. 1952b. Probability, utility and the independence axiom. In Stiglitz 1966.

Savage, L. J. 1954. *The foundations of statistics*. New York: Wiley. Repr. New York: Dover, 1972.

Shackle, G. L. S. 1949a. A non-additive measure of uncertainty. *Review of Economic Studies*, 27(42): 70–74.

Shackle, G. L. S. 1949b. *Expectations in economics*. Cambridge: Cambridge University Press.

Slovic, P. and Tversky, A. 1974. Who accepts Savage's axiom? *Behavioral science* 19: 368–373.

Strotz, R. H. 1953. Cardinal Utility. *The American Economic Review,* XLIII: 384–397.

Sutton, J. 1997. "Gibrat's Legacy". *Journal of Economic Literature*, XXXV: 40–59.

Von Neumann, J. 1957. Bibliography of John von Neumann. In *Complete works* VI. Oxford: Pergamon Press.

Von Neumann, J. and Morgenstern, O. 1944. *Theory of games and economic behavior*. 1947 2nd edn. New York: Wiley. Reprint 1980. Princeton: Princeton University Press.

3 Experimentation, general equilibrium and games

S. Abu Turab Rizvi

> Being denied a sufficiently secure experimental base, economic theory has to adhere to the rules of logical discourse and must renounce the facility of internal inconsistency. A deductive structure that tolerates a contradiction does so under the penalty of being useless, since any statement can be derived flawlessly and immediately from that contradiction.
>
> In its mathematical form, economic theory is open to an efficient scrutiny for logical errors.
>
> Gérard Debreu (1991: 2–3)

3.1 Introduction

The upsurge in the popularity of experimental economics dates from the early to mid-1980s. By 1985 there was enough writing in this area for the *Journal of Economic Literature* to establish a separate bibliographic category, "Experimental Economic Methods" (Roth 1987: 1). This contrasts with the situation in earlier periods. The first review of experimental economics (Rapoport and Orwant 1962) was able to do justice to the field in a single article (Roth in Kagel and Roth 1995: 3). And Roth writes that "...when I began my own experimental work about a dozen years ago, it was most convenient to publish the results in journals of psychology and business" (1987: 1). Thus we can see that prior to the mid-1980s, experimental methods were not an extensive undertaking in economics. Roth's comments further suggest that experimental methods applied to economic topics had a better reception in fields other than economics. This implies that experimentation was not considered to be "really" economics in this earlier time. This essay tries to answer some questions that these thoughts raise. Why was experimentation in economics not popular in economics in earlier times? What accounts for the emergence of experimental economics during the 1980s? How are experimentation and game theory related? (For a further perspective on this last question, in the early years of game theory, consult Dimand's essay in this volume.)

To answer these questions, I try to establish a series of claims. I begin by arguing that economists eschewed experimentation for a variety of reasons, but experimentation particularly did not make sense in the framework of general equilibrium theory, which dominated economics in the postwar period. Allied to this theoretical approach was a related approach to empiricism, econometrics. Neither of these styles of economics was hospitable to experimental economics. In addition, the opposition to experimentation went well beyond general equilibrium theory. Theoretical economics generally, for example the Chicago variant, also did not look to experiments for confirmation. The primary focus in this essay on general equilibrium theory derives from the ideas that while most of axioms of general equilibrium theory are eminently testable, its adherents eschewed experimentation. Moreover, general-equilibrium theory represents the most sought-after theoretical method from 1950 to 1985. Thus I explore key aspects of the demise of general equilibrium theory and its associated econometrics by referring to the Sonnenschein–Mantel–Debreu results on the arbitrariness of aggregate excess demands. These results were published during the 1970s. The arbitrariness theory was codified and its robustness shown by the early 1980s. Economic theory was in the ensuing ten years transformed from the realm of general-equilibrium theory into an amalgam of approaches – and among these were game theory and experimental economics.[1] Thus, once general equilibrium theory ran into trouble – during the late 1970s and early 1980s – experimentation began to flourish. Next, to demonstrate the effectiveness of experimentation, I examine the relation between experimentation and game theory occurring over ten years starting around 1985.[2] Specifically, at this time, experimental evidence called into question bargaining results from rational-choice game theory, and spurred a significant change in the character of the theory, so that evolutionary game theory emerged. I conclude that the role of experimentation in economics has undergone a profound transformation: from a field of investigation that was not in the mainstream of economics, to a method that was an important influence in causing a dominant type of economic theory to be replaced by another. The vicissitudes of general equilibrium theory play a key role in how experimental results have been received by economists, and so we turn to exploring the character of this theory.

3.2 General equilibrium theory

General equilibrium theory combines an axiomatic approach and Walras-inspired theory.[3] From the inaugural activity in the 1950s – Arrow's *Social Choice and Individual Values* (1951), Arrow and Debreu's proof of the existence of a competitive general equilibrium (1954), Koopmans's *Three Essays on the State of Economic Science* on method (1957), and Debreu's *Theory of Value* (1959) – to the consolidation and restatement of Arrow and Hahn's *General Competitive Analysis* (1971), and the 30 years of journal articles surrounding this work, formalist general equilibrium theory reigned supreme in economics. It gave economists a dominant paradigm to work on. In addition, two specific features of general equilibrium theory – the axiomatic, deductive method, and the view that individuals ought to be considered primarily individually, and not in interaction or socially – are crucial. The axiomatic-deductive method was inhospitable to experimental economics, and the competitive-individualist approach was inhospitable to game theory.

Gérard Debreu, the leading figure in general equilibrium theory who is quoted in the epigraph to this chapter, simply considers the experimentation to be unavailable to his approach to economics. By emphasizing the internal consistency of the theory, general equilibrium distances itself from empirical reality (its relation to the empirical world is discussed later in this section). What is clear is that general equilibrium theory in this mode served as the overarching theory for economics. There is ample evidence that formalist general equilibrium theory fits this description of an overarching theory. Perhaps the best example is Arrow and Hahn's *General Competitive Analysis* (1971). In this work, the authors clearly use general equilibrium theory as the basis for a microfoundations project: that is, to see what macroeconomic and other regularities follow from the microeconomic axiom set of formalist general equilibrium theory (Rizvi 1994b). Not only did economists look to this theory for the determinateness of competitive general equilibrium (uniqueness, stability), but they also wanted to use the theory for adequate comparative statics, identification of econometric models, approaches to imperfectly competitive general equilibrium and, importantly, the foundations of macroeconomics. Every subfield of economics, from public finance to international economics, was – in the thirty years of journal articles and monographs surrounding Arrow and Hahn's book – considered poorly grounded unless its results could be derived from the overarching general equilibrium theory. Since all of the formal theory of economics was evidently at the microeconomic level, and formalist general equilibrium theory became microeconomics *par excellence*, no subfield of economics could say it had an adequate foundation without becoming, as it were, an applied field of general equilibrium theory.

It is worth remembering that macroeconomics – as a conceptually distinct field from microeconomics – nearly disappeared, except as serving as a label, during this time (Rizvi, 1994b). This attests to the power of the metatheoretical imperatives of formalist general equilibrium theory. Thus E. Roy Weintraub, in his microfoundations book, stated accurately that "even those few economists who argue that current microeconomics *does not generate* macroeconomics have been extremely shy in their attempts to convince their colleagues of the seriousness of their concerns" (1979: 5). Allan Drazen summarized the view of many economists when he held that "explanations of macroeconomic phenomena will be complete only when such explanations are consistent with microeconomic choice theoretic behavior and can be phrased in the language of general equilibrium theory" (1980: 293).

So we have a situation in which, from an ascent in the early to mid-1950s, and solid dominance in the ensuing three decades, formalist general equilibrium theory served as *the* overarching theory for economics. It is not surprising, given this context, that experimental economics did not thrive during the period of the dominance of general equilibrium theory. A reason for this is that the method of general equilibrium theory is to begin with axioms and to proceed deductively, whereas the typical experimental method is that of induction, where hypotheses are easily reformulated because of new evidence and there is a messy interplay between facts and theorizing. While the axiomatic-deductive method has not been typically allied to experimentation, this does not mean that it cannot be. In fact, there is probably no substantive axiom of general equilibrium theory (or behavioral assumption, such as profit-maximization) that cannot be tested experimentally: May's work on transitivity, discussed below, is a case in point. Thus it is not accurate to state that general equilibrium theory, by its very nature, has few experimentally testable hypotheses. However, as the quotation from Debreu shows, the very clear emphasis in an axiomatic-deductive approach is freeing the axiom set from internal inconsistency, not on experimentally validating the set of axioms: to see if a set of axioms can hang together; if it does not, to use a different set. The axioms, as is established below, are derived from introspection.

Given the self-contained character of formalist theories, and their distance from an empirical substrate, it is difficult to see where evidence, experimental or otherwise, should fit in. Koopmans, in his *Three Essays*, the leading methodological treatise of formalist general equilibrium theory, dealt with this problem. He remarked that while there are different experimental and theoretical specialties in the physical sciences, in the "writings representing the best achievements of economics, we find and expect to find pieces of reasoning and references to facts closely intertwined." Yet by "references to fact" Koopmans meant nothing as systematic as experiment: "The facts of economic life are all around us. Hence much of the factual background of economics can be presupposed without extensive examination or discussion" (1957: 131). For support in this view, Koopmans cites Robbins who had written that "We do not need controlled experiments to establish their [i.e., the postulates'] validity: they are so much the stuff of our everyday experience that they have only to be stated to be recognized as obvious" (Robbins 1935, cited in Koopmans 1957: 131). Thus the facts needed to justify axioms are merely those that are seen introspectively.

Accordingly, Koopmans removed facts from the main business of economic reasoning:

> We can best keep track of the foundation for each statement ... if facts are recognized at the beginning of each piece of analysis by explicitly formulated postulates, and where appropriate at the end by confrontation of conclusions and predictions with additional observations, but are not permitted to enter through a side door when the reasoning proper is in progress.
>
> (1957: 144)

Koopmans was direct about the impropriety of experimentation in economics. He speaks of "the virtual impossibility of experiments under conditions approaching those of real life" and says that "economics is handicapped by severe and possibly unsurmountable obstacles to meaningful experimentation" (1957: 140).

However, eventually, once the reasoning process is through, "conclusions and predictions" might be confronted with observations. How was this to be done? Koopmans discusses a number of empirical approaches, such as input–output methods and "measurement without theory," but the approach that he championed is econometric testing of behavioral (theory-based) models. Along with William Hood, Koopmans was editor of the Cowles Commission monograph *Studies in Econometric Method* (1953) and he published a series of influential publications in econometrics. He joined the Cowles Commission in 1944 and directed it from 1948 to 1954. The Cowles Commission (later named Cowles Foundation) was an important nexus for the development of both formalist general equilibrium theory (Debreu's *Theory of Value* and Arrow's *Social Choice* were both Cowles monographs) and econometrics. Koopmans had followed Jacob Marschak as director of Cowles; Marschak's work (with Andrews 1944) introduced Trygve Haavelmo's foundational ideas on econometrics. These ideas became the basis for the Cowles approach to econometrics, which was the dominant style of econometrics for decades. Haavelmo was very much motivated by making econometrics consistent with experiments – in a certain sense – as Mary Morgan (1990, Ch. 8) has pointed out. Given this development, formalist economics had its own approach to "experimentation" thus defined.

Haavelmo argued that theory "will have an economic meaning only when associated with a design of actual experiments that describes – and indicates how to measure – a system of 'true' variables.... Hypotheses in the above sense are thus the joint implications – and the only testable implications, as far as *observations* are concerned – of a theory *and* a design of experiments" (1944: 8–9). Morgan (1990: 245) notes that Haavelmo saw that this idea of an econometric hypothesis (a theory along with an experimental design) was problematic. He therefore began by distinguishing two sorts of experiment:

> (1) experiments that *we should like to make* to see if certain real economic phenomena – when *artificially isolated* from "other influences"

> – would verify certain hypotheses, and (2) the stream of experiments that Nature is steadily turning out from her own enormous laboratory, and which we merely watch as passive observers.
>
> (Haavelmo 1944: 14)

The first sort of experiment, the controlled laboratory type, is distinguished from what we might not even refer to as an experiment, what the economy – or Nature, as Haavelmo would have it – conducts every day.[4] We can see that experimental economics refers to the first sort of (controlled) experiment. Haavelmo had a further problem since, as he puts it, the more profound economic theories require the first sort of experiment, whereas the data we actually have is of the second, "unplanned", sort (1944: 15). Here he was acknowledging the prevalent view (expressed, for example, by Robbins) that controlled experiments were nonsensical to economists. "Instead, they have to make do with passive observations (those from Nature's experiments) which are influenced by a great many factors not accounted for by the theory" (Morgan 1990: 246). Haavelmo's solution to this problem was to complicate the theoretical representation: "If we cannot clear the data of such 'other influences', we have to try to introduce these influences in the theory, in order to bring about more agreement between theory and facts" (1944: 18). He proposed to do this by making all theoretical relations stochastic, by adding an error term to each, and to do this he employed a microfoundations-based approach, consistent with formalist general equilibrium theory:

> It is on purpose that we have used as an illustration an example of individual economic behavior, rather than an average market relation. For it seems rational to introduce the assumptions about the stochastical elements of our economic theories already in the 'laws' of behavior for the single individuals, firms, etc., as a characteristic of their behavior, and then derive the average market relation or relations for the whole society, from these individual "laws".
>
> (1944: 51–52)

We can now see more clearly why economists eschewed experimental economics for so long, given the nature of the dominant general equilibrium theory and the econometric approach. The "facts" that the axioms of general equilibrium theory were based on were obtained introspectively; the main process of economic reasoning was insulated from facts; and when the conclusions of this reasoning were subjected to "experimental" confirmation, the natural experiments of the economy were explored by an econometrics based on a stochastic version of general equilibrium theory. There was then no space at all for experimental economics, traditionally defined, in any of these procedures.

This conclusion is buttressed by turning from methodological works to a brief look at the reception by economists of experiments during the establishment period of general equilibrium theory. A number of experiments were carried out during this time that were germane to the validity of general equilibrium theory. A relatively well-known experiment that has to do with individual choice is Thurstone's attempt to construct indifference curves from experimental data. The reception of this experiment among economists, in the form of Wallis and Friedman's critique of it, shows the skepticism that economists have felt about experimental methods.[5] Thurstone asked his subjects to rank various combinations of hats and coats and was able to fit (hyperbolic) indifference curves through the data he obtained. Yet even though Thurstone's data gave confirmation for the model of individual choice, Wallis and Friedman objected vehemently to the experiment. They argued that the choices asked to be made were hypothetical, and given the artificiality of the situation – which they felt extended to cover the entirety of experimental methods in economics – "It is questionable whether a subject in so artificial an experimental situation could know what choices he would make in an economic situation; not knowing, it is almost inevitable that he would, in entire good faith, systematize his answers in such a way as to produce plausible but spurious results" (1942: 179–180). This sort of skepticism, based on the artificiality of the experimental setting and its consequent effect on the subject, came to pervade economists' view of experimentation throughout the establishment and dominance periods of formalist general equilibrium theory.[6]

Another example of the reception of experimental data during the establishment of formalist general equilibrium theory is May's (1954) investigation of intransitivity. At the time, many economists including Kenneth Arrow and Gerard Debreu had employed transitivity of preferences in general equilibrium theory as an axiom (Arrow 1951; Arrow and Debreu 1954). As Koopmans, and Robbins before him, emphasized, axioms were established introspectively. However, May, who was a mathematician, decided to see if there existed contrary experimental evidence regarding transitivity. May had long been familiar with the axiom of transitivity since he had been present in 1948 when Arrow publicly presented the first version of his impossibility theorem (Kelly 1987). He consulted Warren McCulloch (the cyberneticist and automata theorist who had been trained in physiology) about such evidence. Based on McCulloch, his own review of the literature and his own experiments, May presented evidence against transitivity. In his experiment, he reported on the preferences of college students for aspects of potential mates (intelligence, wealth, and beauty). Students saw descriptions of pairs of potential mates who had varying amounts of these characteristics and were asked to rank them. Over a quarter of the students showed preferences that violated transitivity. May thought that overall the evidence against the universality of transitivity was strong, and that this axiom's use was questionable. However, consistent with the view that axioms were established introspectively and the bias against experimentation, May's report on intransitivity was ignored. This occurred despite its publication in the main journal of economic theory at the time. It is quite possible that Kenneth Arrow was one of the referees of May's paper.[7, 8] Whether Arrow refereed May's paper or not, it is clear that evidence against transitivity was ignored for a long time. Hugo Sonnenschein, writing in 1971, stated "the economics profession appears to be so well indoctrinated with the concept of transitive preference that statements about behavior arising from intransitive preferences are sometimes interpreted as making no sense. Indeed, such behavior is referred to as 'irrational.' Suffice it to say that the rationality of consumer behavior is not based on empirical observation." Instead, "Empirical observations or experimental results frequently indicate intransitivities of choices" (223). Sonnenschein's comment is interesting since one interpretation is that it served the interests of general equilibrium theorists to ignore evidence against transitivity just because transitivity was at that time thought to be an important axiom to the general equilibrium project. If this is so, it buttresses the idea that the imperatives of general equilibrium theory acted against the acceptance of experimental results.

During the period of the establishment of formalist general equilibrium theory, then, experimental work was not given much attention by economists, even when it directly contradicted their theoretical presuppositions.[9] This deflection of experiment and its subservience to theory was supported by methodological ideas that were developed by Koopmans and others. With this background in mind, it is easier to understand why interactions between experimentalists (largely from a psychology background) and economic theorists yielded so little. An instance of this mutual misunderstanding took place at the Santa Monica seminar of 1952.[10] The seminar was partly funded by a Ford Foundation grant to an interdisciplinary group from the University of Michigan on the theme of "The Design of Experiments in Decision Processes." The group, with members from economics, mathematics, philosophy, psychology and sociology had been meeting regularly at Michigan since 1950. Thirty-seven scholars sponsored by Ford, RAND, the Cowles Commission and the Office of Naval Research attended the seminar, and it turns out that they presented 37 papers. There are 19 papers in Thrall *et al.* (1954), which represents the proceedings of the conference, if we include the two introductory ones.[11] The participant list is impressive and clearly interdisciplinary (Smith 1992: 260); it includes (if one doesn't quibble too much with disciplinary categorization) from psychology, Bush, Coombs, Estes, Festinger, and Simon; from mathematics, Karlin, Nash, Shapley and von Neumann; from economics, Debreu, Hildreth, Koopmans, Marschak, Radner and Morgenstern; and from statistical decision theory, Mosteller and Raiffa.

Yet the possibility of rich interaction between experimentalists and theorists did not come about. In Smith's assessment:

> What the supporters of the Santa Monica seminar hoped was to provide a presentation-discussion forum that would stimulate empirical research and further theory development; quantitatively, its success in stimulating experiment must be judged much more modest than in furthering theory. The seminar's integrating theme was not experimental design, but the use of mathematics in the social sciences. (1992: 261)

In this emphasis, the Santa Monica seminar presaged the practice of economists in the decades to follow.

By focusing on the considerable resistance to experimentation in the character and aims of general equilibrium theory, I do not mean to imply that there was no such resistance elsewhere in economics. Indeed, the discussion so far already indicates a broader resistance to experimentation among economists. For example, Wallis and Friedman were not general equilibrium theorists. However, their idea – seen in the Chicago approach – that the basic framework of economics has a self-evident character that does not need support from experimentation fits well with the general equilibrium objections. Similarly, while Robbins's ideas on introspection did not derive from general equilibrium theory, its adherents such as Koopmans adopted them. It is certainly fair to say that opposition to experimentation ranged widely among economists. The focus here on general equilibrium theory is important, however, since general equilibrium theory came to dominate the methodological aspirations of most economists. Thus precepts associated with it also came to be widespread.

3.3 The demise of general equilibrium theory

General equilibrium theory's ascendancy was not to last. The developments leading to the decline of general equilibrium theory are worth considering.

While general equilibrium theory in its formative state concentrated on establishing the existence of competitive general equilibrium, this was not enough. Other important desiderata were the uniqueness and stability of competitive equilibrium, a coherent comparative statics, identification of econometric models, the existence of imperfectly competitive general equilibrium, and the microfoundations of macroeconomics. All of these topics were addressed, in a confident tone implying that positive results were forthcoming, in Arrow and Hahn's *General Competitive Analysis* (1971). For a theory that purported to underpin the whole of economics, such progress was required. Yet this progress never came and the confidence proved to be unfounded.

This realization occurred as a result of the spectacular series of impossibility results that I have called Sonnenschein–Mantel–Debreu (SMD) theory after its main promulgators (Rizvi 1994b, 1997, where details are provided). In the 1970s, these authors and their collaborators established that despite the availability of well-behaved axioms at the individual level, the aggregate excess demands arising in Walrasian formalist general equilibrium models were essentially arbitrary, except that they satisfied Walras's Law and a form of continuity. These latter two properties were needed to establish existence of the general equilibrium solutions, but all of the Arrow–Hahn desiderata mentioned in the previous paragraph required well-behaved aggregate excess demands. So economists gradually realized there could be no general results on uniqueness (Mas-Colell 1977), stability (Sonnenschein 1973), comparative statics (Kehoe 1985), econometric identification (Diewert 1977; Stoker 1984a, 1984b), imperfectly competitive general equilibrium (Roberts and Sonnenschein 1977; Grodal 1996) and microfoundations of macroeconomics (Rizvi 1994b). Thus the SMD papers showed that formalist general equilibrium theory had reached a dead end: no general results beyond existence were possible.

Consequently, when SMD theory became well known by the early 1980s, it became obvious to many that formalist general equilibrium theory could no longer serve as an overarching theory for economics. The great promise of formalist general equilibrium theory that had been dangled in front of economists for 30 years was finally dashed. This event had serious and unsettling consequences. Hildenbrand writes that:

> When I read in the seventies the publications of Sonnenschein, Mantel and Debreu on the structure of the excess demand function of an exchange economy, I was deeply consternated. Up to that time I had the naïve illusion that the microeconomic foundation of the general equilibrium model, which I had admired so much, does not only allow us to prove that the model and the concept of equilibrium are logically consistent (existence of equilibria), but also allows us to show that the equilibrium is well determined. This illusion, or should I say rather, this hope, was destroyed, once and for all, at least for the traditional model of exchange economies.
>
> (1994: ix)[12]

Once the status of general equilibrium theory as a basis for economics as a whole was called into question by SMD theory, a stage of pluralism in economics ensued (Rizvi 1994a: 2–6; 1997: 275–276). It is in the early to mid-1980s that we see the rise of rational-choice game theory and experimental economics along with other trends. In each case, there were no significant theoretical or methodological innovations that would have caused this upsurge. Rather, with general equilibrium theory vacating the scene, there was more "space" for these alternative approaches to develop and to receive a hearing on issues that the previous theory could not address.

As an example of this dynamic, the rise of rational-choice game theory can be seen as a response to the SMD troubles. In a comment on Oliver

Hart's review of attempts to found an adequate theory of imperfect competition on general equilibrium, Sonnenschein wrote that "the Negishi line [which attempted this founding], which builds on the Arrow–Debreu–McKenzie theory, has been pretty much played out" (1985: 175). Here Sonnenschein refers to his own work with John Roberts which showed how the SMD results blocked progress along Negishi's lines (Roberts and Sonnenschein 1977). Instead, Sonnenschein writes that he "will *not* confine [his] attention to general equilibrium theory." He then argues that "recent results" in game theory (Rubinstein's work on repeated games and a Nash approach to auctions) "are useful for the theory of monopolistic competition. This is the 'new blood' that I believe is much needed" (Sonnenschein 1985: 175). He even provides a list of questions in game theory that need to be answered for the approach to make headway, and he refers to his graduate students who have since led the way in game theory (Dilip Abreu, Vijay Krishna, David Pearce, Motty Perry and Leo Simon).[13]

With breaches in the general equilibrium fabric as large as the one created by the adoption to game-theory methods, the eschewing of experimental approaches – as in Debreu's remark – no longer made sense. To understand the interaction between game theory and experimentation, we need to examine some of the problems rational-choice game theory faced, and to which experimentation was germane. As will be seen in the next two sections of this essay, experimental methods were able to shape the direction of theoretical development. This importance contrasts with the ignoring of experimentation during the dominance period of general equilibrium theory (as in the "response" to May's results). The demise of general equilibrium theory leads, then, to a period of pluralism. In this period, game theory and experimental economics, in a close relationship, thrive. It is this sense in which the demise of general equilibrium theory leads to a flowering of experimental economics. For hand-in-hand with general equilibrium theory went the view that experimentation was not relevant. Once general equilibrium theory, with its methodological dictates not favoring experimentation, was no longer at center stage, experimentation could come to the fore.

3.4 Experimental economics and rational-choice bargaining theory

The period of pluralism in economic theory beginning around 1985 was typified by a reliance on game theory in its rational choice and evolutionary variants. And game theory, in both of these modes has been closely associated with experimental economics. Experimentation works well with game theory in a way that is not imaginable with general equilibrium theory.[14] Games can have a simple structure with few players, are based on individual decision-making, and are thus conducive to experiment. Moreover, game theory has never had a settled, overarching style, in the way that general equilibrium theory does. These features of game theory have conspired with the atmosphere of pluralism to give experimentation a boost. In fact, experimentation has played a crucial role in how rational-choice game theory has been received and in the rise of evolutionary game theory. In order to see the recent effectiveness of experimentation, it helps to set the stage by considering the state of rational-choice game theory, to which experimentation became germane.

While rational-choice game theory became a favored tool of economist during the latter half of the 1980s, it faced some significant problems (Rizvi 1994a). The focus in this essay is clearly on the experimental results and the theoretical transformation they occasioned. However, it may be relevant to emphasize briefly that the difficulties with rationality in game theory – that its common solution concepts (prescriptions as to how to play a game) such as Nash equilibrium are burdened with knowledge assumptions that are implausible and which make the notion of strategizing hard to maintain; that the concept of rational play itself becomes suspect in games with a dynamic structure; and that the folk theorem and related results mean that there are too many equilibria, so that almost anything goes – have themselves had a great impact on the move to evolutionary game theory. (Rizvi 1998, on which the following relies heavily, has details on these issues and references to other work.)

While there was not a well-established formulation of game-theoretic rationality overall, one type of conception became immensely influential and popular. This was the subgame perfect equilibrium. It is one of the refinements of the concept of Nash equilibrium.[15] Consider the following illustration of the celebrated bargaining model of Rubinstein (1982) that can be said to usher in the rational-choice game-theory era. In particular, consider bargaining over a fixed sum – the cake division problem. As is well appreciated, every division of cake (that uses it all up) between two players is a Nash equilibrium, and thus the concept seems to contribute very little to an analysis. For Rubinstein, though, there are two innovations. First, as regards the structure of bargaining, he imagines offers of cake-division alternating between two players until the other party accepts an offer. Also, since there is passage of time, the payoff (cake) is discounted. Nevertheless, there is a whole host of Nash equilibria. So, to proceed, Rubinstein employed a stronger solution concept. This is the second innovation. Rubinstein was able to show that there is a unique subgame perfect equilibrium. This is because a subgame perfect equilibrium prescribes optimal behavior in each equilibrium and out-of-equilibrium situation. Thus a player cannot increase a demand (beyond the proposed unique solution) that will cause the other player to prefer to reject that offer. Consequently, the optimal offer will be one that leaves the opponent just indifferent.

A serious problem for bargaining model is incompatible experimental evidence. An alternating-offer bargaining game that ends after one period is known as the ultimatum bargaining game if, when the offer is rejected, the game ends with neither player receiving a division. The game has the unique subgame perfect equilibrium in which the player moving first proposes a maximally advantageous allocation (all or nearly all of the cake) and the second player accepts. This is a clear prediction that lends itself easily to experimental test. Yet it fails that test badly (Güth *et al.* 1982; Camerer and Thaler 1985; Güth and Tietz 1990; Davis and Holt 1993: ch. 5; Roth 1994). The first player in the experiments typically offers to keep between one-half and two-thirds of the cake, not anywhere close to all of the cake. A player offering to keep two-thirds of the cake stands an equal chance of having this offer rejected. If the game has two stages, the evidence as to what will be done is not so clear-cut, with some experiments reproducing subgame perfect equilibrium and others not.

What is clear, though, is that this experimental evidence upset the centrality of the Rubinstein bargaining model and its variants (as well as the concept of subgame perfection). In fact, the discussion of these results was quite interesting and led to further confusion. Initially, a number of authors maintained that the form of preferences assumed of players might simply have been wrong: perhaps the players "played fair" and did not seek to maximize personal gain. If this is so, the experimental evidence may yet reflect a subgame perfect equilibrium being played, though with preferences that reflect fairness concerns (Camerer and Thaler 1988; Thaler 1988; 1992). This development opened the gate to evolutionary-type reasoning, which is amenable in principle to a multiplicity of player types (own-gain maximizers and those preferring equality, for example). What resulted was a debate between those assuming strict self-interest and those advocating a presumption of a norm of fairness. Neither side had decisive arguments in what promised to be an endless back-and-forth. The fairness doctrine did not "win" since, among other things, the diligence with which the norm of fairness that was held by experimental subjects was shown to vary in successive plays of the game (Ochs and Roth 1989; Bolton 1991). If preferences are indeed unstable, any constellation of data can be explained with a suitably specified set of preferences, and one particular "norm" – self-interest or fairness – cannot be the guide to explaining choice. At this point, some theorists threw up their hands and tried to regroup. Neither self-interest rationality nor equality-preferring rationality was proving to be powerful in handling experimental evidence in the ultimatum game. In the words of Samuelson (1996: 26), on which this review is based, the response to this morass was "to abandon the model of rational players optimizing against stable preferences" of whatever sort. "The result has been the development of evolutionary game theory."

For at least two broad reasons, then – those having to do with the problems in the abstract expressions of game-theoretic rationality and those resulting from dramatic experimental nonconfirmations of some of the most popular models and refinements of rational-choice game theory – it was obvious by the early 1990s that rational-choice game theory was in trouble. It was exactly in this situation that evolutionary game theory found a foothold in economics and began its ascent. Evolutionary game theory, from its inception, had a close relation to experimentation.

3.5 Experimental economics and evolutionary game theory

Evolutionary game theory (despite its own difficulties) succeeded in many areas where rational-choice game theory had problems (Samuelson 1996; Rizvi 1998). For us, though, the issue is to see what role experimentation played in its interaction with evolutionary game theory. As with rational-choice game theory, there seems to be a close involvement between experimentation and evolutionary game theory, an involvement that flourished in the pluralistic atmosphere following the problems with general equilibrium theory.

Evolutionary game theoretic models conformed well to experimental evidence. For example, the experimental evidence regarding the ultimatum game indicated that players' choices form a Nash equilibrium but are not subgame perfect, as the Rubinstein bargaining analysis would suggest. In other words, there was a difference between the prediction of a theory and what happened in an experimental setting. To rectify this situation, evolutionary game theorists sought a model that selected strategies such as those observed in the experimental setting. Binmore *et al.* (1995) did this. They were able to show the survival of strategies that give a substantial portion of the cake to the second player – the one who is in the position of replying to an offer. In addition, this equilibrium was stable.

Binmore and Samuelson (1992) took up the idea of boundedly rational players in an evolutionary model. They assumed that agents were supposed to have lexicographic preferences: in the first instance they preferred higher payoffs, and in the second place algorithms that are less complex. The latter they modeled as the number of states of an automaton. For a dynamic they chose a modification of an evolutionarily stable strategy and applied this to an infinite-horizon alternating-offer bargaining game to see what strategies would be selected (Binmore *et al.* 1993). They found that the strategy selected (in a limiting case) turns out to be the Rubinstein bargaining outcome from rational-choice theory as the discount factor increases. As Samuelson (1996) notes, the "subgame-perfect equilibrium in infinite-horizon bargaining games is then rescued by evolutionary models from ... its most problematic features." In shorter, finite games such as the ultimatum game, the results are not subgame perfect but are closer to the experimental results.

Samuelson (1996) identifies two issues in interpreting these findings. There is still the ambiguity of whether fairness concerns on the part of the players are triggering the outcomes. That is, rational-choice game theory using fairness preferences could also explain the experimental outcomes. This concern is allayed since, as we have seen, the norm of fairness was not adhered to well in repetitions of the relevant game. In addition, the verification of experimental outcomes does not follow the usual method of empirical economics. That method is to obtain a comparative static result and then to test whether a change in an exogenous variable affects an endogenous variable in the predicted manner. The method used in the bulk of the experimental literature, on the other hand, is simply to assert the compatibility of a model outcome with an experimental outcome. Be this as it may, the evolutionary approach – whatever its shortcomings – does better than the rational-choice approach (using self-interest) since it at least does demonstrate this compatibility. Moreover, the fairness method did not gain very wide acceptance for a number of reasons. First, for many economists, there was a strong presumption to maintain an assumption of self-interested behavior. Second, and related to this, was another presumption, that of the Stigler–Becker approach, which was to favor a change in the constraints that agents face rather than to allow preferences that are presumed to have to be altered. This, Stigler and Becker argued, was so that there was some backbone to the maximizing model: otherwise, any result could be explained by a suitable change of preferences. Third, as related earlier, the norm of fairness was not adhered to consistently in experiments: in this sense, the fairness approach did less well than the evolutionary approach in conforming to the evidence. For all of these reasons, incorporating fairness into preferences did not seem to provide a viable alternative to the evolutionary approach.[16]

Despite these problems, it is impressive that evolutionary game theory was able to challenge (and surpass in important respects) rational-choice game theory on the strength of its ability better to conform to experimental evidence.[17] As we have seen, this has not always been a criterion for the success of an economic theory.

3.6 Conclusion

We can now plausibly account for the alterations in the popularity of experimental work among economists. During the ascendance and dominance periods of formalist general equilibrium theory (the 30-odd years following 1950), experimental economics was in a hiatus. Economists, who felt the overarching theoretical force of general equilibrium theory, were unreceptive to a method that was inductive and which upset the axiom–result–econometrics model of economic investigation. The axioms were given introspectively, and were not subject to disconfirmation by experimental data; the results followed directly from axioms without the intervention of data; and the econometrics relied on "natural" rather than controlled experiment. Theoretical economists outside the general equilibrium mold, such as those in the Chicago tradition, also did not look to experiments for confirmation. Even confirmatory work – Thurstone's – was argued against, and many experiments and experimental reports, such as May's, were ignored. When the SMD results caused a breach the confidence economists had in general equilibrium theory, however, the floodgates were open to many currents of alternative approaches. In this atmosphere of methodological pluralism, experimental economics grew rapidly. Experiments fit easily with game theoretic methods, which thrived in this atmosphere. Now, experiments proved crucial in transformation of economic theory, as the success of evolutionary game theory shows.

Even if this interpretation of experimentation is plausible, in other ways it is preliminary and tentative. There is certainly scope for asking what other sorts of evidence can be brought to bear on the concerns of this essay. For example, many of the principals involved in this narrative could be interviewed. It would be interesting to ask the economists involved what their motivations and intentions were, as opposed to focusing on the written record, as is done here, since the written record can only partially give insight into the themes which are of concern. The relation between experimentation and game theory, not just in the past fifteen years, but throughout the postwar period is another form of inquiry that is worth pursuing.

Acknowledgments

I would like to thank Esther-Mirjam Sent for her comments and the editors for their suggestions.

Notes

1 I have explored some of these issues in other work, on which I rely in this chapter: the arbitrariness results and their impact (Rizvi 1994b), the rise of rational-choice game theory (1994a), the ascendance of evolutionary game theory (Rizvi 1998), and the search for an alternative to microfoundations in the European work on market demand (Rizvi 1997). Mirowski discusses the alternatives to general equilibrium theory under the rubric of "cyborg sciences" (2002), and Sent (2004) investigates the related resurgence of the concept of bounded rationality in the economics literature from the 1980s onward.

2 The relation between game theory and experimentation has often been mutually supporting. However, experimentation in economics has also occurred independently of game theoretic formulations as well, e.g., Thurstone's work on experimentally derived indifference curves, or May's work on transitivity (Thurstone 1931; May 1954).

3 By general equilibrium theory I mean the neo-Walrasian work associated with the names of Arrow, Debreu and McKenzie and their followers.

4 This view is echoed by Oskar Morgenstern as discussed in Innocenti and Zappia in this volume.

5 Thurstone remarks on the genesis of his research (1931, p. 139):

> The formulation of this problem is due to numerous conversations about psychophysics with my friend Professor Henry Schultz of the University of Chicago. It was at his suggestion that experimental methods were applied to this problem in economic theory. According to Professor Schultz, it has probably never before been subjected to experimental study.

Interestingly, the Wallis and Friedman (1942) critique appears in a *Festschrift* for Henry Schultz.

6 An editor points out, correctly, that this critique is a reaction to a particular experiment rather than to experimentation as a whole. Indeed, there is an experimental literature that follows on Thurstone's work which tries to rectify problems in his experimental set-up (e.g., Rousseas and Hart 1951). However, the ideas that experimentation is too artificial and manipulative to be of use continued to color economists' views of experimentation taken as a whole.

7 The details in the next note are from Box 015 of collection B83-0023 (Kenneth Ownsworth May) at the University of Toronto Archives. I have not consulted these, but base my account on Bartlow (2000).

8 May submitted his paper to *Econometrica* after presenting it to a meeting of the Econometric Society in December 1952. In June 1953 the editor, Robert Strotz, informed him that the referees had not understood his paper. Strotz offered to send the paper to a fourth referee. May defended his paper, and made suggestions for new referees including Arrow. The paper then appeared in January 1954. May's experience predates Vernon Smith's similar frustration with uncomprehending referees (Smith 1992: 244–247); yet he likewise had a kind editor (Harry Johnson) and this resulted in the publication of an experimental paper (Smith 1962) in the *Journal of Political Economy*.

9 As an editor of this collection points out, the hostility to experimentation was not exclusively from general equilibrium theorists. Robbins and Friedman – in their work that is quoted – are not part of general equilibrium program. Yet their attitudes in this regard were adopted by the general equilibrium theorists.

10 This seminar is discussed in more detail in an earlier version of this essay, Rizvi (1999). For more background on the Santa Monica seminar, including the larger intellectual currents that resulted in it, consult Leonard (forthcoming, chapter entitled "Into the Labyrinth: Social Science and the Present Danger, RAND 1946–1960"). Innocenti and Zappia in their chapter and Dimand in his, also discuss this seminar.

11 Moreover, the editors included some papers that were not presented at the seminar, but which they held were relevant (Thrall *et al.* 1954: v). The participant and papers lists appear in the appendices to the book.

12 This is now a generally accepted conclusion. Christopher Bliss, who earlier had defended general equilibrium theory, wrote at around the same time, "The near emptiness of general equilibrium theory is a theorem of the theory" (1993: 227). He was referring to the SMD results. The idea of using representative agent models, as a way around the problem, has been effectively criticized by Alan Kirman (1992).

13 For more on the rise of rational-choice game theory, consult Rizvi (1994a), from which this is drawn.

14 This point was emphasized by an editor, to whom I am grateful.

15 This concept was developed by Selten (1965, 1975) and requires that Nash equilibrium hold not only in the original game but also in every subgame of the original game. Thus what results is a Nash equilibrium that involves no threats that would not actually be carried out if the players' bluffs were called. That is, the strategies chosen specify only actions that players would want to follow if

called on to do so. The whole refinements project has come to a halt. Refinements refer to plausible strengthenings of Nash equilibrium that reduce the multiplicity of equilibria with the goal of uniqueness. Uniqueness (in game theory as opposed to non-strategic economics) is more than just a nice feature: without it players cannot coordinate on the same equilibrium. Yet Norde *et al.* (1996) have shown that there is no solution concept that provides a unique equilibrium for each finite strategic game that is also consistent. Van Damme, the author of key works on refinements (1991, 1992), candidly comments on this: "I don't know how to deal with this" (Aumann and van Damme 1997: 28). It is also by now broadly realized that the refined equilibria are extraordinarily fragile with respect to changes in the underlying data of the problem and hence to misspecifications of them (Mas-Colell 1996: 184–185).

16 Despite these explanations it may seem odd, as an editor has emphasized, that it was easier for some economists to jettison fairness-based maximization – for all of its problems – in favor of no maximization at all.

17 It may seem that this is inevitable since evolutionary game theorists intended to find models that conformed to the experimental evidence. However, the conforming of their models to the experimental evidence is still a considerable achievement. First, it demonstrates the greater flexibility of the modeling in the evolutionary approach that this desired conformity can be achieved within it. This was not possible in the rational-choice model on the assumption of self-interested preferences. Second, economists using the rational-choice model incorporating fairness did also try to conform to the experimental evidence, and they were less successful in this attempt than the evolutionary game theorists.

References

Arrow, K. 1951. *Social Choice and Individual Values*. New York: John Wiley.

Arrow, K. and G. Debreu. 1954. "Existence of an Equilibrium for a Competitive Economy," *Econometrica* 22: 265–290.

Arrow, K. and F. Hahn. 1971. *General Competitive Analysis*. San Francisco: Holden Day.

Aumann, R.J. and E. van Damme. 1997. "On the State of the Art in Game Theory: An Interview with Robert Aumann." In W. Albers, W. Güth, P. Hammerstein, B. Moldovanu and E. van Damme, eds, *Understanding Strategic Interaction: Essays in Honor of Reinhard Selten*, pp. 8–34. (Interview date: June 30, 1995.)

Bartlow, Thomas L. 2000. "Kenneth O. May and the Theory of Social Choice." http://www66.homepage.villanova.edu/thomas.bartlow/history/SocialChoice/KOMay.htm (accessed April 12, 2001).

Binmore, K., J. Gale and L. Samuelson. 1995. "Learning to Be Imperfect: The Ultimatum Game," *Games and Economic Behavior* 8: 56–90.

Binmore, K., M. Piccione and L. Samuelson. 1993. "Evolutionary Stability in Alternating-Offers Bargaining." Mimeo, University of Wisconsin.

Binmore, K. and L. Samuelson. 1992. "Evolutionary Stability in Repeated Games Played by Finite Automata," *Journal of Economic Theory* 57: 278–305.

Bliss, C. 1993. "Oil Trade and General Equilibrium: A Review Article," *Journal of International and Comparative Economics* 2: 227–242.

Bolton, G.E. 1991. "A Comparative Model of Bargaining: Theory and Evidence," *American Economic Review* 81: 1096–1136.

Camerer, C. and R.H. Thaler. 1985. "Anomalies: Ultimatums, Dictators and Manners," *Journal of Economic Perspectives* 9: 209–220.

Davis, D.D. and C.A. Holt. 1993. *Experimental Economics*. Princeton, NJ: Princeton University Press.

Debreu, G. 1959. *Theory of Value*. New York: John Wiley.

Debreu, G. 1991. "The Mathematization of Economic Theory," *American Economic Review* 81: 1–7.

Diewert, W.E. 1977. "Generalized Slutsky Conditions for Aggregate Consumer Demand Functions," *Journal of Economic Theory* 15: 353–362.

Drazen, A. 1980. "Recent Developments in Macroeconomic Disequilibrium Theory," *Econometrica* 48: 283–306.

Grodal, B. 1996. "Profit Maximization and Imperfect Competition." In Beth Allen, ed., *Economics in a Changing World: Volume 2. Microeconomics*. New York: St. Martin's Press, 3–22.

Güth, W., R. Schmittberger and B. Schwarze. 1982. "An Experimental Analysis of Ultimatum Bargaining," *Journal of Behavior and Organization* 3: 367–388.

Güth, W. and R. Tietz. 1990. "Ultimatum Bargaining Behavior: A Survey and Comparison of Experimental Results," *Journal of Economic Psychology* 11: 417–419.

Haavelmo, T. 1944. "The Probability Approach in Econometrics," *Econometrica* 12: 1–118. Supplement.

Hildenbrand, Werner. 1994. *Market Demand: Theory and Empirical Evidence*. Princeton, NJ: Princeton University Press.

Hood, William C. and Tjalling C. Koopmans. 1953. *Studies in Econometric Method* (Cowles Commission Monograph 14). New York: Wiley.

Kagel, J. and A. Roth. 1995. *The Handbook of Experimental Economics*. Princeton, NJ: Princeton University Press.

Kehoe, Timothy J. 1985. "Multiplicity of Equilibria and Comparative Statics," *Quarterly Journal of Economics* 100: 119–147.

Kelly, Jerry S. 1987. "An Interview with Kenneth J. Arrow," *Social Choice and Welfare* 4: 43–62.

Kirman, Alan P. 1992. "Whom or What Does the Representative Individual Represent?" *Journal of Economic Perspectives* 6: 117–136.

Koopmans, T. 1957. *Three Essays on the State of Economic Science*. New York: McGraw-Hill.

Marschak, J. and W. Andrews. 1944. "Random Simultaneous Equations and the Theory of Production", *Econometrica* 12: 143–205.

Mas-Colell, A. 1977. "On the Equilibrium Price Set of a Pure Exchange Economy," *Journal of Mathematical Economics* 4: 117–126.

Mas-Colell, A. 1996. "The Determinacy of Equilibrium 25 Years Later." In B. Allen, ed., *Economics in a Changing World: Volume 2, Microeconomics*. New York: St. Martin's, 182–189.

May, Kenneth O. 1954. "Intransitivity, utility, and the aggregation of preference patterns," *Econometrica* 22(1): 1–13.

Mirowski, P. 2002. *Machine Dreams: Economics Becomes a Cyborg Science*. Cambridge: Cambridge University Press.

Morgan, Mary S. 1990. *The History of Econometric Ideas*. Cambridge: Cambridge University Press.

Norde, H., J. Potters, H. Reynierse and D. Vermeulen. 1996. "Equilibrium Selection and Consistency." *Games and Economic Behavior* 12: 219–225.

Ochs, J. and A.E. Roth. 1989. "An Experimental Study of Sequential Bargaining," *American Economic Review* 79: 355–384.

Rapoport, Anatol and Carol Orwant. 1962. "Experimental Games: A Review," *Behavioral Science* 7: 1–37.

Rizvi, S.A.T. 1994a. "Game Theory to the Rescue?" *Contributions to Political Economy* 13: 1–28.

Rizvi, S.A.T. 1994b. "The Microfoundations Project in General Equilibrium Theory," *Cambridge Journal of Economics* 18, 357–377.

Rizvi, S.A.T. 1997. "Responses to Arbitrariness in Contemporary Economics," *History of Political Economy* 29 (annual supplement): 273–288.

Rizvi, S.A.T. 1998. "The Evolution of Game Theory." Paper presented to the Erasmus Institute of Philosophy and Economics, Erasmus University.

Rizvi, S.A.T. 1999. "Two Episodes in Experimentation and Game Theory." Paper presented at the European Conference on the History of Economics titled "The 'Experiment' in the History of Economics." Paris, April 22–24.

Robbins, Lionel. 1935. *An Essay on the Nature and Significance of Economic Science*, second edition. London: Macmillan.

Roberts, John, and Hugo F. Sonnenschein. 1977. "On the Foundations of the Theory of Monopolistic Competition," *Econometrica* 45: 101–114.

Roth, A.E. 1987. "Introduction and Overview," in A.E. Roth, ed., *Laboratory Experimentation in Economics: Six Points of View*. Cambridge: Cambridge University Press, 1–13.

Roth, A.E. 1994. "Bargaining Experiments," in J. Kagel and A.E. Roth, eds, *Handbook of Experimental Economics*. Princeton, NJ: Princeton University Press.

Rousseas, Stephen W. and Albert G. Hart. 1951. "Experimental Verification of a Composite Indifference Map," *Journal of Political Economy* 59: 288–318.

Rubinstein, A. 1982. "Perfect Equilibrium in a Bargaining Model," *Econometrica* 50: 97–109.

Samuelson, L. 1996. "Bounded Rationality and Game Theory," *Quarterly Review of Economics and Finance* (Special Issue) 36: 17–35.

Selten, R. 1965. "Spieltheoretische Behandlung Eines Oligopolmodells Mit Nachfragetragheit," *Zeitschrift fur die gesamte Staatswissenschaft* 12: 301–324.

Selten, R. 1975. "Reexamination of the Perfectness Concept for Equilibrium Points in Extensive-Form Games," *International Journal of Game Theory* 4: 25–55.

Sent, E.-M. 2004. "The Legacy of Herbert Simon in Game Theory," *Journal of Economic Behavior and Organization* 53(3): 303–317.

Smith, Vernon L. 1962. "An Experimental Study of Competitive Market Behavior," *Journal of Political Economy* 70: 111–137.

Smith, Vernon L. 1992. "Game Theory and Experimental Economics: Beginnings and Early Influences," in E. Roy Weintraub, ed., *Toward a History of Game Theory* (Annual Supplement to Volume 24, *History of Political Economy*). Durham, NC: Duke University Press, 241–282.

Sonnenschein, Hugo F. 1971. "Demand Theory without Transitive Preferences," in John S. Chipman, Leonid Hurwicz, Marcel K. Richter, and Hugo F. Sonnenschein, eds, *Preferences, Utility and Demand: A Minnesota Symposium*. New York: Harcourt Brace Jovanovich Inc.

Sonnenschein, Hugo F. 1973. "Utility Hypothesis and Market Demand Theory," *Western Economic Journal* 11: 404–410.

Sonnenschein, Hugo F. 1985. "Comment," in K.J. Arrow and S. Honkapohja, eds, *Frontiers of Economics*. Oxford: Blackwell.

Stoker, Thomas M. 1984a. "Completeness, Distribution Restrictions, and the Form of Aggregate Functions," *Econometrica* 52: 887–907.

Stoker Thomas M. 1984b. "Exact Aggregation and Generalized Slutsky Conditions," *Journal of Economic Theory* 33: 368–377.

Thaler, R.H. 1988. "Anomalies: The Ultimatum Game," *Journal of Economics Perspectives* 2: 195–206.

Thaler, R.H. 1992. *The Winner's Curse*. Princeton, NJ: Princeton University Press.

Thrall, R.M., C.H. Coombs, and R.L. Davis (eds). 1954. *Decision Processes*. New York: Wiley.

Thurstone, L.L. 1931. "The Indifference Function," *Journal of Social Psychology* 2: 139–167.

van Damme, Eric. 1991. *Stability and Perfection of Nash Equilibria*, second edition. Berlin: Springer Verlag.

van Damme, Eric. 1992. "Refinements of Nash Equilibrium," in J.J. Laffont, ed., *Advances in Economic Theory: Sixth World Congress*, Volume 1. New York: Cambridge University Press, 32–75.

Wallis, W. Allen and Milton Friedman. 1942. "The Empirical Derivation of Indifference Functions," in O. Lange, F. McIntyre, and T.O. Yntema, eds, *Studies in Mathematical Economics and Econometrics in memory of Henry Schultz*. Chicago, IL: University of Chicago Press, 175–189.

Weintraub, E. Roy 1979. *Microfoundations*. Cambridge: Cambridge University Press.

4 Thought- and performed experiments in Hayek and Morgenstern

Alessandro Innocenti and Carlo Zappia

The necessary consequence of the reason why we use competition is that, *in those cases in which it is interesting*, the validity of the theory can never be proved empirically. We can test it on conceptual models, and we might conceivably test it in artificially created real situations where the facts which competition is intended to discover are already known to the observer. But in such cases it is of no practical value, so that to carry out the experiment would hardly be worth the expense ... The peculiarity of competition – which it has in common with the scientific method – is that its performance cannot be tested in particular instances where it is significant, but is shown only by the fact that the market will prevail in comparison with any alternative arrangements.

(Friedrich A. Hayek 1968, p. 180)

...experiments are designed to enable us to predict outcomes under controlled conditions and to make it possible to conclude from those to wider applications. There are, of course, limits to experiments in economics, but in a sense any variation in taxation, in foreign exchange rates, in tariffs, etc. etc., can be viewed as a coarse experiment whose result can lead to new theories and hence to better prediction when the new occasion comes around.

(Oskar Morgenstern 1972, p. 710)

4.1 Introduction

It has been argued that the emergence and early progress of experimental economics are related to the work of Oskar Morgenstern (Schotter 1992). Although he did not publish any experimental findings, Morgenstern became involved in the development of experiments in economics in at least two ways. First, most of his contributions to economics, from the 1928 volume on economic prediction to the 1970 work on the predictability of stock prices, were devoted to various aspects of empirical research, including the promotion of both econometrics and statistical analysis. Second, in conjunction with John von Neumann, he created game theory, whose way of modeling the process of decision-making lent itself to experimental applications. Morgenstern was an unconventional kind of thinker, tending to anticipate "unexpected" turns in the evolution of mainstream science, rather than contribute to its systematization. And experimental economics has, indeed, been viewed as a development that has initiated an important thread in the criticism of neoclassical economics, the full implications of which are still to be drawn (Smith 1989).

However, curiously, Morgenstern's early contributions as an economist were characterized by the view that economics as a science was mainly deductive, in the sense associated with the Austrian construction of the thought experiment (Moss 1997).[1] The "method of imaginary construction," or "thought experiment," typical of the Austrian tradition, can be seen as a method to help economists avoid facing complexity in the initial steps of analysis. Morgenstern (1954, p. 484) describes thought experiments as the method of "imagining conditions that differ from the known conditions and then attempting to identify the proper factor to which the imagined variations could be ascribed." The method proves valuable mainly when the role of a single important element of a complex system is to be ascertained, for example the role of the alert entrepreneur in the Austrian theory of the competitive market.[2] The method was intended by Austrian economists as an instrument for drawing logical lessons with empirical content from imaginary constructions. In Morgenstern's (1954, p. 484) words, "this procedure consists in the drawing of implications and like other experiments may lead to the discovery of new facts." For instance, Friedrich A. Hayek considered general equilibrium theory as a thought experiment aimed at identifying the causes of intertemporal discoordination (Hayek 1941, p. 26).[3]

This essay argues that a comparative analysis of Hayek's and Morgenstern's contributions can suggest why methods as different as thought- and performed experiments have been advocated in economics. In the mid-1930s, the two Austrian economists shared the view that the empirical content of economics was to be sought outside equilibrium theory, by applying the deductive method. In the 1950s, Morgenstern's renewed call for empirical analysis actually signaled a shift towards an inductive approach, endorsing the methodological value of direct, performed experiments, in contrast to Hayek's persistent reliance on a deductive approach to empirical analysis, and on the thought experiment as its main instrument. Essentially, we maintain that they held a common methodological stance in the 1930s, but Morgenstern later embraced an inductive approach while Hayek continued to reject it.[4] It is worth specifying that, in stressing the contrast between Hayek and Morgenstern as exponents of diverging methodologies, our assessment of their respective positions inevitably neglects other differences between the two authors.[5]

We shall consider Morgenstern's definition of a thought experiment, quoted above, as a point of reference. It is certainly a clear-cut, but also quite restrictive, definition. Morgenstern, it seems, had in mind qualitative results concerning the movements of endogenous variables with respect to controlled variations in data, something which might resemble an exercise in comparative statics in a formal model. It is true that the methodology of thought experiment has been applied by Austrian economists not only to comparative statics but also to comparisons between the competitive market and imaginary alternative frameworks.[6] However, to contrast the routes taken by the two Austrian economists, we have found it preferable to embrace Morgenstern's definition.

The essay is structured as follows. Section 4.2 argues that a specific episode in the middle of the 1930s, namely a quite subterranean discussion about the assumption of perfect foresight in economics, was indicative of the two writers' growing dissatisfaction with the concept of equilibrium. The outgrowth of the exchange between Hayek and Morgenstern is interpreted as a plea, shared by both, for empirical analysis. Section 4.3 contends that, in spite of the deductive approach shared by the two economists, their respective articles on perfect foresight (Morgenstern 1935, and Hayek 1937) laid the basis for future disagreement on experiments. Section 4.4 deals mainly with Morgenstern's later turn towards an inductive approach and his recommendation of experimental investigation in economics, as opposed to the canonical use of thought experiments. There follows an examination of the intellectual process leading to Morgenstern's position, as stated in the passage quoted at the beginning of the essay. Section 4.5 considers Hayek's reliance on a deductive approach in his subsequent analysis of the market process and of competition as a discovery procedure. The rationale of Hayek's faith in the method of thought experiment in the 1960s, with specific regard to his contention that complex phenomena cannot be dealt with by means of empirical analysis in the form of performed experiments, is briefly investigated.

4.2 Perfect foresight and thought experiments in the 1930s

In the 1920s and 1930s, the role of time in economic theory was controversial, especially in the Austrian circles of Ludwig von Mises and Hans Mayer. These were two distinct groups of young economists, including Hayek and Morgenstern respectively.[7] Both groups were aware that a better understanding of the way individuals plan their actions in an intertemporal setting was required if the shortcomings of stationary equilibrium were to be overcome. In Lachmann's (1990) words, the economists working on the Austrian variant of the neoclassical approach in the 1930s, after dealing with the subjectivity of values, were striving to incorporate the subjectivity of expectations into economic theory.

Despite the common origin of Hayek's and Morgenstern's efforts to make room for expectations by incorporating a time dimension, their investigations produced conflicting results. Hayek, who is hailed as the first economist to introduce the notion of intertemporal equilibrium (see Milgate 1979, who refers to Hayek 1928), made his first attempt at explicitly incorporating expectations in equilibrium theory in his 1933 Copenhagen Lecture on "Price Expectations, Monetary Disturbances and Malinvestment" (published in German in 1935). From the very beginning of this essay, he was at pains to define the conditions for expectational equilibrium:

> It has become clear that, instead of completely disregarding the time element, we must make very definitive assumptions about the attitude of persons toward the future. The assumptions of this kind which are implied in the concept of equilibrium are essentially that everybody foresees the future correctly and that this foresight includes not only the changes in objective data but also the behaviour of all other people with whom he expects to perform economic transactions.
>
> (1935, pp. 139–140)[8]

This passage struck Morgenstern, who, in his essay "Perfect Foresight and Economic Equilibrium" (1935, p. 171), considered it as an exemplar of the erroneous opinion, prevailing among those dealing with the time element, that "the theoretical perfection of equilibrium could not be obtained without the assumption of complete foresight by the economic subjects and the entrepreneurs."[9] Engaged as he was in reformulating equilibrium through the application of time and expectations (see section 4.3 below), Morgenstern argued that, despite being generally viewed as a prerequisite for equilibrium over time, the meaning of "full," "perfect" or "correct" foresight was far from obvious.[10] Morgenstern's statement of what perfect foresight means in equilibrium theory is worth quoting:

> The individual exercising foresight must thus not only know exactly the influence of his own transactions on prices but also the influence of every other individual, and of his future behaviour on that of the others, especially of those relevant for him personally.... The impossibly high claims which are attributed to the intellectual efficiency of the economic subjects immediately indicate that there are included in this equilibrium system not ordinary men, but rather, at least to one another, exactly equal demi-gods, in case the claim of complete foresight is fulfilled ... If "full" or "perfect" foresight is to provide the basis of the theory of equilibrium in the strict specified sense ... then a completely meaningless assumption is considered. If limitations are introduced in such a way that the perfection of foresight is not reached, then these *limitations are to be stated very precisely*.
>
> (Morgenstern 1935, p. 173)[11]

Here, Morgenstern is not simply questioning the realism of perfect foresight; he is also interested in examining "somewhat closely the conditions which result if full foresight is posited and *especially if there results recipro-*

cal inclusion of foresight about the probable behaviour of others." Morgenstern seems to accept that the hypothesis of perfect foresight can be a useful tool for analyzing the behavior of an individual taken in isolation. But once the "Robinson Crusoe economy" is left aside and the interactive aspects of economic action are considered, Morgenstern strikes a skeptical note:

> The fact is that a calculation of the effects of one's own future behaviour always rests on the expected future behaviour of others, and *vice versa. This can be observed empirically every time*. However, the chain of surmised mutual 'reactions' breaks off comparatively soon; often too, they play no excessive role because of the power of external data of a physical nature. This may be the case on certain markets, for example as the stock-exchange. With unlimited foresight, it is something else.
>
> (1935, p. 173)

At this point, Morgenstern (1935, pp. 173–174) takes up the paradox of Holmes and Moriarty[12] featuring in a previous work of his. The paradox is an argument in support of the view that "an endless chain of reciprocally conjectural reactions and counter-reactions . . . can never be broken by an act of knowledge but always only through an arbitrary act – a resolution." It follows that "unlimited foresight and economic equilibrium are thus irreconcilable with one another." Morgenstern's use of the paradox clearly evokes the methodology of thought experiment. The analysis of Holmes's chain of deductions is intended to show that the "empirical" information obtained from a mental, not a performed, experiment allows the theorist to rule out certain theoretical conjectures, which, in this instance, concern how equilibrium is to be defined in an interpersonal decision problem over time. The unfolding paradox is essential for Morgenstern's claim that it is logically inconsistent to attempt to solve the problem of strategic interaction over time by assuming perfect foresight.

To move on to how Hayek reacted to Morgenstern's allegations, the relevant text is "Economics and Knowledge." Hayek presents this article as an attempt to make equilibrium analysis applicable to intertemporal price relationships. After giving the celebrated definition of equilibrium as a state of coordination of individual plans,[13] Hayek (1937, p. 42) comments: "These considerations seem to throw considerable light on the relationship between equilibrium and foresight, which has been somewhat hotly debated in recent times." The footnote reference is to Morgenstern's 1935 paper. It is arguable, therefore, that the discussion on the meaning of correct foresight which follows is, at least in part, an answer to Morgenstern:

> Correct foresight is then not, as it has sometimes been understood, a precondition that must exist in order that equilibrium may be arrived at. It is rather the defining character of a state of equilibrium. Nor

> need foresight for this purpose be perfect in the sense that it need extend into the indefinite future or that everybody must foresee everything correctly. We should rather say that equilibrium will last so long as the anticipations prove correct and that they need to be correct only on those points, which are relevant for the decisions of individuals. But on this question of what is relevant foresight or knowledge, more later.
>
> (Hayek 1937, p. 42)

As regards Hayek's partial revision of the relationship between equilibrium and foresight, announced in the 1939 English reprint of the 1933 lecture, two points of clarification are brought forward. On the one hand, correct foresight is now precisely viewed as neither an assumption nor a pre-condition for equilibrium, but as the defining characteristic of equilibrium itself. On the other hand, correct foresight is not equivalent to perfect foresight, for the requirements for correct foresight are, in a sense, less strict. Both these arguments implicitly refer to the questions raised by Morgenstern. In particular, the second point hints at the limited cognitive and computational capabilities of individuals; hence "demi-gods" are not necessarily involved. This clarification can be interpreted as entailing that, *contra* Morgenstern, accuracy in the anticipation of all future events is not required. It is only necessary to anticipate the events that could imperil the validity of the theories of the workings of the economy held by individuals.[14] However, Hayek did not endorse Morgenstern's point concerning the logical inconsistency of equilibrium with perfect foresight. Hayek's revision of the notion of equilibrium shows how the "tautological propositions of pure equilibrium analysis" regarding the actions of a single individual could consistently be applied to the explanation of economic interrelations.

Hayek also refers to Morgenstern's paper in the 1946 essay "The Meaning of Competition." He states that "complete knowledge of the relevant factors on the part of all participants in the market" is the most "critical and obscure" condition assumed by the theory of perfect competition. On this, Hayek concludes with a remark on Morgenstern's point which one cannot find in the 1937 paper: "I shall here not go into the familiar paradox of the paralysing effect really perfect knowledge and foresight would have on all action." It is apparent that Hayek is maintaining that the logical problems associated with the notion of equilibrium with "really" perfect foresight do not concern his own 1937 notion of equilibrium with correct foresight. In particular, he continued to use equilibrium with "correct" foresight as a useful logical instrument in *The Pure Theory of Capital*, that is, in his last attempt to formulate the model of real economy on which his theory of the trade cycle was based (Hayek 1941).

Although with different emphases, in their essays of the mid-1930s both Hayek and Morgenstern, after dealing with the notion of equilibrium over time, explicitly addressed the question of the empirical content of economic theory. They shared the view that this empirical content was to be sought outside equilibrium theory. In fact, they seem to outline a two-step procedure to develop economics. The first step of the procedure aimed to make economics an exact science: the typical neoclassical practice of using, in Morgenstern's (1935, p. 169) words, "neither exact nor complete statements about the assumptions underlying the theory of general equilibrium" should be replaced with a method of reasoning, such as the axiomatic method, which allowed for an exact recognition of all the implications of a given set of propositions, as well as an exact derivation of theorems from propositions. As has been noted (Leonard 1995, p. 313), the 1935 essay signals that, under the influence of a new mentor, Karl Menger, Morgenstern was eventually escaping the influence of Mayer, who, following the Austrian tradition of Carl Menger, firmly opposed the use of mathematics in economics.[15] Even if, unlike Morgenstern, he did not contribute directly to this development, Hayek (1937, p. 35) pointed to the same issue when he explained that

> my criticism of the recent tendencies to make economic theory more and more formal is not that they have gone too far but they have not yet carried far enough to complete the isolation of this branch of logic and to restore to its rightful place the investigation of the causal processes, using formal economic theory as a tool in the same way as mathematics.

The second step of the procedure aimed to specify the empirical content of economics. However brilliant the development of equilibrium theory by means of the axiomatic method, the process through which equilibrium can be obtained in actual economies remains to be investigated; and this task necessarily entails an examination of what foresight and knowledge mean for individuals acting in actual economies (see in particular Morgenstern 1935, p. 178, and Hayek 1937, p. 46).[16]

In the 1930s, however, Hayek and Morgenstern differed with respect to the way in which this empirical content was to be investigated. A first point to note is that both authors were deductive in approach. In particular, they were trying to deal with the assumption of incomplete knowledge in actual economies by applying mental chains of deductions and conjectures. That is to say, both were thinking in terms of thought experiments: they altered one relevant variable at a time and then speculated on the effects on the economy. But they assumed different starting points for their thought experiments. On the one hand, Hayek relied on his own definition of equilibrium as a state of plan coordination over time, a reliance which made the exercise sensible, in a way not unlike comparative static analysis. On the other hand, Morgenstern was not convinced at all that a plausible notion of equilibrium with foresight could be devised; thus he showed limited confidence in the mental deductions he was drawing from the assumption of incomplete knowledge.

4.3 In search of a role for empirical analysis in economics

Although Morgenstern's 1935 essay is usually referred to for its critical part, it features a constructive part as well. Morgenstern is aware that, if equilibrium theory is to be preserved, an alternative formal structure must be devised to deal with the intricate relationships between economic phenomena involving interpersonal decisions.[17] As will be substantiated below, *Theory of Games and Economic Behavior*, to which Morgenstern contributed mainly through his criticism of neoclassical economics in the first chapter, can be interpreted as the chief outcome of Morgenstern's search for "exactness" in the analysis of market interactions among individual agents. However, the 1935 essay contains no substantive hint at the formal representation emerging later. Here Morgenstern (1935, pp. 175–179) devises an informal model in which he assumes, first, individual agents endowed with different degrees of knowledge. These agents are interested in subsets of the environment and constantly adjust their "opinion" about the environment, until "there is no longer any improvement in the sense of constant welfare." Second, Morgenstern postulates the existence of highly knowledgeable individuals endowed with "purely theoretical knowledge of [economic] relationships," who are able to evaluate the "overall" consequences of their behaviour. But he fails to explain how this purely theoretical knowledge differs from perfect foresight.[18]

Although Morgenstern (1935, p. 175) states his intention to investigate the importance of foresight and knowledge for actual economies, he brings forward only vague suggestions.[19] Individuals endowed with a certain "degree of foresight," which is based on varying amounts of insight into economic relationships, usually revise expectations in response to environmental changes. This means that expectations should be viewed as data of the economy and that, as for other data, comparative statics are necessary to understand their role in actual economies. Thus, Morgenstern was groping for a research strategy that ultimately resembles an exercise in comparative statics without any consistently defined state of equilibrium to start from. Moreover, after the "cogent examination" of interpersonal decision problems in *Theory of Games and Economic Behavior*, Morgenstern seemed no longer interested in defining, and, what is more important, using a notion of general equilibrium over time for analysing the empirical content of economic theory.

After 1945, Morgenstern switched his attention to the second step of the procedure. Arguably, one reason for this change of interest can be found in the 1935 essay, which concludes with a reference to the need for a more inductive approach supported by statistical data:

> a great number of empirical studies may have to be made ... in order to obtain some kind of a picture about the range of the element of expectations ... It would, for example, be quite conceivable to submit as the adequate data concrete transactions, going on to prove what this result would be, compared with the actual, had different coefficient of expectations been set up.... On the basis of these empirical studies and by means of the materials of experience ... concrete theorems may be handled in such a way that there are discovered expectations and foresight factors, which have been included but generally unexpressed.
>
> (Morgenstern 1935, p. 183)

As will be argued in the following section, Morgenstern's endorsement of the experimental turn in economics derived from the methodological option he favored in the process of giving economic theory empirical content.

As for Hayek's approach, his viewpoint is clearly stated at the very beginning of "Economics and Knowledge:"

> I shall contend that the empirical element in economic theory – the only part which is concerned not merely with implications, but with causes and effect, and which leads therefore to conclusions which, at any rate in principle, are capable of verification (or rather falsification) – consists of propositions about the acquisition of knowledge.
>
> (Hayek 1937, p. 33)

In Hayek's view, economics can claim the status of empirical science only to the extent that it is capable of analyzing the conditions under which "the knowledge and the intentions of the different members of society are supposed to come more and more in agreement" (Hayek 1937, p. 45), as the economy is supposed to be, by assumption, in equilibrium. Indeed, it is in the 1937 essay that one first finds Hayek's claim about the importance of dispersed non-price knowledge, as well as of its diffusion through the market process; this was to become a main recurrent theme not only of his work (Hayek 1946, 1968), but of the modern Austrian school in general (Vaughn 1994, Ch. 4).

Hayek's investigation of the disequilibrium process through which individual knowledge is used, and through which it changes, can be considered as his version of the second step of the two-step procedure. However, although he makes constant reference to the empirical aspect of his analysis, Hayek never sets out to verify (or falsify by means of empirical counterexamples) the propositions put forward. In fact, he advocates (1937, p. 55) a strictly deductive approach:

> in stressing the nature of the empirical propositions of which we must make use if the formal apparatus of equilibrium analysis is to serve for

> an explanation of the real world, and in emphasising that the propositions about how people will learn, which are relevant in this connection, are of fundamentally different nature of those of formal analysis, I do not mean to suggest that there opens here and now a wide field for empirical research. I very much doubt whether such investigation would teach us anything new.

Here, Hayek's lasting faith in the principles of the Austrian school (as compared to Morgenstern's "heterodoxy") is clearly expressed. As briefly recalled in the introductory section, deductivism has been a feature shared by almost all scholars of the Austrian school, beginning with Carl Menger's attack on the German historical school.[20] In Hayek's case, he commits himself to a deductive approach even in the pursuit of the empirical content of economic theory.[21] The rationale for Hayek's commitment to deductivism was the subject of elaboration and revision in later works, as shown in section 4.5.

4.4 Morgenstern and the postwar rise of performed experiments

The postwar debate on the relation between theory and empirics in economics was influenced by the first performed experiments. The Santa Monica conference of 1952 played a crucial part in this story; it has been viewed as the birthplace of experimental gaming.[22] The conference, in which game theorists met experimenters associated with the Rand Corporation, was promoted by the Ford Foundation and Michigan University under the title "The Design of Experiments in Decision Processes." Among the nineteen essays published in Thrall *et al.* (1954), two deserve mention for their influence on subsequent developments, especially in experimental methodology: the essay by Estes (1954) and that by Kalisch *et al.* (1954). Estes's essay, which aimed to show that learning could be represented as a converging stochastic process, triggered off a debate on the informational and computational capacities of economic agents. This debate featured Flood (1954), Simon's *Models of Man* (1957), and Sidney Siegel, who in the early 1960s carried out a laboratory experiment proving the importance of monetary incentives to the behavior of experimental subjects.[23] "Some Experimental n-Person Games" by Kalisch *et al.*, although far from conclusive, showed how game theory allowed translation of the hypotheses to be tested into simple and precise models. The experimental subjects were first instructed in the main principles of game theory and then submitted to the experiment with predetermined time; payments consisted of tokens that were converted into dollars at the end of the experiment. The discussion of results took into account both informational and environmental conditions and the different personalities of the subjects.

These contributions did not go unnoticed by Morgenstern, who attended the conference. In his presentation, Morgenstern (1954, p. 484) argued that performed experiment should have a place in the economist's toolbox:

> I do believe that there exist great opportunities for direct experiments now and in the future. I am thinking of the actual, *physical*, experiment, i.e., one in which physical reality is being subjected to desired conditions, as distinguished from the so-called "thought-experiment."

Morgenstern's confidence in the usefulness of experimentation in social sciences was strengthened by the ensuing experimental activity, which he correctly perceived as an outgrowth of game theory. In the 1950s there were two different approaches to experimentation: the socio-psychological one, represented by experimental gaming, and the economic-managerial approach, expressed by business games.[24] These approaches shared two main features: firstly, the object of verification was usually represented by games in normal form; secondly, their theoretical background related to economics only indirectly, with other social sciences having the lion's share.[25] In business games, in particular, a multiplicity of factors (like the subjects' intellectual ability, patterns of learning, personality traits, and social origin) matched a variety of types of economic behavior to be considered "rational" or "maximizing." As Hoggatt (1959, pp. 192–195) put it: "we focus on using game situations as a research tool for studying the behavior of human beings in conflict situations ... [our aim is] to observe how the subject's actual behavior compares with various types of maximizing behavior as these are visualized in economic theory."

Hoggatt's business game was intended to point out the complexity of human behavior, which did not conform to neoclassical maximizing behavior but was shown to be the outcome of a mixture of conflicting maximum problems. This conclusion closely resembled the view Morgenstern made explicit in the first chapter of *Theory of Games*:

> If two or more persons exchange goods with each other, then the result for each one will depend in general not merely upon his own actions but on those of the others as well. Thus each participant attempts to maximize a function (his above-mentioned "result") of which he does not control all variables. This is certainly no maximum problems, but a peculiar and disconcerting mixture of several conflicting maximum problems. Every participant is guided by another principle and neither determines all variables that affect his interest.
>
> (von Neumann and Morgenstern 1944, p. 11)

Therefore, it is not surprising that, in 1962, Morgenstern, in assessing the meaning of the interplay between game theory and business, noted that "game theory has clearly established the experimental character of economics. Although in a certain sense a by-product only, this nevertheless heralds a new outlook, a new attitude from which economics in general cannot fail to profit" (Morgenstern 1962, p. 11). The 1972 passage quoted in opening this essay, where Morgenstern acknowledges that experiments were basic both to the establishment and application of new economic theories, amounted to a reference to this development.

The tangle of claims and assumptions from which game theory originated is relevant to this story. The collaboration with von Neumann had a momentous effect on Morgenstern's approach to economics. When the two authors met in Princeton, they shared the view that neoclassical theory was not rigorous enough. The "Austrian" Morgenstern embraced von Neumann's mathematical rigor, but, at the same time, went further than von Neumann in arguing for the application of game theory to economics (Mirowski 1992; Rellstab 1992; Schotter 1992; Leonard 1995). Taking advantage of his pre-war criticism of neoclassical theory, Morgenstern claimed that game theory had the potential for a radical change in both the mathematical and the theoretical foundations of economic science. In particular, game theory could remove the simplifications of the Walrasian system. But, while in the 1950s economists promptly assimilated von Neumann's new mathematical concepts, they neglected Morgenstern's claim that the neoclassical postulate of maximization had to be either weakened or abandoned.[26] The application of game theory to economics was characterized by an emphasis on formal aspects until the 1970s, at least, when the identification of game theory with the theoretical analysis of competitive markets weakened. The heterodox potentialities of game theory have been developed only recently, chiefly through the rejection of that crucial neoclassical postulate, the coincidence between rational choice and the solution of a well-defined maximization problem. In the 1950s, Morgenstern was already aware that game theory was incompatible with the principle of constrained maximization. Dispensing with this essential hypothesis would lead economists to focus on empirically meaningful models of behavior.

In Morgenstern's view, game theory represented the appropriate foundation for a new analysis of the empirical processes of economic exchange. Building on the basis of von Neumann's mathematical apparatus of *Theory of Games*, game theory could provide both an abstract environment for empirical and experimental analysis and counterexamples leading to a re-examination of the basic postulates of the neoclassical approach. In the papers of the 1930s discussed in the previous section, Morgenstern maintained that neoclassical theory made improper use of mathematics. In particular, the formulation of problems was too inaccurate to render their translation into axiomatic terms possible, statements were often treated as proofs, and references to actual economic life were confused and offered no clue as to the relation between theory and empirical evidence.[27] In order to correct these methodological flaws, Morgenstern (1936) proposed the introduction of Hilbertian logic into economics. He intended this type of logic as a formal tool capable of identifying all implications of any proposition with exactitude. As already mentioned, *Theory of Games and Economic Behavior* presented what Morgenstern meant to be the first step of the procedure outlined in the previous section – the definition of economics as an exact science. In arguing in favor of a "process of mathematization" of economics, von Neumann and Morgenstern (1944, p. 4) maintained that the chief reason why mathematics had not been widely used in economics was that "economic problems are not formulated clearly and are often stated in such vague terms as to make mathematical treatment *a priori* appear hopeless." Clearly enough, Morgenstern's agenda did not change over the decades, with the need for empirical analysis intertwining with that for axiomatization, and both stemming from a comprehensive critique of neoclassical economics.

A reconstruction of Morgenstern's contribution to *Theory of Games* that stresses continuity with his previous work might appear to overemphasize Morgenstern's intellectual consistency.[28] However, our point here is that the formal framework emerging from the collaboration with von Neumann constitutes one possible alternative (indeed, the main alternative; see Myerson 1999) to general equilibrium with perfect foresight, and that it signals the definitive turn of modern economic theory towards axiomatics, as Morgenstern advocated. But, at the same time, both a call for methodological "modesty"[29] and the preponderant role of von Neumann's mathematics had the effect of postponing progress in the analysis of the empirical content of economic theory. Nevertheless, it remains true that von Neumann and Morgenstern's (1944, pp. 4, 5) contention is that "the empirical background of economic science is definitely inadequate," and that though "the aim of this book lies not in the direction of empirical research," it may be hoped that "as a result of the improvement of scientific technique and of experience gained in other fields, the development of descriptive economics will not take as much time as the comparison with astronomy would suggest."

Morgenstern followed this line of inquiry in his post-*Theory of Games* activity, starting with his 1950 volume *On the Accuracy of Economic Observations*, an investigation into the reliability of economic data. The book aimed to found a new research area on the measurement of error; its second chapter listed many sources of errors in economic statistics, and the first of these sources was the lack of designed experiments.[30] This deficiency was considered as the main cause of an essential difference between natural and social sciences: while, in the natural sciences, the theorist could confidently rely on the methods by which data were collected, in the social sciences, this confidence was lacking, because the collector and user of data were often different people (Morgenstern 1950, p. 17). Consequently, given the goal of making the interplay between theory and data collection in economics as close as it was in physics, it was necessary to add performed experiments to the tools commonly employed by economists for the empirical verification of their models.

In 1954, Morgenstern's took up the point on experiment in "Experiment and Large Scale Computation in Economics," which addressed two issues: "first the occasional appearance of strictly planned experiments and second the ability to compute on large scale (with the aid of electronic computers) by making use of currently available theory" (Morgenstern 1954, p. 493). Both these new tools suggested the failings of thought experiments:

> [The thought experiment] is legitimate but exceedingly difficult to handle, hence the numerous times when it has given rise to poor results. It is often restricted to qualitative considerations. When one thought-experiment follows another new difficulties may arise. Length of chains of deduction can itself become a serious logical problem as can be seen from the difficulty of deciding in some mathematical proofs whether the proof is correct or not, if only because it is of "great" length.
>
> (Morgenstern 1954, p. 484)

It is noteworthy that while in the 1930s Morgenstern took issue with the logical consistency of the Walrasian system by means of a typical thought experiment, in the 1950s, he questioned the efficacy of the method of thought experiment through a criticism of the feature previously resorted to, namely, the length of chains of conjectural reactions and counter-reactions, carried *ad infinitum*. This was employed to show, in the 1930s, that perfect foresight prevented any definitive equilibrium resolution, and, in the 1950s, that the use of thought experiments involved serious logical problems. If, in the 1930s, Morgenstern's escape from the indeterminacy of equilibrium was an arbitrary decision breaking the chain of conjectures, in the 1950s, the way out of the indefinite deductive procedure of thought experiment was to perform a laboratory experiment.[31]

To summarize, Morgenstern made an effort to implement a more realistic attitude in economics. Besides methodological pronouncements and analytical groundwork, this effort consisted of writings on temporal data series, statistical errors, and dynamic growth models. Within this framework, he regarded performed experiments as one of the ways to improve the empirical side of economic analysis. But, in his view, scientific enterprise should also have targeted a revision of the theoretical models with which analysis begun. In fact, the conventional conception of economic behavior proved sharply different from that entailed by game theoretical models. This discrepancy has been demonstrated by laboratory experimentation to a degree that goes well beyond Morgenstern's original insights; collecting evidence in simple choice settings like games has disclosed, in Morgenstern's words (1954, p. 496), "some properties of a nature hitherto unknown."

4.5 Empirical research in deductive terms: Hayek's position

In Morgenstern's case, his intention to uncover the critical points of neoclassical theory, in combination with his eagerness to provide economics with fresh empirical content, resulted in an inductive approach, which explains his advocacy of experimental methods of analysis. On the contrary, Hayek's search for the empirical content of economic theory after "Economics and Knowledge" shows lasting confidence in the deductive approach. Starting with the debate on socialist calculation, though, Hayek's work became much more wide-ranging than the pure economic analysis he had pursued in the early 1930s. In this respect, the 1942–44 essay "Scientism and the Study of Society" is of crucial importance, because it can be argued that nearly all of Hayek's mature methodological views are put forward in this essay (Caldwell 1994).

Hayek's essay on scientism lays the basis for a new argument in favor of the deductive method. The main point is that scientism in social sciences, defined as the application of the method and language of natural sciences, is fruitless because the subject matter of the two forms of scientific knowledge is fundamentally different. Namely, the human beliefs studied by the social sciences cannot be reduced to any "objective fact" about the external world, though they constitute a fundamental component of the "external" world to be analyzed by a single individual:

> the facts of social sciences are merely opinions, views held by the people whose actions we study. They differ from the fact of physical sciences in being beliefs or opinions held by particular people, beliefs which as such are our data ... and which we can recognise from what they do and say merely because we have ourselves a mind similar to theirs.
>
> (Hayek 1942–44, p. 47)

As a result:

> It is only by the systematic and patient following up of the implications of many people holding certain views that we can understand, and often even only learn to see, the unintended and often uncomprehended results of the separate and yet interrelated actions of men in society.
>
> (Hayek 1942–44, p. 58)

As anticipated through the excerpt from "Economics and Knowledge" quoted near the end of section 4.3, even this evolved version of Hayek's methodology lends no support to empirical analysis, as the term is commonly intended. Hayek's deductive method still consisted in obtaining, by means of an effort of imagination, what empirical analysis could, allegedly, not provide by itself. In this sense, thought experiments had a "purely pedagogic" purpose, as Moss (1997, p. 157) points out. But they also represented a tool designed to fill the gap between theory and reality, according to an approach that Hayek would define more clearly in the 1950s and 1960s, building on the basis of the essay on scientism. Actually, the full development of this methodological conception had to await Popper's contribution.[32]

Hayek (1955) holds that the aim of any model is confined to the definition of a certain range of phenomena, supposedly produced by the type of situation under consideration. According to this account, "the selection and application of the appropriate theoretical scheme thus becomes something of an art where success or failure cannot be ascertained by any mechanical test" (Hayek 1955, p. 18). Such a vision of scientific work distanced Hayek from the inductive method based on experiments. According to Hayek, in the social sciences, theories are particularly difficult to prove or disprove. The multiplicity of factors determining any situation prevents the validity of deductive reasoning from being established by direct observation. Therefore, deduction remains the single way to limit the range of phenomena to expect. Deduction relies upon the application of our existing knowledge, which is also a base for new knowledge: "that certain conclusions are implied by what we know already does not necessarily mean that we are aware of these conclusions, or are able to apply them whenever they would help us to explain what we observe" (Hayek 1955, p. 7).[33]

Later, Hayek (1964) coined a specific word to define this kind of theorizing. He argued that the complexity of social phenomena required that analysis concentrated on the recurrence of abstract patterns:

> Such a theory destined to remain "algebraic," because we are in fact unable to substitute particular values for the variables, ceases then to be a mere tool and becomes the final result of our theoretical efforts. Such a theory will, of course, in Popper's terms, be one of small empirical content, because it enables us to predict or explain only certain general features of a situation which may be comparable with a great many particular circumstances.... The advance of science will thus have to proceed in two different directions: while it is certainly desirable to make our theories as falsifiable as possible, we must also push forward into fields where, as we advance, the degree of falsifiability necessarily decreases. This is the price we have to pay for an advance into the field of complex phenomena.
>
> (Hayek 1964, pp. 28–29)

From our perspective, this means that, if theory tackles subjects so abstract and many-sided that they exclude meaningful predictions, the only viable alternative is to rely upon imagination to distinguish between what is possible and what is not. Hayek's corollary, as expressed in the quotation that opens this essay, was that the usefulness of performed experiment was invalidated by the consideration that it could be employed only for facts "already known to the observer" (Hayek 1968, p. 180).

Indeed, Hayek based his analysis of the market process and of competition as a discovery procedure mostly on deduction and thought experiments. A substantial continuity characterizes his approach, as is exemplified by its relationship to the Walrasian equilibrium model. In the 1930s, Hayek pointed out its conceptual and methodological flaws for the analysis of the competitive process in conditions of dispersed knowledge. In the perspective of the "Scientism" essay, as well as of the following methodological essays, a Walrasian system of equations is not capable of mastering the patterns which emerge when certain conditions are satisfied, because it is designed to provide "point explanations" like those provided by the natural sciences; but the subject matter of economic analysis is, by its very nature, different from that of the natural sciences. In fact, when complex phenomena are investigated, only "explanations of the principle" can be sensibly formulated. As a result, the notion of spontaneous order (Hayek 1968) is offered as an alternative to Walrasian general equilibrium for the analysis of pattern coordination through the market process. Its purpose is to elucidate the very general conditions under which coordination holds. But its application necessarily entails overlooking the particular circumstances that determine pattern coordination. In this abstract environment, thought experiments can perform their distinctive function, that is, discovering empirical information through experiments that cannot be carried out, but only imagined.[34]

4.6 Concluding remarks

This essay has analyzed how two Austrian economists, Hayek and Morgenstern, dealt with the relationship between thought- and performed experiments. We have maintained that, prior to the 1940s, both Hayek and Morgenstern applied the deductive procedure of thought experiment. On such a basis, they claimed that economics could improve its methodological status if it developed according to a two-step procedure. The first step was to become an exact science thanks to the analytical power guaranteed by the adoption of the axiomatic method; the second step amounted to a careful and precise definition of the empirical content of economics.

After the 1940s, and in particular after the advent of game theory, Hayek and Morgenstern dealt with the empirical content of economics in different ways. On the one hand, Hayek relied on his own definition of empirical analysis as a purely deductive investigation into the process by which individual knowledge changes. Experiments designed to test "artificially created real situations" would not work, because the phenomena of economic life were complex and irreducible to "objective data." On the other hand, Morgenstern promoted the introduction of experimental methods into economics, to take place through the adoption of laboratory procedures transposed from the natural sciences. This change of perspective was a consequence of the flourishing of experimental activities stimulated by game theory. An overview of the early years of experimental economics shows, first, that game theory allowed translation of models into verifiable hypotheses concerning simple choices, and, second, that it created an appropriate setting for experiments, disclosing properties of human behavior that challenged certain basic assumptions of neoclassical economics. These two considerations explain why Morgenstern, contrary to Hayek, changed his mind about thought experiments, and encouraged performed experiments as a useful tool to carry out the empirical step of economic inquiry.

Acknowledgments

We would like to thank Marcello Basili, Roberto Romani, Stefano Vannucci, two anonymous referees and the editors for comments. This essay is part of a research project on "Experiment in Economics" for which financial assistance from the University of Siena is gratefully acknowledged.

Notes

1 The place of Morgenstern in the history of economics is the subject of very different, and sometimes opposite, assessments. For instance, Boettke (1994, p. 2), who considers Mises and Hayek as the main representatives of the Austrian school, and views it as an alternative approach to mainstream economic theory, argues that "individuals like Schumpeter, Haberler, Machlup, Morgenstern and Robbins would carve out their own unique place within economics for their theoretical nuances (due in large part to Austrian themes of imperfect knowledge, dynamic market process, the importance of time and methodology), but they were still viewed by most other economists, and most importantly by themselves, as mainstream neoclassical economists." In the same volume, Schotter (1994, p. 556) opens his essay on social institutions and game theory by observing that "even a casual reading of the introduction of their book indicates that von Neumann and Morgenstern viewed game theory as a unifying theory for the social sciences and not as a narrow replacement for neoclassical economic theory." That Morgenstern's main contribution to economics is the abandonment of the orthodox conception of economic behavior is argued for in Innocenti (1995). Morgenstern's contribution to the theory of games is dealt with in Leonard (1995).

2 This is well exemplified by Mises's "evenly rotating economy." In Mises's work (1963, pp. 244–250), the role of entrepreneurship emerges through a contrast with individuals operating in a timeless, static economy in equilibrium.

3 For a recent, similar viewpoint on equilibrium models see Hahn (1996). The relation between general equilibrium theory and experimentation is discussed at length in Rizvi's chapter.

4 As will be shown, this holds true in spite of both Morgenstern's contribution to the axiomatization of economics in *Theory of Games and Economic Behavior* and Hayek's empirically oriented analysis of alternative institutional environments.

5 We are referring to their different political positions, underlying personal rivalry. On this aspect see Leonard (forthcoming, Ch. 3). It is likely that political views helped to shape their different attitudes towards economics since the 1930s. Since this essay focuses on methodological themes strictly intended, these questions will not be considered in what follows.

6 For instance, Hayek, in the tradition of Wieser, repeatedly referred to an imaginary centrally planned economy in order to highlight the beneficial effects of having decisions decentralized among individual agents in actual economies (in particular, see Hayek 1945).

7 On the relationships between the two circles, and especially on Morgenstern's late dissatisfaction with Mayer's causal-genetic approach, see Böhm (1992). On the Austrian circles in the inter-war period see also Craver (1986) and Kirzner (1994).

8 In the 1935 essay, Hayek's main goal was to show how a theory of business cycle could be based on "expectations inevitably doomed to disappointment." The essay was a reply to Myrdal's allegation that there was no role for expectations in Hayek's trade-cycle theory. This focus on trade-cycle theory may explain why Hayek did not elaborate further the notion of "correct foresight." When the essay was translated into English (1939), Hayek added a footnote to the paragraph just quoted, remarking that "Economics and Knowledge," published in 1937, contained a more elaborate and "partly revised" analysis of the relationship between equilibrium and foresight. As will be argued later, this footnote originated from Morgenstern's attack on this point.

9 Morgenstern quoted the entire passage in the text of his article. Since Morgenstern's article was translated into English (by F. Knight) before the English version of Hayek's article was released, there are some minor differences between the passage as cited from Hayek (1935) and the version given in Morgenstern (1935).

10 Moreover, in Morgenstern's view, the implicit assumption that "there is *identity* between *foresight and the expectation of the future*" shows that those economists were unaware of the difficulties stemming from the introduction of the expectation element. In this connection, Hayek's 1935 essay is quoted once more as a (negative) example.

11 It is appropriate to remark that the term "demi-gods" is largely equivalent to both those of "superoptimizer," as in Winter (1985), and "homo-rationalis," as in Aumann (1985). These terms are used to indicate the knowledge abilities attributed to individual agents in current general equilibrium theory and game theory respectively.

12 The paradox concerns the paralyzing effect on actual action of thinking strategically in a two-person game. The example is that of Moriarty's attempt to induce Holmes to leave London in order to catch him in Dover. Holmes's option to get off the train to Dover at an intermediate stop gives birth to a chain of mental reactions to the expected behavior of the other player. However, Morgenstern's reasoning does not consider the possibility of using mixed strategies. On this point see Bicchieri (1993).

13

> For a society, then, we *can* speak of a *state* of equilibrium at a point in time – but it means only that the different plans which the individuals composing it have made for action in time are mutually compatible. And

> equilibrium will continue, once it exists, so long as the external data correspond to the common expectations of all members of the society.
> (Hayek 1937, p. 41)

14 In modern equilibrium theory, this point has been made explicit by Hahn (1984). It has been convincingly argued that Hahn's definition of equilibrium, which still sets the standard in current equilibrium theory, is nothing but a stochastic version of Hayek's definition (Littlechild 1982). On Hayek's notion of equilibrium as a state of mutual compatibility of plans, see Zappia (1996).

15 Morgenstern's endorsement of the axiomatic method figures one year later in the essay "Logistic and the Social Sciences:" "Beside the axiomatic method there is the genetic method which may even have a higher didactic value. But in order to gain rigorous insight into the state of any science, the use of the axiomatic method cannot be dispensed with" (1936, p. 396). It hardly needs observing that this shift of approach culminates in the introductory chapter of *Theory of Games and Economic Behavior*.

16 To assess the relevance of this task to current economic theory, compare Arrow's remarks (1996, pp. xiii–iv), introducing a recent volume on the status of the rationality hypothesis:

> Interactive rationality is relevant when the payoff of any agent depends on the action of others. In general, then, the best choice of action by A depends on the actions of B and *vice versa*. But how can A know the actions of B? Is it possible to have knowledge (even probabilistic knowledge) of the actions of another? Competitive equilibrium theory provides an answer to this conundrum, game theory (Nash equilibrium) another, each with its own assumption. But the deeper logical question is, how do either of these equilibrium concepts come into being? And, of course, the second question is, are the answers empirically convincing?

17 Morgenstern (1935, p. 174) argues:

> The resulting events are so extremely complicated that only far-reaching employment of mathematics could help to suggest reciprocal dependencies. The relationship between human behaviours dependent on one another, even without the assumption of perfect foresight, is almost inconceivably complicated, and it requires cogent examination.

18 It has been noted that Morgenstern's 1935 essay anticipated the rationale of rational expectations hypothesis (amongst others, see Arrow 1986, and Schotter 1992). This is certainly correct if reference is made to the informal model just mentioned. Morgenstern (1935, p. 177) perceptively observes that if it is maintained that, in order to have equilibrium, "it is enough if every individual belonging to the economy concerned simply knows what the concrete situation will be on a certain future market," then this is incorrect because "it is also posited by the theory that individual acts *rationally*. However, this " 'rationality' posits, in its turn, that the economic subjects themselves perceive the connections and dependencies – that they really see through the relationship to a certain degree." Nevertheless, Morgenstern seems unaware that the requirement of "rationality" attributed to Walrasian (and Paretian) equilibrium, which he understands as something more than individual rationality, is the equivalent of the perfect foresight assumption in a context of uncertainty. If the actions of individual agents vary continuously with foresight and the future realization of relevant variables is a continuous function of actions, it is possible to show that there exists a foresight that would cause itself to be true, as happens with a rational expectations equilibrium. Apart from the information requirement

that the rationality of agents is common knowledge, this theorization is equivalent to Morgenstern's argument on rationality (Radner 1989). As a result, the logical impossibility of a rational expectations equilibrium cannot be argued on these grounds.

19 In an attempt, admittedly provisional, to clarify the meaning of "degree of foresight," Morgenstern proceeds by distinguishing between an individual's insight into mutual relationships, which he terms "technical foreseeability," and "effective foresight," that is "knowledge of individual historical events and occurrences" (1935, p. 179). But the discussion of these two different notions of foresight makes it clear that at this juncture Morgenstern did not have a probabilistic notion of perfect foresight, which he actually considered as a synonym for effective foresight. True, a genuinely probabilistic view of the introduction of time into equilibrium theory cannot equally be found in other contemporary authors, such as Hayek, Hicks, and Myrdal, to mention those referred to by Morgenstern. However, in Morgenstern's case, this absence has damaging implications because he does not seem to grasp that, in the 1930s, the generally accepted meaning for perfect foresight is more similar to "technical" than to "effective" foresight. A better understanding of the requirements for equilibrium over time emerges from Hayek's (1937, p. 42) definition of "correct foresight," to which consideration has already been given. This point is dealt with in detail in Zappia (1999).

20 The achievements and shortcomings of historical empiricism and inductivism, as opposed to Austrian deductivism, have been recently assessed in Grimmer-Solem and Romani (1999).

21 One point should be made before moving on. Hayek's deductivism is substantially different from Mises's apriorism. Mises based his aversion to empirical testing on the methodological viewpoint that the fundamental postulates of economic behavior are to be considered true independently of real experience, that is, they are Kantian synthetic a priori propositions. Hayek, on the contrary, does not deny that a priori propositions by and large reflect structures and connections among objects of economic reality; nevertheless, he maintains that these propositions can be discovered as a result of a mostly deductive theoretical effort (see Smith 1994).

22 For the history of experimental economics, see Smith (1992), Roth (1993, 1995), and Rizvi's essay in this volume. A detailed analysis of the Santa Monica conference can be found in Dimand's essay.

23 The influence of Siegel on experimental economics is discussed in Smith (1992).

24 Experimental games were performed mainly by social scientists (psychologists, sociologists, philosophers and decision theorists) belonging to a closely knit community, chiefly financed by the military. Deutsch (1958), Flood (1958), Loomis (1959), and Scodel *et al.* (1959) tested the Prisoner's Dilemma; Vinacke and Arkoff (1957) verified the coalition theory proposed in *Theory of Games and Economic Behavior*; Mosteller and Nogee (1951), Allais (1953), Edwards (1953), Flood (1955) and Davidson *et al.* (1957) conducted experimental tests of the utility function proposed by von Neumann and Morgenstern in *Theory of Games*; Stone (1958) and Schelling (1958, 1959) verified Nash's bargaining theory and the theory of focal points. Business games, on the other hand, were developed by business-school economists as tools for training and selecting managers. The first business game was performed by a group of economists and managers directed by Richard Bellman, and it was published in 1957. Later, Andlinger and Greene set up a "business management game" (Andlinger 1958), and a group of IBM researchers organized a laboratory to make experiments in decision analysis (International Business Machines 1958a and 1958b). Finally, Hoggatt (1959) used a business game to test Cournot's model.

25 The first feature has been documented by an exhaustive review of experimental gaming in the 1950s (Rapoport and Orwant 1962). The article discusses over forty experiments and shows how each of them can be represented as the verification of a game in normal form. The second feature has been corroborated by an authoritative observer, Herbert Simon: "I do not think that the impetus for experimentation within a game-theoretical framework initially came from economists, but rather from psychologists (particularly those who had begun to build mathematical learning theory), statisticians, and interdisciplinary types close to cybernetics and management science" (quoted in Smith 1992, pp. 253–254).

26 On Morgenstern's attitude towards this issue, see Innocenti (1995). Von Neumann's way forward in the process of abandonment of the neoclassical postulate is discussed at length in Mirowski (2002).

27 See in particular Morgenstern's (1941) harsh review of Hicks's *Value and Capital.*

28 From both a theoretical point of view (e.g., the static, un-Austrian nature of von Neumann's solution to the problem of individuals' interaction), and a biographical one (Morgenstern's moving to the United States due to the degenerating political situation in Austria), there occurred dramatic changes which are not accounted for in our reconstruction.

29

> The field covered in this book is very limited, and we approach it in the sense of modesty. We do not worry at all if the results of our study conform with views gained recently or held for a long time, for what is important is the gradual development of a theory, based on a careful analysis of the ordinary everyday interpretation of economic facts.
>
> (von Neumann and Morgenstern 1944, p. 7)

30 Among these sources, Morgenstern (1950) indicates deliberate hiding of information, low training of observers, failure of questionnaires, aggregation of data, lack of definition or classification, errors of instruments, consideration of discrete rather than continuous intervals of time, and interdependence or stability of errors.

31 In the 1954 article, Morgenstern stresses that the validity of direct experiments rest on their similarity with the experiments performed in physical sciences. In this light, while Chamberlin's (1948) early experiment can be useful "for pedagogical purposes" only, both Mosteller and Nogee's (1951) and Edwards's (1953) experiments on gambling situations are praised because they can provide "a theory of utility of a truly scientific character, removed from the realm of pure speculation." And these experiments, Morgenstern (1954, p. 502) contends, "are on a borderline of economics; they connect with fields where experience with experiments has already been obtained." Again, it was a comparison between economics and natural sciences that led Morgenstern to consider performed experiments as a useful tool for economists.

32 However, see Caldwell (1992) for a different viewpoint.

33 Cartwright's essay in this volume discusses the rationale and limits of the use of deduction in mainstream economic theory. In particular, her discussion of the way economic models can teach us "genuine truths about empirical reality" (p. 137) is reminiscent of Hayek's.

34 Boettke (2000) has argued that Hayek's interest in the impact of alternative institutional environments on the process of coordination of individual plans can be interpreted as an empirical investigation in its own right. In Boettke's view, the fact that Hayek is not in principle averse to both prediction of "patterns" and the empirical recognition of economic regularities allows for a comparison between the implications of a theory and the observation of these regularities.

References

Allais, M. 1953. "Le Comportement de l'homme rationnel devant le risque: critique des postulats et axiomes de l'école américaine." *Econometrica*, XXI: 503–546.

Andlinger, G. R. 1958. "Business Games – PLAY ONE!," *Harvard Business Review*, 36(2): 115–125.

Arrow, Kenneth J. 1986. "Rationality of Self and Others in an Economic System." In Robin M. Hogarth and Martin W. Reder, eds, *Rational Choice. The Contrast between Economics and Psychology*. Chicago: University of Chicago Press.

Arrow, Kenneth J. 1996. "Introduction." In Kenneth J. Arrow, Enrico Colombatto, Mark Perlman and Christian Schmidt, eds, *The Rational Foundations of Economic Behaviour*. Basingstoke: Macmillan.

Aumann, Robert J. 1985. "What is Game Theory Trying to Accomplish?" In Kenneth J. Arrow and Seppo Honkapohja, eds, *Frontiers of Economics*. Oxford: Basil Blackwell.

Bellman, Richard, Charles E. Clark, Donald G. Malcom, Clifford J. Craft and Franc M. Ricciardi. 1957. "On the Construction of a Multi-stage Multi-person Business Game," *Operations Research*, 5(4): 469–503.

Bicchieri, Cristina. 1993. *Rationality and Coordination*. Cambridge: Cambridge University Press.

Boettke, Peter J. 1994. "Introduction." In Peter J. Boettke, ed., *The Elgar Companion to Austrian Economics*. Aldershot: Edward Elgar.

Boettke, Peter J. 2000. "Which Enlightenment, Whose Liberalism? Hayek's Research Program for Understanding the Liberal Society." In Peter J. Boettke, ed., *The Legacy of F. A. Hayek: Politics, Philosophy and Economics*. Cheltenham: Edward Elgar.

Böhm, Stephan. 1992. "Austrian Economics Between the Wars: Some Historiographical Problems." In Bruce J. Caldwell and Stephan Böhm, eds, *Austrian Economics: Tensions and New Directions*. Boston: Kluwer.

Caldwell, Bruce J. 1992. "Hayek the Falsificationist? A Refutation," *Research in the History of Economic Thought and Methodology*, 10: 1–15.

Caldwell, Bruce J. 1994. "Four Theses on Hayek." In Marina Colonna, Harald Hagemann and Omar Hamouda, eds, *Capitalism, Socialism and Knowledge. The Economics of F. A. Hayek*. Vol. II. Aldershot: Edward Elgar.

Chamberlin, Edward H. 1948. "An Experimental Imperfect Market," *Journal of Political Economy*, 56(4): 95–108.

Craver, Earlene. 1986. "The Emigration of the Austrian Economists," *History of Political Economy*, 18(1): 1–32.

Davidson, David, Patrick Suppes and Sidney Siegel. 1957. *Decision Making. An Experimental Approach*. Stanford: Stanford University Press.

Deutsch, Morton. 1958. "Trust and Suspicion," *Journal of Conflict Resolution*, 2: 265–279.

Edwards, Ward. 1953. "Probability-Preferences in Gambling," *American Journal of Psychology*, 66(3): 349–364.

Estes, W. K. 1954. "Individual Behavior in Uncertain Situations: An Interpretation in terms of Statistical Association Theory." In R. M. Thrall, C. H. Coombs and R. L. Davis, eds, *Decision Processes*. New York: John Wiley.

Flood, Merrill M. 1954. "On Game-Learning Theory and Some Decision-Making

Experiments." In R. M. Thrall, C. H. Coombs and R. L. Davis, eds, *Decision Processes*. New York: John Wiley.

Flood, Merrill M. 1955. "A Group Preference Experiment." In *Mathematical Models of Human Behavior*. Stanford: Dunlap Associates.

Flood, Merrill M. 1958. "Some Experimental Games," *Management Science*, 5(1): 5–26.

Grimmer-Solem, Erik and Roberto Romani. 1999. "In Search of Full Empirical Reality: Historical Political Economy, 1870–1900," *European Journal of the History of Economic Thought*, 6(3): 333–364.

Hahn, Frank H. 1984. "On the Notion of Equilibrium in Economics." In *Equilibrium and Macroeconomics*. Oxford: Basil Blackwell.

Hahn, Frank H. 1996. "Rerum Cognoscere Causas," *Economics and Philosophy*, 12(2): 183–193.

Hayek, Friedrich A. 1928. "Das Intertemporal Gleichgewichtssystem der Preise und die Bewegungen des 'Geldwerts.'" *Weltwirtschaftliches Archive*. Vol. 28. (English translation, "Intertemporal Price Equilibrium and Movements in the Value of Money," in Hayek 1984: 71–117.)

Hayek, Friedrich A. 1933. *Monetary Theory and the Trade Cycle*. London: Jonathan Cape.

Hayek, Friedrich A. 1935. "Preiserwartungen, Monetare Storungen und Fehlinvestitionen." *Nationalokonomisk Tidsskrift*. Vol. 73. (English translation, "Price Expectations, Monetary Disturbances and Malinvestments," reprinted in *Profit, Interest and Investment and Other Essays on the Theory of Industrial Fluctuations*. London: Routledge & Kegan Paul, 1939: 135–156).

Hayek, Friedrich A. 1937. "Economics and Knowledge," reprinted in Hayek 1948: 33–56.

Hayek, Friedrich A. 1941. *The Pure Theory of Capital*. Chicago: University of Chicago Press.

Hayek, Friedrich A. 1942–44. "Scientism and the Study of Society," reprinted in Hayek 1952.

Hayek, Friedrich A. 1945. "The Use of Knowledge in Society," reprinted in Hayek 1948: 77–91.

Hayek, Friedrich A. 1946. "The Meaning of Competition," reprinted in Hayek 1948: 92–106.

Hayek, Friedrich A. 1948. *Individualism and Economic Order*. Chicago: University of Chicago Press.

Hayek, Friedrich A. 1952. *The Counter-Revolution of Science: Studies on the Abuse of Reason*. Glencoe: Free Press.

Hayek, Friedrich A. 1955. "Degrees of Explanation," reprinted in Hayek 1967: 3–21.

Hayek, Friedrich A. 1964. "The Theory of Complex Phenomena," reprinted in Hayek 1967: 22–42.

Hayek, Friedrich A. 1967. *Studies in Philosophy, Politics and Economics*. Chicago: University of Chicago Press.

Hayek, Friedrich A. 1968. "Competition as a Discovery Procedure," reprinted in *New Studies in Philosophy, Politics, Economics and the History of Ideas*. Chicago: University of Chicago Press, 1978: 179–190.

Hayek, Friedrich A. 1984. *Money, Capital and Fluctuations: Early Essays*. Chicago: University of Chicago Press.

Hoggatt, Austin C. 1959. "An Experimental Business Game," *Behavioral Science*, 4(3): 192–203.

Innocenti, Alessandro. 1995. "Oskar Morgenstern and the Heterodox Potentialities of the Application of Game Theory to Economics," *Journal of the History of Economic Thought*, 17(2): 205–227.

International Business Machines. 1958a. *IBM Management Decision-Making Laboratory, Model 1: Administrator's Reference Manual*. IBM.

International Business Machines 1958b. *IBM Management Decision-Making Laboratory, Model 1: Instructions For Participants*. IBM.

Kalisch, G. K., J. W. Milnor, J. F. Nash and E. D. Nering. 1954. "Some Experimental n-Person Games." In R. M. Thrall, C. H. Coombs and R. L. Davis, eds, *Decision Processes*. New York: John Wiley.

Kirzner, Israel M. 1994. "Introduction." In M. Kirzner, ed., *Classics in Austrian Economics: A Sampling in the History of a Tradition. The Interwar Period*. London: Pickering.

Lachmann, Ludwig 1990. "G. L. S. Shackle's Place in the History of Subjectivist Thought." In Steven F. Frowen, ed., *Unknowledge and Choice in Economics*. Basingstoke: Macmillan.

Leonard, Robert J. 1995. "From Parlor Games to Social Science: von Neumann, Morgenstern, and the Creation of Game Theory 1928–1944," *Journal of Economic Literature*, 33(6): 730–761.

Leonard, Robert J. (forthcoming). *From Red Vienna to Santa Monica: von Neumann, Morgenstern and Social Science 1925–1960*, mimeo.

Littlechild, Stephen. 1982. "Equilibrium and the Market Process." In I. M. Kirzner, ed., *Method, Process and Austrian Economics*. Lexington: Lexington Books.

Loomis, J. L. 1959. "Communication, the Development of Trust and Cooperative Behavior," *Human Relations*, 12(3): 305–315.

Milgate, Murray. 1979, "On the Origin of the Notion of Intertemporal Equilibrium," *Economica*, 46(1): 1–10.

Mirowski, Philip. 1992. "What Were von Neumann and Morgenstern Trying to Accomplish?" In Weintraub 1992: 113–149.

Mirowski, Philip. 2002. *Machine Dreams: Economics Becomes a Cyborg Science*. Cambridge: Cambridge University Press.

Mises, Ludwig von. 1963. *Human Action: A Treatise in Economics*. New Haven: Yale University Press.

Morgenstern, Oskar. 1928. *Wirtschaftsprognose, Eine Untersuchung ihrer Voraussetzungen und Möglichkeiten*. Wien: J. Springer.

Morgenstern, Oskar. 1935. "Vollkommene Voraussicht und wirtschaftliches Gleichgewicht," *Zeitschrift für Nationalökonomie*, 6: 337–357. (English translation, "Perfect Foresight and Economic Equilibrium," in Schotter 1976: 169–183.)

Morgenstern, Oskar. 1936. Logistik und Sozialwissenschaften. *Zeitschfrift für Nationalökonomie*, 7, 1–24 (English translation, "Logistics and Social Sciences," in Schotter 1976, 389–404).

Morgenstern, Oskar. 1941. "Professor Hicks on Value and Capital," *Journal of Political Economy*, 49(2): 361–393.

Morgenstern, Oskar. 1950. *On the Accuracy of Economic Observations*. Princeton: Princeton University Press.

Morgenstern, Oskar. 1954. "Experiment and Large Scale Computation in Economics." In Oskar Morgenstern, ed., *Economic Activity Analysis*. New York: John Wiley.

Morgenstern, Oskar. 1962. "On the Application of Game Theory to Economics." In *The Recent Advances in Game Theory*, papers delivered at a Meeting of the Princeton University Conference, October 4–6, 1961: 1–12.

Morgenstern, Oskar. 1972. "Descriptive, Predictive and Normative Theory," *Kyklos*, 25(4): 699–714.

Moss, Laurence S. 1997. "Austrian Economics and the Abandonment of the Classic Thought Experiment." In W. Keizer, B. Tieben and R. van Zijp, eds, *Austrian Economics in Debate*. London and New York: Routledge.

Mosteller, Frederick and Philip Nogee. 1951. "An Experimental Measurement of Utility," *Journal of Political Economy*, 59(5): 371–404.

Myerson, Roger B. 1999. "Nash Equilibrium and the History of Economic Theory," *Journal of Economic Literature*, 37(3): 1067–1082.

Radner, Roy. 1989. "Uncertainty and General Equilibrium." In John Eatwell, Murray Milgate and Peter Newman, eds, *The New Palgrave: General Equilibrium*. London: Macmillan.

Rapoport, Anatol and Carol Orwant. 1962. "Experimental Games: A Review," *Behavioral Science*, 7(1): 1–37.

Rellstab, Urs. 1992. "New Insights into the Collaboration between John von Neumann and Oskar Morgenstern on the *Theory of Games and Economic Behavior*." In Weintraub 1992: 77–94.

Roth, Alvin E. 1993. "On the Early History of Experimental Economics," *Journal of the History of Economic Thought*, 15(4): 184–209.

Roth, Alvin E. 1995. "Introduction to Experimental Economics." In John H. Kagel and Alvin E. Roth, eds, *The Handbook of Experimental Economics*. Princeton: Princeton University Press.

Schelling, Thomas C. 1958. "The Strategy of Conflict: Prospectus for a Reorientation of Game Theory," *The Journal of Conflict Resolution*, 2(3): 203–264.

Schelling, Thomas C. 1959. "For the Abandonment of Symmetry in Game Theory," *The Review of Economics and Statistics*, 41(3): 213–224.

Schotter, Andrew, ed., 1976. *Selected Economic Writings of Oskar Morgenstern*. New York: New York University Press.

Schotter, Andrew. 1992. "Oskar Morgenstern's Contribution to the Development of the Theory of Games." In Weintraub 1992: 95–112.

Schotter, Andrew. 1994. "Social Institution and Game Theory." In Peter J. Boettke, ed., *The Elgar Companion to Austrian Economics*. Aldershot: Edward Elgar.

Scodel, A., J. S. Minas, P. Ratoosh and M. Lipetz. 1959. "Some Descriptive Aspects of Two-Person, Non Zero-Sum Games. I," *Journal of Conflict Resolution*, 3(2): 114–119.

Simon, Herbert A. 1957. *Models of Man. Social and Rational*. New York: John Wiley.

Smith, Barry. 1994. "Aristotelism, Apriorism, Essentialism." In Peter J. Boettke, ed., *The Elgar Companion to Austrian Economics*. Aldershot: Edward Elgar.

Smith, Vernon L. 1989. "Theory, Experiment and Economics," *Journal of Economic Perspectives*, 3(1): 151–169.

Smith, Vernon L. 1992. "Game Theory and Experimental Economics: Beginnings and Early." In Weintraub 1992: 241–282.

Stone, Jeremy J. 1958. "An Experiment in Bargaining Games," *Econometrica*, 26(2): 286–296.

Thrall, R. M., C. H. Coombs and R. L. Davis eds. 1954. *Decision Processes*. New York: John Wiley.

Vaughn, Karen I. 1994. *Austrian Economics in America: the Migration of a Tradition*. Cambridge: Cambridge University Press.

Vinacke, Edgar W. and Abe Arkoff. 1957. "An Experimental Study of Coalitions in the Triad," *American Sociological Review*, 22(4): 406–414.

von Neumann, John and Oskar Morgenstern. 1944. *Theory of Games and Economic Behavior*. Princeton: Princeton University Press (second edition, 1947).

Weintraub, Roy E., ed. 1992. "Toward a History of Game Theory," *History of Political Economy*, 24 (annual supplement).

Winter, Sidney G. 1985. "Comment on Arrow and Lucas." In Robin M. Hogarth and M. W. Reder, eds, *Rational Choice. The Contrast between Economics and Psychology*. Chicago: University of Chicago Press.

Zappia, Carlo. 1996. "The Notion of Private Information in a Modern Perspective. A Re-assessment of Hayek's Contribution," *European Journal of the History of Economic Thought*, 3(1): 107–131.

Zappia, Carlo. 1999. "The Assumption of Perfect Foresight and Hayek's Theory of Knowledge," *Revue d'Economie Politique*, 106 (6): 833–846.

5 Social comptabilism and pure credit systems

Solvay and Wicksell on monetary reform

Mauro Boianovsky and Guido Erreygers

5.1 Introduction

In the 1890s the Belgian industrialist Ernest Solvay launched the idea of replacing the existing "mechanism of money" by a new device, which would preserve the benefits of the old system, but would avoid its inconveniences, such as the instability of the price level. He coined the new system "social comptabilism". It would consist of the abolition of (metallic) money and its replacement by a system of accounts. All economic transactions would be mediated by appropriate inscriptions on the debit or credit side of the accounts of those involved. Solvay not only launched the idea, he also devoted great effort to disseminating it. He founded and financed the *Institut des Sciences Sociales* to examine the system in a scientific way. His collaborators studied the Post Office Saving Bank of Vienna, considered to be a prototype of a social comptabilist institution, and drafted a law proposal aimed at the creation of a similar bank in Belgium. A pamphlet aimed at securing their support was sent to famous economists, including Léon Walras. Solvay himself described in detail how one could gradually move from the old to the new system, and gave numerous speeches in the Belgium Senate in a vain attempt to win support for his plans.

A similar proposal was formulated in the late 1890s by the Swedish economist Knut Wicksell. In Chapter 6 of his book *Interest and Prices*, Wicksell introduced the "purely imaginary case" of a "pure credit economy", in which money does not circulate and "all domestic payments are effected by means of the Giro system and bookkeeping transfers". Wicksell had advanced the notion of a pure credit economy in manuscript form in 1889 (see Wicksell 2001 [1889]). Wicksell returned to this idea more than once in later works, including Volume II of his 1906 *Lectures*. With a background quite different from Solvay's, Wicksell conceived of the pure credit economy as part of his study of the demand for money and its velocity of circulation, which he considered to be a crucial element in the explanation of the determinants of the price level. He came to the conclusion that the existing monetary system of his time was gradually approaching the pure credit case, where the price level is decided only by the rate of interest, since what we now call the "real balance effect" is absent from every market. Wicksell pointed out that such a process was being delayed by the use of gold as the standard of value (which was in contradiction with its replacement by credit as store of value and medium of exchange) and suggested the abandonment of the gold standard, to be followed by a law giving power to the central bank to attract interest-earning deposits and make loans at the same rate of interest, which itself would become the basic rate of interest of the system. As discussed below, according to Wicksell, price-level stability could be a feature of a pure credit economy with a central bank, in contrast with a laissez-faire pure credit system.

Solvay's and Wicksell's view that the existing monetary system should be reformed is consistent with the importance of "experiments" in their frameworks, albeit for different reasons, as we shall see below. We will also consider the links between Solvay's and Wicksell's monetary views and those expressed in the 1980s as part of the "New Monetary Economics".

5.2 Solvay's social comptabilism

5.2.1 Solvay on experiments

The young Ernest Solvay must have had a great confidence in the experimental method. In his earliest recorded writing on social questions he wrote, "You choose the positive, sure, egalitarian way, the *experimental method*, the foundation of all modern scientific advances" (1871; *NLD*, II, p. 9).[1] This attitude may have been influenced by his successful experiments with chemical processes. Solvay amassed a huge fortune on the basis of a number of patents that he obtained from 1861 onwards for the industrial fabrication of soda (sodium carbonate, Na_2CO_3) by means of ammoniac. Solvay did not "invent" the process, but he was the first to find a way to exploit the process on an industrial scale. He managed to do so by a combination of intuition and tenacity (Elkhadem and Mayer, 1997, p. 143) and a number of trials and errors in the gas factory of his uncle. Solvay & Cie, the company founded by Ernest and his brother Alfred in 1863, had a difficult start, but began to thrive in the 1870s.

In the late 1870s, Solvay launched himself fully into investigations of a purely scientific character. As he recalled much later, in 1858 he arrived at an intuition that gripped his mind with "une intensité extraordinaire" (*NLD*, I, p. 280):[2] not only matter has mass, but also heat (energy). For about twenty years, he kept the idea to himself, but then he decided both to submit the idea to at least one renowned scientist – the Belgian chemist Jean Servais Stas, who reacted quite sceptically – and to try and prove it by means of experiments. A first experiment consisted of provoking, in a closed copper cask, a chemical reaction releasing an enormous amount of heat; the cask exploded, however, as described in detail in a paper by Ernest Solvay and René Lucion (1877). Other experiments soon followed, one of which involved a specially constructed "shocking machine" (a description is given by Lucion and Brichaux, 1924; cf. also Dony-Hénault, 1942). All of these experiments failed, however: it seemed impossible to prove that energy had a material support and to determine by measurement that the production of energy went together with a loss of mass. As he explained later in his secret *mémoire* of 1896:

> These unsuccessful attempts did not discourage me. On reflection, the experiences which I had done proved once more that the material equivalent of heat could not be detected in the circumstances in which I had been working, nothing more. On the other hand, various considerations led me to think that this equivalent had to be so small that only reasoning, aided by calculations, would allow it to be determined, if it can be determined at all.
>
> (*NLD*, I, pp. 282–283)

This episode in Solvay's life is interesting in three respects. First, it raises the question of whether he, in some sense, anticipated the basics of the relativity theory of modern physics. After his death, Lorentz and Herzen – both active members of Solvay's Conseils de Physique, the first as its president and the second as one of Solvay's close collaborators – politely judged that his guess was a "fortunate intuition" (*NLD*, I, p. 283). In the light of present-day scientific criteria, Isabelle Stengers (1997, p. 154) has characterized it more bluntly as a "simple homonym". Secondly, the episode reveals Solvay's lifelong preoccupation with the notion of energy. In the later stages of his life, he maintained that energetics was the fundamental science, the science upon which all other sciences had to be based. Around the turn of the century, he began to describe his views on social questions first as "social productivism" and then as "social energetics". He found an ally in Wilhelm Ostwald, the 1909 laureate of the Nobel Prize in Chemistry, who dedicated his book *Energetische Grundlagen der Kulturwissenschaft* (1909) to Solvay. When Max Weber reviewed this book, however, he included a truly devastating footnote of five pages long on Solvay's energetic approach.[3]

Thirdly, we believe that Solvay's disappointing experience with scientific experiments pushed him in the direction of research primarily based upon deduction, a preference that he retained until the end of his life. This is clearly illustrated by his declarations on the occasion of the first Conseil de Physique, held at Solvay's invitation in Brussels between 29 October and 3 November 1911. He handed over to the participants – the leading physicists of the time – a note with his "théorie gravito-matérialitique" (Solvay, 1911b). In the opening address, he declared that he had followed the deductive method, and candidly described his approach as "physical philosophy":

> (. . .) this study is more of the nature of physical philosophy than of ordinary physics. For over forty years I have advanced the opinion that with regard to the *essential* mental reconstitution of the active Universe, on which all of us are working with conviction, the last word of supreme enlightenment will be spoken by the philosopher rather than by the experimenter: on this road, as a general rule it will no longer be experience that will continue to incite calculation, but from now on it will mainly be calculation that will incite experience.
>
> (Solvay, 1911a; *NLD*, I, p. 117)

He was convinced that the role of the experimental method in the "science of principles" was transitory or at least of secondary importance, and that the lead would soon be taken by the "chastened philosophical method". Nevertheless, closing the Council, he expressed the wish that the experiments he had in mind for the confirmation or rejection of hypotheses could take place, and he kindly invited the specialists to help him with this (*ibid.*, pp. 120–121).[4]

Solvay's position and wealth allowed him to adopt what he considered to be the high and comfortable position of a pure theorist and to relegate to his collaborators the low tasks of experimentation and verification.[5] He could easily afford to define and pursue his own research projects without having the need to conform to the scientific habits then prevailing. Both in his physical and social and economic research, he was proud of his independence. In an article in which he summarized his views on the social question, he stressed: "I have worked impartially and without prejudice, but nevertheless having a feeling of the result that I should obtain: I have acted like an experimenter in his laboratory" (Solvay, 1898b; *NLD*, II, p. 212). Taken in isolation this quotation could suggest that Solvay gave prominence to the experimental method in his social and economic research, but this is certainly not the case. The message he wanted to convey was that his research was guided by principles in which he strongly believed, and which he had adopted after a long period of internal reflection, rather than on the authority of an external instance. As soon as his convictions were solid enough, he announced the general principles of his thoughts and let his collaborators deal with the facts. The foundation of the Institut des Sciences Sociales in 1894 serves as an example of this approach.[6] In May 1894, Solvay had urged the Minister of Finance to create a specialized organism to study social and economic questions (Solvay, 1894a; *NLD*, II, pp. 71–72). Since the Minister did not take any initiative in that direction, Solvay decided to do it all by himself, taking charge of all the expenses. Perhaps he rushed things somewhat; later he would declare that he had founded the Institut des Sciences Sociales "à titre d'essai", characterizing it as "provisional" in comparison to the "definitive" Institut de Sociologie, founded in 1901 (Dejongh and Hanssens, 1901, p. 17). Nonetheless, he intended the Institute to be heavily oriented towards his own preoccupations, and more precisely to complement his own deductive way of reasoning with a more inductive approach:

> Independently of more general studies, extending to the whole of sociology, this institute will undertake, by means of the observation and study of facts, to examine impartially and thoroughly the *a priori* notions which I believed I had to formulate, and to submit them to the scrutiny of the inductive method.
>
> (Solvay, 1894b, p. 3)[7]

5.2.2 The initial social comptabilist proposal

Among the issues that Solvay put on the agenda of the Institut des Sciences Sociales, his idea for the reform of the monetary system known as "social comptabilism" ranked very high. Contemporaries such as May (1896) and Walras (1897) perceived the Institute as a think tank founded mainly to study and to prepare the practical realization of Solvay's social comptabilism. Although Solvay's initial plan was somewhat broader, it is true that social comptabilism dominated the activities of the Institute. Solvay, who was at that time a senator for the liberal party, entrusted the direction of the Institute to three famous Belgian socialists (and scientists): Guillaume De Greef, Hector Denis and Emile Vandervelde. Other collaborators included Henri La Fontaine, the 1913 laureate of the Nobel Peace Price, and Paul Otlet, the famous bibliographer. The foundation of the Institute was accompanied by the creation of a new journal, the *Annales de l'Institut des Sciences Sociales*, in which the results of ongoing research were published. All in all, 33 issues, or 6 volumes, of the *Annales* came out, covering the period from 1894 to 1900.[8]

No systematic study of the activities of the Institut des Sciences Sociales exists. We have partial information gathered by a contemporary observer – an 1897 article by Dick May, the pseudonym of Miss J. Weill – and another by a later collaborator of Solvay, Warnotte (1946, pp. 520–529). More recent accounts have been provided by de Bie (1988, pp. 61–90) and Crombois (1994, pp. 25–33). Vandervelde (1895, p. 230) indicated that, certainly in the beginning, Solvay and his collaborators at the Institute worked 'collectively' around Solvay's research programme. From La Fontaine's notes, we can indeed infer that the members of the Institute met for discussions on a weekly basis, but it is also clear that Solvay rarely, if ever, attended the meetings. Apparently he communicated his views mainly by means of intermediaries. Despite his absence at the meetings, he was certainly doing his part of the thinking. Compared to what he published on social questions before 1894, Solvay's output in the period 1894–1900 exploded. In the *Annales* he published altogether 17 notes and articles, while his collaborators at the Institute and others contributed about 20 notes and articles which are more or less connected with Solvay's ideas.

In the very first article published in the *Annales*, "Comptabilisme et proportionnalisme social", Solvay strongly connected his ideas on money to the issues of inheritance and inheritance taxation. It was not the first time that he made this link;[9] he also stressed it in a speech before the Belgian Senate, in which the first reference can be found to "un certain comptabilisme social" (Solvay, 1894a; *NLD*, II, p. 68). The main proposition of "Comptabilisme et proportionnalisme social" is that, in order to have the intended effect, the introduction of an inheritance tax has to be combined with the abolition of "exchange money" ("monnaie d'échange"). As regards inheritance tax, Solvay had in mind a very ambitious project. He proposed in fact to replace all existing taxes by a single tax on bequests (in later articles, he specified that the inheritance tax should be progressive with relation to the number of generations between the original creator of the capital and the inheritor, the so-called "impôt successoral réitéré"). It is in the course of an examination of the criticisms that might be raised against his proposal that money appears. Two of those critiques were that high inheritance tax rates might encourage fraud on a large scale, and that a system based on a single tax might be inferior to a system based on multiple taxes, since in the second case the errors and the inequalities caused by fraud compensate one another in a certain degree. Yet Solvay was not impressed by these critiques and thought that it would be possible to find a way to eliminate fraud. The miracle solution, so to speak, would be to replace the existing monetary system by a system of accounts managed by the state:

> in order for fraud to become completely impossible, and for the single tax to appear to be practically feasible, it is necessary that the citizens have a direct interest in making known the exact amount of their assets. This leads us to our second formula: *the replacement of money by a system of accounts introduced by the State.*
>
> (Solvay, 1894b, p. 14)

Solvay's idea was to introduce a system that would enable the state to perfectly monitor the economic transactions of its citizens, and hence to determine exactly the wealth of each individual. In Solvay's own words, the system would be "une sorte d'appareil enregistreur de toutes les transactions, qui permettrait de constater à chaque instant, avec une exactitude suffisante, le droit et l'avoir de chacun" (*ibid.*, p. 5).

5.2.3 The mature proposal

In 1896, however, Solvay began to have second thoughts and openly regretted the "premature" publication of the article "Comptabilisme et proportionnalisme social". He therefore decided to return to the question, but this time "en restant sur le terrain monétaire et comptabiliste pur"

(Solvay, 1896; *NLD*, II, pp. 229–230). The resulting article, "Principe et raison d'être du comptabilisme social", is a key reference for Solvay's social comptabilism.[10] Although, in the following years, Solvay refined his propositions on several occasions, the basic ideas remained the same. The main question that he tried to answer in the article was the following:[11]

> Would it be possible, in a society constituted as ours is, to replace the agency of money by another agency which would have its advantages without its inconveniences, and which could be considered as theoretically perfect, – in other words would it be possible to replace the agency of money by a system which would be the final expression of possible improvement in this matter and the definitive point to which social economics ought necessarily to tend?
>
> (Solvay, 1897a, p. 1)

The main inconvenience of the monetary system to which Solvay alluded is that it entails the use of a unit of measure that is variable over time. In a gold-based monetary system, gold serves as the unit of value. Since gold is a commodity, it is subject to variations in value in response to shortage or excess of the money supply, or due to speculation. The "real value" of the unit of measurement therefore changes over time.[12] Hence, the change in the *money value* of a good does not adequately reflect the change in its *real value*, which is determined by the state of supply and demand for that good. The use of commodity-based money, therefore, entails confusion and distortion; it is a "defective instrument" (*ibid.*, p. 11) which should be replaced by something better.

The alternative to the money system should be a system with an invariable unit of value. Solvay maintained that such a system could be devised by choosing a unit of value at a given moment of time, $t=0$, say, and expressing all values at all dates in terms of this once-and-for-always unit of measurement. Society could for example decide to take the value of gold at time $t=0$ as unit of value. This would eliminate any distortion between the ratio of actual prices and the ratio of real values. Put differently, Solvay argued that in order to avoid the distortions related to the use of money, it would be necessary to use a unit of measurement which had a material existence at the moment when the unit of value was defined, but which lost its material support thereafter:

> it will be seen how absurd it becomes to persist in the custom of representing materially a unity which should be detached from the support which has served to define it at a given moment, and which no longer appears as anything but an abstraction permitting in a homogenous manner the arithmetical representation by figures, of the value of things, relatively and individually. This abstract unity ought to be detached from every material tie.
>
> (*ibid.*, p. 8)

But would it really be possible to replace the monetary system by a new system based upon an invariable unit of value? Solvay's answer is based upon an analysis of the functions of money. He attributed two functions to money: first, it is "an indispensable instrument for effecting transactions which are not mere acts of barter", and second, "it presents itself as having rendered possible ... the registering, the writing down or account-keeping of the transactions, if one may say so, which barter did not permit" (*ibid.*, p. 2). In other words, Solvay stressed the role of money as a "means of transaction" and as a "means of accounting", but neglected its role as a "store of value". As a result he believed that, in order to replace the existing monetary system, it would suffice to find an alternative way to perform the first two functions, which is exactly what he thought his social comptabilism would do.

The central idea of social comptabilism is that every economic transaction be mediated by appropriate entries on the accounts of those involved in the transaction. A central organization ("le comptable général", e.g. the National Bank) would be entitled to attribute these accounts; everyone who proves to be solvent would have the right to obtain such an account. All economic transactions would be recorded as debit and credit operations. Solvay stressed that the replacement of the monetary system by social comptabilism would not be a revolutionary development, but the accomplishment of a tendency already present in the actual system:

> It is evident that in this way society as it is at present organised, can demonetize the precious metals and establish social comptabilism without in principle having to make any revolution whatever in its present position, it has only largely to increase a portion of its machinery, already existing and in full swing. To sum up, it is a question of a simple change in the machinery of transactions and all society is interested in the realization of such a progress purely mechanical and functional, which moreover has no connection with any doctrine, opinion or party, and is no new invention whatever.
>
> (*ibid.*, p. 13)

By way of example, as a first approximation of a comptabilist institution, Solvay referred to the Post Office Bank of Vienna (Austria), which had links with all the post offices in the Austro-Hungarian Empire.[13] Hector Denis wrote an article about this bank for the *Annales* ("Le service de chèques et de virements à la caisse d'épargne postale de l'Empire d'Autriche"), and drafted a parliamentary bill with the aim of creating such a bank in Belgium too.[14]

5.2.4 The Walras critique

By 1896, then, a few modest steps were taken in the direction of a comptabilist experiment in Belgium. At the same time, the theoretical examination of social comptabilism continued, and in 1897 it even shifted to a higher level when the Institute decided to send the brochure *Le Comptabilisme Social* to a number of economists who might be interested in Solvay's theory. In Volume 3, issues 4 and 5, of the *Annales*, the reactions of Charles Gide, John K. Ingram, Ladeslas Zaleski and Léon Walras were reproduced. Gide's response was brief, but very positive; he indicated that Solvay's propositions were quite close to his own: "I think that this is the system of the future.... in advance I am in favour of the thesis of Mr Solvay" (Gide, 1897, p. 220).[15] The reactions of Ingram and Zaleski, on the other hand, were negative. Ingram stressed the "indispensable" character of metallic money and concluded: "...I do not share any of the ideas that are expressed in it. In my opinion, the abolition of metallic money is not only undesirable, but also impracticable" (Ingram, 1897, p. 311). Zaleski (1897, p. 312) referred to the Russian situation and predicted that both international trade and national conflicts would endanger the comptabilist system.

The most stimulating reaction came from Walras. In his letter, he congratulated Solvay for his efforts:

> I shall express in one word what I really think about the importance and the interest of such a creation by saying that it was no exaggeration to found an "Institute of Social Sciences" with the sole purpose of studying this principle and its implications, and that Mr Solvay deserves at the same time our highest esteem for having launched this idea into science and our most sincere gratitude for having prepared its practical realization.
>
> (Walras, 1897, p. 219)[16]

Moreover he promised to think more thoroughly about Solvay's propositions and to communicate his observations to the Institute.

Walras's reflections were published in the article "La Caisse d'épargne postale de Vienne et le comptabilisme social" in the *Revue d'économie politique* of 1898.[17] Although Walras recognized a high degree of similarity between his own monetary equations and those provided by Solvay, he challenged the validity of Solvay's assumptions. Walras rejected, in particular, the hypothesis that the value of the monetary unit – even if it were a purely conventional unit – could be fixed once and for all.[18] He argued that the value of any monetary unit (be it gold, paper, or simply a unit of account) was directly proportional to its utility (as money), and inversely proportional to its quantity. In this connection, Walras easily spotted a weakness in Solvay's reasoning, since he affirmed that an excess of comptabilist units would have no effect on prices, while a shortage would lead to a fall (Solvay, 1897a, p. 10). According to Walras (1898, p. 213), Solvay's position contradicted the quantity theory of money precisely in the case where it was the most incontestable. Walras furthermore predicted that the introduction of social comptabilism *à la* Solvay would lead to a *cours forcé* of the unit of account. As soon as a war or a major crisis occurred, people would be tempted to convert their assets into precious metals. As a result, the unit of account would depreciate and account-holders would be ruined and lose all faith in the future. In short, the comptabilist system would collapse and economic life would be seriously damaged.

> This perspective suffices for me, along with the economists, to refuse to follow Solvay with regard to the mobilisation of the entire social wealth or with regard to the *cours forcé* of the money of account. But moreover I have reasons not to follow the economists themselves with regard to the mobilisation of circulating capital or of paper money.
>
> (Walras, 1898, p. 218)[19]

Walras's critique was taken very seriously at the Institute. The discussion centred around the third section of Walras's article, entitled 'Le comptabilisme social: l'unité fixe de valeur' (*ibid.*, pp. 210–215). A substantial part of Volume 4, issue 4, of the *Annales* was devoted to Walras's analysis. Apart from a reproduction of the relevant section of Walras's article, it contained an article by Solvay (1898a) on the invariable unit of value, and critical remarks by Denis (1898), Henri Vanderrydt (1898) and Paul Otlet (1898). These articles were reprinted in a pamphlet called *A Propos du Comptabilisme Social*, published by the Institute in 1898. In his reaction, Solvay noted that others seemed to have three difficulties with his theory; it appeared to be hard to understand (i) that the value of goods is "absolutely independent" of money, (ii) that, in society, money is in principle "absolutely useless", and (iii) what the exact function of money happened to be. Solvay did not modify his position but reaffirmed his previous statements. For him, commodity-money was in essence a "means of transaction":

> The money object thus became a means of transaction, the tool of the transaction. It has no other function and, basically, no other grounds for existence. If transactions were not required, there would be no need for money; if people could make transactions just as well in another way, it would become useless.
>
> (Solvay, 1898a; *NLD*, II, pp. 258–259)

He thought it would be possible to perform economic transactions without using commodity-money at all. The system of accounts introduced by social comptabilism would make commodity-money simply obsolete.

The main point of divergence between Solvay and Walras concerned the possibility or impossibility of having a comptabilist unit of account with a constant value. Solvay was not impressed by Walras's critique:

> The mathematical fiction that I used to prove, in my previous notes, the invariability of the comptabilistic unit was legitimate. It is true that a being with unlimited capacities could, at an exact moment in time, fix at every place the value – *a value which is evidently constant for an infinitely short time* – of an indefinite number of things with variable value, in relation to the value of one of those things chosen as a unit. From then onwards, this unit which is chosen and used in that way and *which has indeed got nothing but an instantaneous reality*, would remain nevertheless indestructible in time and in space. It would be the *abstract unit* that we have tried to define and that could be used in the future, in a constant and indefinite way, to register the relations of the variable values of things, to account all transactions while radically excluding the notion and the act of exchange.
>
> (*ibid.*, p. 261)

Moreover, he was of the opinion that Walras had misunderstood his position on the asymmetric effects of an excess and a shortage of monetary units. Yet Solvay simply reaffirmed what he had written before, adding only that under a comptabilist regime it would be highly unlikely that there would ever be a shortage (*ibid.*, pp. 269–270). On this issue, Denis dissented from both Solvay and Walras. Denis agreed with Walras that Solvay's position was in conflict with the quantity theory of money, but he disagreed with Walras on the practical possibility of an excess or a shortage. According to Denis, the issue that divided Solvay and Walras would never be pertinent:

> I think, however, that in Mr Solvay's comptabilistic system – completely leaving aside the issue of its realisation – neither *independent* quantitative variations of comptabilistic money in the direction of an excess (*hausse*), nor *independent* quantitative variations in the direction of a shortage (*baisse*), are conceivable. Mr Walras's formula, which in itself is indisputable, would have no application *in practice*.
>
> (Denis, 1898, p. 284)

Denis was convinced that under social comptabilism the emission of monetary units would be subordinate to the number and the value of economic transactions. The quantity of monetary units would *always* be exactly sufficient to cover the needs of exchange and production; in Walras's terms, comptabilist money would have a constant and invariable *rareté*. Denis concluded:

> In fact the relationships of causality are definitely and irrevocably fixed. The supply of comptabilistic money is from now on always determined and measured by the quantities of commodities and services which are exchanged. Under the comptabilistic hypothesis, the servant – money – definitely follows the master – the resources and services which are exchanged –, thereby finally putting into practice Boisguillebert's profound idea.
>
> (*ibid.*, p. 285)

Denis's explanation might be seen as an attempt to reconcile Solvay's and Walras's views, and as an invitation to further reflection. But apart from Walras's acknowledgement that Denis had apparently very well grasped his monetary theory (see Jaffé, 1965, vol. III, p. 28), the discussion was not pursued.

5.2.5 The final phase

At least partially as a result of the Walras critique, enthusiasm at the Institute for social comptabilism cooled down. Solvay himself continued to advocate his proposal, but he became more and more isolated. In 1899, he wrote a series of three "open letters" to the members of the Belgian Parliament, to inform them about the aims of social comptabilism and suggest practical ways of realizing it.[20] But the letters did not have the intended effect. In a speech delivered on 22 March 1900 before the Belgian Senate, Solvay acknowledged his failure to convince his fellow members of parliament – not really unexpected in view of the fact that Solvay belonged to the opposition. More significantly, he even admitted that he had serious difficulties in directing the research of his collaborators at the Institut des Sciences Sociales towards "a truly comptabilist application", and launched an offer to financially support "any competent researcher who would produce a serious work on the realization of comptabilism" (Solvay, 1900a; *NLD*, II, p. 121). He thought that his ideas were not as appreciated as they should have been, and he was certainly frustrated by the lack of any practical result. Not surprisingly, soon thereafter he decided to cease the activities of the Institut des Sciences Sociales and to replace it by the Institut de Sociologie, under the command of his new protégé Émile Waxweiler. This also put an end to all attempts to bring about a comptabilist experiment. However, Solvay was apparently unaware that a similar exercise in monetary theory and monetary experiments was being conducted at the time in Sweden by Knut Wicksell (1898), in a book that, in contrast with Solvay's own contributions, would become a classic a few decades later.

5.3 Wicksell on monetary reform experiments

5.3.1 Wicksell on experiments

Wicksell discussed experiments in economics in his inaugural lecture on "Ends and Means in Economics" delivered at the University of Lund in September 1904 (1958 [1904], pp. 58–60). That lecture was, to a great extent, an attack on the methodology of the German Historical School and its criticism of abstract economic theory in general. After stating the case for the methodology of verificationism in economics (see Henriksson, 1991, p. 35), Wicksell disputed the claim, put forward by "both friends and foes of systematic or theoretical economics", that it is in general impossible "to give a strict verification of the propositions or rules which we formulate as hypotheses, as tentative abstractions from experience, because it is impossible to isolate economic phenomena to the extent necessary for such verification. Unlike the natural sciences, economics is not in a position to carry out experiments, they say." Wicksell did not accept these early displays of "methodological dualism" and sustained that experiments are often made in economics, albeit in a specific form:

> It seems to me that this contention is to a great extent exaggerated; as a matter of fact, such experiments are constantly being made in the realm of our science and they are of the most incisive character conceivable, because one economic element is altered discontinuously while everything else remains the same – and the experimenter is the economic legislator. These experiments are frequently even direct and quite deliberate: the measures introduced by the legislation are based upon the supposition that some abstract proposition or other is valid, and the result is either confirmation or refutation of the proposition in question.
>
> (1958 [1904], pp. 58–59)

Wicksell did not name the "friends of economic theory" who had questioned the possibility of carrying out experiments, but he probably had in mind J.S. Mill's (1992 [1844], pp. 146–147) statement that moral sciences, in contrast with physical sciences, cannot make controlled experiments, which means that they cannot generally obtain what Francis Bacon used to call an *experimentum crucis*, and, by that, cannot be based on inductive methods (see also Blaug, 1980, pp. 64–69; see, however, section 6.3 of Cartwright's essay in this volume for the broad argument that Mill's notion of "stable tendencies" is compatible with the importance of experiments in economic theory). It should be noted that Wicksell was not the first to regard changes in economic legislation as equivalent to experiments. John Neville Keynes (1973 [1891], pp. 182–184) entertained that notion, but dismissed it in the end, on the feeble grounds that "it is not the case that the primary object of every new law is to afford means of studying the effects which a change of conditions or the introduction of a new agency is capable of producing". He conceded, however, that what Jevons (1883, pp. 253 ff.) had called "tentative legislation" could be regarded as experiments; the former being tentative measures that introduce new economic legislation only temporarily or in a few sectors or regions of the economy "with the express object of gaining insight into their social and economic effects" (see also Ferber and Hirsch, 1982).

It is remarkable that all instances of economic experiments given by Wicksell in his 1904 lecture (1958 [1904], pp. 59–60) belong to the realm of monetary theory and policy (e.g. Gresham's Law; the success of the Austrian government in keeping its inconvertible paper money, by means of the purchase and sale of public bonds, at a higher value than that of the silver into which it was once redeemable; the increase of the value of silver currencies in Holland and India in relation to gold by means of the expedient of ceasing to mint silver coins on private account). This can be ascribed to Wicksell's view that, in contrast to relative prices, the conditions that decide the price level are defined by the monetary system set up by society and its government:

> In all other economic spheres other circumstances, such as technique, natural conditions, individual or social differences, play a role which science can only imperfectly survey and control. But, with regard to money, everything is determined by human beings themselves, i.e., the statesmen, and (so far as they are consulted) the economists; the choice of a measure of value, of a monetary system, of currency and credit legislation – all are in the hands of society, and natural conditions (e.g., the scarcity or abundance of the metals employed in the currency, their chemical properties, etc.) are relatively unimportant. Here, then, the rulers of society have an opportunity of showing their economic wisdom – or folly.
>
> (1935 [1906], pp. 3–4)

While attempts to change relative prices (by means of tariffs, state subsidies, export bounties, and so on) "almost inevitably involve some loss of utility to the community" and should, by that, "be regarded as opposed to all reason", money prices "are a matter in the last analysis of pure convention, depending on the *choice of a standard of price* which it lies within our own power to make" (Wicksell, 1936 [1898], p. 4).[21] Wicksell's monetary thought was aimed at the study of the determination of the price level, which provided the analytical basis for his suggestions as to how to stabilize the price level through a reform of the gold-standard system. The choice of the monetary system and of the goals and instruments of monetary policy was, therefore, understood as a socially controlled experiment designed by economists and policy makers.

A few years after his 1904 inaugural lecture, Wicksell again mentioned economic experiments as part of an article on the verification of the law of diminishing returns to land, published in the German *Thünen Archiv* in 1907. According to Wicksell, it was difficult to confirm the law by observing the actual yield of agriculture in different estates, for

> either an economy is managed in a rational way, in which case its intensity has already reached the limit of profitability and one never obtains information on the amount by which the relative gross yield would increase as a consequence of a decrease in the degree of intensity . . . or the economy is not managed in a rational way, in which case it is obviously impossible to decide to what extent the lack of knowledge of the management, *independently of the intensity-level chosen*, has caused a smaller relative gross yield.
>
> (1998 [1907], p. 117)

The way out is to carry out controlled experiments: "The only reliable method would be to *conduct experiments* or to compare the agricultural results of *two* or more *countries*, where the basic conditions of agricultural *profitability*, i.e., the level of wages or the level of product prices, differ widely – if one is not willing to accept the logic common sense as the basis of the law" (*ibid.*). Here, in contrast to Wicksell's 1904 emphasis on the connection between experiments and economic legislation, experiments are used to establish a proposition in economic theory, concerning the influence of "natural" or physical conditions on production. In a passage added in 1911 to the second Swedish edition of Volume I of his *Lectures*, Wicksell discussed again the problems involved in the attempt to verify the law of diminishing returns to land, and pointed out that it could be done only by means of controlled experiments: "It must, indeed, be quite easy to prove it by *direct experiment*, and in so far as such experiments have been made – unfortunately all too few and on too small a scale – the results undoubtedly tend to confirm the law" (Wicksell, 1934 [1901], p. 122). Hence, the notion of economic experiments was an important element of Wicksell's methodology, both in the realm of monetary economics and in the theory of production. Wicksell's rejection of the opposition between economics and natural sciences was shared by Solvay, as discussed above, and was a common feature underlying their respective proposals to carry out experiments in the monetary field.

5.3.2 The pure credit economy

In order to tackle Wicksell's concept of a "pure credit economy" and the monetary reform proposal associated with it, it is necessary to discuss briefly how it grew out of his study of money demand and its relation to the determination of the price level. The main feature of Wicksell's approach to price-level determination is the investigation of the development of credit as a means of superseding the function of money (gold) as store of value, based on four models of a monetary economy: "pure cash", "simple credit", "organized credit" and "pure credit" (1936 [1898], Chapter 6; see also Boianovsky, 1998, Sections II and III). In the case of the "pure cash economy" there are no bonds; the size of cash balances is decided by the need to meet anticipated future purchases and to have a reserve for unforeseen liabilities (what we now call "transactional" and "precautional" demand for money; cf. Laidler, 1991, p. 125). The stability and determinacy of money prices depend on the existence of what Don Patinkin (1965) would later call a "real balance effect" in the markets for commodities. Assuming a monetary economy with "simple credit between private individuals" (Wicksell, 1936 [1898], pp. 61–62), the necessity for holding cash balances can be reduced as far as anticipated expenditures are concerned, but this does not normally affect the precautionary demand for money. The real balance effect can now also be found in the bond market.

In the case of an "organized (or developed) credit economy", individuals keep most of their transactions and precautionary balances as interest-earning deposits with the competitive banking system. In contrast with "simple credit", in an organized credit system the "subjective element of risk [of not recovering the money entrusted] disappears in proportion as the wealth which affords the guarantee is great in relation to the amount at stake, so that only the mathematical risk remains" (Wicksell, 1935 [1906], p. 72). Building on Francis Edgeworth (1888; see Wicksell, 1936 [1898], p. 66, n. 1), Wicksell explains that, thanks to the "Law of Large Numbers" of probability theory[22] and to the fact that quite often the bank's customers have business relations with one another, the bank's demand for cash reserves will be just a fraction of its liabilities (1935 [1906], pp. 83–84; 1936 [1898], pp. 66–68), which means an increase in the "virtual" velocity of circulation of money (gold) when compared with both the pure cash and simple credit economies. A fortuitous increase of the price level in a developed credit economy brings about a higher demand for cash, which will in part provoke an "immediate reaction against the price movement" to the extent that individuals reduce their demand for commodities in order to restore their real cash balances. But the reaction comes "above all" in the form of the effects of an increase in the demand for loans (supply of bonds) on the reserves of the banking system. The reaction is not "immediate", but after a period of time banks will be forced to raise their rate of interest in order to protect their reserves, which helps to bring money prices back to their original and stable level.[23]

Wicksell's last and quite influential model of a monetary economy is the "pure credit economy", where there is no demand for outside currency and all payments are carried out by means of transfers in bank accounts.

Banks, which are supposed to be connected by a common clearing house, do not demand reserves for domestic cash payments. Nevertheless, since Wicksell is still assuming a gold standard economy, they must maintain a stock of gold in order to meet foreign and industrial demand for gold. "For the sake of simplicity", Wicksell (1936 [1898], p. 71) imagines that the whole monetary system of a country is in the hands of a single "Bank". He further assumes that the average value *R* of the Bank's gold reserve "comprises the property of the bank itself". On this assumption, as far as domestic transactions are concerned, "the Bank's claims on the public must be exactly equal to its debts to the public. If the sum of the credit balances is *K*, the sum of the debit balances must be *K*, or rather –*K*; so that the algebrical sum of all balances always remains equal to zero". The stability of money prices under these circumstances, however, does not result from the demand by the non-banking public for gold as store of value, but (assuming a closed economy) from the industrial demand for gold as a commodity, as Wicksell explains on p. 113 of *Interest and Prices*. Assuming that the credit system has been "fully developed in every country", a fortuitous increase of the price level "discourages the production of gold, and, other things being equal, it increases the consumption of gold in industry. As soon as consumption began to outstrip production, the deficiency would have to be supplied out of the banks' stocks, for no other source is allowed for". This long process would eventually prompt banks to raise their interest rates and bring money prices back to their original level. This mechanism was behind Wicksell's criticism of the view – put forward by Adolf Wagner (1862, p. 127) and other supporters of "free banking" – that one could dispense with gold as a means of payment and a reserve of value and base the monetary system on credit alone (see also Hernandez-Aramburo, 1996, pp. 264–266):

> It is sometimes said to be feasible to *base* a monetary system upon gold and yet to dispense entirely, or almost entirely, with the employment of gold both in circulation and in the banks' reserves. This would be done by extending the use of cheques, by the issue of notes of which the cover is of a purely banking nature, and so on. This view, which is held by some of the most prominent writers on monetary questions, must be regarded as utopian. In such a system the value of money would be *directly* exposed to the effects of every fortuitous incident on the side of the production of the precious metals and every caprice on the side of its consumption. It would undergo the same violent fluctuations as do the value of most other commodities. But it would be quite possible to maintain a stable value of money without the use of reserves of a precious metal. Only would be necessary for the *metal to cease to serve as a standard of value*.
>
> (Wicksell, 1936 [1898], pp. 34–35, see also p. 46; and Wicksell, 1935 [1906], pp. 123–124)

According to Wicksell, the progressive replacement of gold as store of value as the economy converges to a pure credit system would make the price level behave increasingly as a relative price, since the monetary demand for gold tends to nil. This "contradiction" could only be overcome by "completely divorcing the value of money from metal, or at any rate from its commodity function, by abolishing all free minting, and by making the ... unit employed in the accounts of the credit institutions both the medium of exchange and the measure of value" (Wicksell, 1935 [1906], p. 126). Nevertheless, still assuming a competitive banking system formed by profit-maximizing banks, such a pure credit economy without a material substance as standard of value would feature indeterminacy of the price level, as Wicksell (1914, pp. 145–146) made clear. Under these circumstances, the equilibrium of general prices "can occur for any level they may have" and "should be constructed on the analogy with the so-called neutral equilibrium in mechanics: it does not change by itself, but nor do any fortuitous changes in it generate forces which would necessarily establish again its previous condition". What is behind Wicksell's contention that bank loans increase together with the price level (so that the rate of interest does not move and prices do not come back to their original level) is the implicit assumption that the credit-supply function of profit-maximizing banks is homogeneous of degree zero in nominal values (cf. Sweeney, 1988, pp. 160–162, 173, 180; see also Hawtrey, 1934 [1919], pp. 11–13).

The level of prices in pure credit economies after the monetary reform depicted above is decided entirely by the bank rate of interest, according to Wicksell's well-known "cumulative process" of price change as a result of the difference between the bank rate and the "normal rate of interest" (that is, the interest rate that equilibrates saving and investment). However, the profit-maximizing banks described by Wicksell would have no incentive to set their interest rates at a level consistent with price stability. Such a monetary policy can be carried out only if a central bank is introduced into the picture.[24] Assuming there is no outside currency in circulation (banknotes, coins, etc.) – and, by that, no opportunity for the central bank to affect through open-market policy the interest rate charged by private banks – a public central bank could be introduced as an institution that remunerates its deposits at the same rate charged for its loans (Wicksell, 1917, 1919a). In a competitive banking system, the difference between the rate of interest that is paid on deposits (including current accounts) and the rate charged on loans covers the banks' running costs, the holding of "liquid securities which carry only a moderate of interest", the holding of a stock of metallic money which earns no interest, and, above all, the "trouble and risk involved" (Wicksell, 1936 [1898], pp. 139–140). According to Wicksell (1919a), the margin between these two rates far exceeded that amount in the post-war Swedish financial system. This reflected not only the circumstances surrounding the war, but also the natural tendency to "concentration" in the bank business because of economies of scale.[25] Wicksell (1919a, p. 185) was aware that if central banks were allowed to remunerate their deposits at the same rate charged for their loans, in principle nobody would be able to lend at a higher rate or to deposit money at a lower rate of interest, which means that there would be no margin of profit for commercial banks. The intermediation of credit would apparently be completely in the hands of the central bank. But, as Wicksell points out, this conclusion is precipitate, since there would still be opportunity for private financial intermediation in areas and sectors of the economy where risk evaluation by the central bank is difficult. Such intermediaries would then be able to charge a rate of interest higher than the central bank's, which becomes the basic rate of the pure credit system (see also 1917, p. 182; cf. 1936 [1898], pp. 74–75).[26]

5.3.3 A "pure credit" experiment

In April 1917, Wicksell was invited to give a lecture at the Norwegian Economic Association. The topic of his talk was the "Scandinavian Monetary System", and it included a proposal to implement a pure credit economy. Wicksell (1917, p. 184) described the exercise as a "*thought experiment*" ("tankeexperiment"), but at the same time pointed out that it was motivated by the cessation of free minting of gold and by the end of the central bank's obligation to accept gold at a fixed price in the Scandinavian countries since February 1916. He explained the transition to pure credit using as an example the balance sheet of the central bank of Norway, which is supposed to be, for now, the only bank of the economy. For the sake of illustration, Wicksell (p. 179) imagines that the bank has before the reform assets consisting of gold reserves (100 million krona) and claims (200 million krona), and liabilities in the form of deposits (100 million krona, which also includes the capital of the bank) and notes in circulation (200 million krona). With the permission of the Norwegian parliament, the central bank calls in its notes; half is paid out to note holders in gold and the other half is put down as a deposit at the individual's bank account, on which he or she has the right to draw cheques. Cheques cannot be paid out in cash (gold or notes), but only be transferred to other accounts. At the same time, the bank stops issuing notes and accepting gold as deposit or in payment. The bank's total assets have now been reduced by 100 million krona (the gold reserves that were given out) and comprise, on one side, claims (200 million krona, as before) and, on the other, deposits (200 million krona, including the bank's capital). That sum can increase through new loans (which bring about directly or indirectly corresponding deposits in the bank) and can be reduced through payment of debts to the bank. Wicksell acknowledges that at the beginning gold coins would probably be used as means of payment between individuals, but – since they are no longer received by the bank, nor ("let us assume") held as cash balance – they would soon cease to be used as means of payment and, instead, be melted down and absorbed by industry. In such an economy, "*money* means henceforth only the *unit in which the bank's accounts are kept*" (1917, pp. 180–181). Under these circumstances, the only "regulator" of the price level (and of the exchange rate as well against other countries) is the level of the bank's rate of interest.

One of the main features of pure-credit economies is the absence of outside currency. This is true not only of coins, but also of banknotes, which "can be obtained only on payment of interest (or in exchange for commodities), but they earn no interest for their owners. Private individuals are therefore unwilling to stock them in large quantities, and they flow back to the banks in the shape of deposits or are lent to others on return for interest" (Wicksell, 1936 [1898], p. 69). Nevertheless, Wicksell (1935 [1906], pp. 88–91) was aware that not all payments can be made by cheque and mentioned often that bank notes are "far more convenient" for small payments (see, e.g., 1936 [1898], p. 70). More importantly, the use of credit "presupposes a certain amount of confidence" that is lacking in times of "crises", when the demand for medium of payment turns more to hard cash (see 1935 [1906], p. 90; and especially 1902, p. 40).[27] Wicksell acknowledged the existence of inconvertible notes issued by a central bank in his more "realistic" scenarios for monetary reform. In this case, the measure of value is the central-bank paper money, which is the unit employed in the accounts of the banking system (1935 [1906], p. 126), but the bank rate of interest (on deposits and loans alike) is still the key instrument to regulate the amount of notes in circulation and the price level, as in the pure-credit economy (see 1917, p. 184 and 1919a, pp. 183–185; see also Woodford's (2003, pp. 112–114) notion of a "cashless limiting economy" in which the money balances held to facilitate transactions become very small relative to national income and inflation is a function of the Wicksellian gap between the natural and market rates of interest).

Wicksell's 1917 "thought experiment", published in Swedish in a relatively unknown journal, has never been mentioned by commentators and it evoked no reactions from his contemporaries. However, as discussed below, his 1898 model of a pure-credit economy has had a significant influence on the development of monetary economics, especially after the realization that the post-gold-standard monetary system was gradually coming closer to the framework envisaged by Wicksell in his thought experiment. In 1934, during the successful policy carried out in Sweden to stabilize the price level and counteract the effects of the world economic depression, Bertil Ohlin wrote an article entitled "Knut Wicksell – Father of the Swedish Monetary Experiment". According to Ohlin (p. 161), "Knut Wicksell was the originator of this development of ideas", based on the abandonment of the gold standard in 1931 and the implementation of a monetary policy based on the use of the bank rate of interest as an instrument to stabilize the price level, as opposed to the stabilization of the rate of exchange.

5.4 The influence of Solvay's and Wicksell's monetary ideas

5.4.1 Differences in appraisal

Solvay's social comptabilism and Wicksell's pure credit have many points in common, and yet they never referred directly to one another. Wicksell did notice that the "ideal banking system" (a phrase Wicksell sometimes used to describe the pure-credit economy) had "in recent times engaged the attention of many writers under the name of 'universal comptabilism', and various proposals for its realization have been made" (1935 [1906], p. 87). Both Wicksell and Solvay mentioned the Austrian Post Office Savings Bank as an important illustration of payments by bookkeeping transfers, or the "Giro system".[28] Nevertheless, they drew different conclusions from their respective theoretical constructions, as far as the stabilization of the price level is concerned. While Wicksell stressed bank interest-rate policy, Solvay insisted that social comptabilism would make possible the definition of an "abstract unit of account" separated from the medium of exchange, which apparently would be enough to render the price level constant.

The respective fates of Solvay's social comptabilism and Wicksell's pure credit have been quite different, as far as economic theory is concerned. Wicksell's construction has been used as a benchmark in monetary economics by authors such as von Mises, Lindahl, Hicks and Patinkin, among others (see Trautwein, 1995), while Solvay's concept has remained largely unknown to the profession (or strongly criticized whenever mentioned, as witnessed by Rist's (1938) reference to the "Solvay School"). This is well illustrated by von Mises's classic *Theory of Money and Credit*, which refers to Solvay and to Wicksell in connection with social comptabilism and pure credit. Von Mises (1980 [1912], p. 112) labelled Solvay a "money crank" who thought that an elastic credit system automatically adapted to the need for currency is "the cure to all human ills". Von Mises suggested that Solvay's theory was an application of the monetary views of the English "Banking School" of Tooke and Fullarton, and maintained that "the rejection of schemes such as Ernest Solvay's 'social comptabilism' is to be attributed solely to the practical man's timidity and not to any strict proof of the weakness of the schemes, which has indeed not been forthcoming". But, despite writing that "Solvay's theories also contain various other fundamental errors", von Mises did not come back to that in the rest of his book and did not provide any "strict proof" of the weakness of social comptabilism, other than a general criticism of the Banking School. Von Mises's (pp. 394–395) reference to Wicksell's "hypothetical bank" in a pure-credit economy was, on the other hand, accompanied by a detailed examination of the "limits" to the creation of credit by the banking system in these circumstances, which became part and parcel of his explanation of the upper turning point of the business cycle (and was, by the way, rejected by Wicksell; see Boianovsky, 1995, Section 5).

Another example of an economist criticizing Solvay is Pareto (1965 [1903], pp. 280–284), who used the terms "fundamental error", "illusion" and "sophism" when analysing Solvay's theory. He concluded that the proposed system might have perverse effects, and that its formulation was the result of an ignorance of the laws of economics:

> What is wrong in the projects that we have been talking about, are the difficulties that spring from the abuses of the issuing of a new sort of money. These difficulties can be observed where paper money is issued that pushes gold completely out of circulation.
>
> The issuing of paper money has in general as a result that it permits the rich to despoil the poor, for a more or less long time, and it is a curious thing to see how some persons, who claim to have and who really have a sincere desire to do the right thing for the people, propose measures that would contrive to despoil it. This is a consequence of not knowing the laws of economics.
>
> (*ibid.*, p. 284)

Loria (1902, pp. 119–122) also strongly doubted that social comptabilism would be feasible.

In all fairness, we must add that a more positive attitude towards social comptabilism was displayed by a number of less well-known authors in the French and German literature on money of the beginning of the twentieth century. In a book in which he tried to show that a socialist system of exchange cannot co-exist with a non-socialist system of production, Marc Aucuy (1908, pp. 276–349) devoted a whole chapter to a discussion of social comptabilism and even annexed to it a short unpublished paper by Solvay (*Note inédite de M. Solvay sur le comptabilisme*, dated 6 September 1906, pp. 349–354). Like many others, Aucuy too thought that the impossibility of fixing an invariable unit of measurement was one of the main weaknesses of social comptabilism. Furthermore, he compared and contrasted Solvay's monetary ideas with those of Robert Owen, François Vidal, François Haeck and Pierre-Joseph Proudhon. In the same line of thought are the comments of Roche-Agussol (1903, pp. 90–114) and Poudou (1919, pp. 308–315). In the German-speaking countries, Solvay's "comptabilité sociale" was mentioned in Joseph Schumpeter's (1917–1918, p. 637) review of monetary theory. Walter Wegelin (1921, pp. 34–37, 48–56, 90), and to a lesser degree also Hans Langelütke (1925, pp. 12–13, 40, 82n), compared Solvay's social comptabilism with the monetary theories of Silvio Gesell and Pierre-Joseph Proudhon. Arthur Wolgang Cohn (1920, pp. 90–92) noted parallelisms between social comptabilism and some proposals of Friedrich Engels, Edward Bellamy and Justus Recht.[29]

5.4.2 The new monetary economics

From the perspective of the history of economic thought, an interesting comparison can be made between, on the one hand, the concepts of social comptabilism and pure credit advanced by Solvay and Wicksell and, on the other, the ideas put forward by Black (1987 [1970]), Fama (1980), Greenfield and Yeager (1983, 1989) and Cowen and Kroszner (1994), all of which have attracted attention under the label "New Monetary Economics". According to the New Monetary Economics, in completely unregulated payment systems all media of exchange would be bank-issued or "inside" money, which would be separated from the unit of account, defined as a single commodity or, preferably, as a commodity bundle. In such a system, its proponents claim, the price level would be stable and the quantity of money would be demand determined at its optimal amount. Accordingly, the New Monetary Economics has been associated with thought experiments involving reform of the currently regulated monetary system.

The historical survey of the (pre)history of the New Monetary Economics carried out by Cowen and Kroszner (1994, Part III) considers Wicksell's pure credit, but overlooks Solvay's contribution and the French literature in general. Nevertheless, there are strong similarities between the New Monetary Economics and the proposals put forward by Solvay and Wicksell (especially as far as Solvay's notion of an "abstract" unit of account is concerned), as well as important differences, including their divergent views towards laissez-faire payment systems. In the following two sub-sections we briefly analyse two aspects of the relationship of Solvay and Wicksell with the New Monetary Economics.

The Kitson connection

On the issue of the invariable unit of value, there is a striking resemblance between the work of Solvay and that of his contemporary Arthur Kitson (1859–1937), who, as an inventor with over 500 patents (including work with Thomas Edison on the electric light), was not far from Solvay's notion of experiments in monetary economics and elsewhere. This was already noticed by two of Solvay's close collaborators at the Institut des Sciences Sociales. Not only De Greef (1899, pp. 35, 94, 127, 129), but especially Denis (1901), drew attention to the similarity between the monetary ideas of Solvay and those of Kitson. Denis wrote an extensive study of Kitson's (1895a) book and, although he never said so explicitly, it may well be that he was more impressed by Kitson's arguments than by Solvay's.[30] More recently, the interpretation of Kitson (1895b) by Cowen and Kroszner perhaps applies even better to Solvay:

> An abstract medium of account can be defined by setting the value of any commodity on a given day equal to "one" and pricing all commodities in terms thereof. For all succeeding market periods, however,

> this link is severed and only the abstract medium remains. Market participants set prices (in terms of abstract media) by reference to the abstract medium-denominated prices of the preceding period. The abstract medium is derived from a sequential process which ultimately refers back to an original commodity value.
>
> (1994, p. 126)[31]

Different opinions have been voiced on the precise nature of the unit of account suggested by Kitson (see especially Sumner, 1990, p. 114). In contrast to Solvay, however, Kitson did at least once attempt to define the unit of account explicitly (Kitson, 1895b, pp. 6–7; see also Bilgram, 1895, p. 2). Solvay failed to state clearly that his proposed abstract unit of account should be defined by a bundle of commodities with a fixed price of 1 unit. Solvay's ambiguity on this crucial aspect of his plan for monetary reform may explain the difficulty that commentators experienced when trying to make sense of his "abstract unit". Walras was by no means the only economist who considered this to be a major stumbling block. Achille Loria (1902, p. 120) pointed out that the measure of value in Solvay's system "is fixed by the determination beforehand of the value of a given good at a particular time. But this initial value, how is it expressed?" Instead of purchasing power in terms of a given basket of commodities *à la* Kitson, Loria suggested that the "initial value" of the commodity should be measured in labour time. According to Loria, convertibility in terms of labour time was essential in avoiding nominal changes in the amount of credit in Solvay's economy.

Whatever the difficulties, it is clear that on this issue Solvay and Kitson were, to a much greater extent than Wicksell, close to the view put forward in the 1980s by the New Monetary Economics that the key to price-level stabilization is the separation of the function of money as the unit of account from its function as the medium of exchange in pure accounting systems of exchange. On at least one other issue there are important differences. Both Kitson and the New Monetary Economics supported "free banking", with banknotes issued competitively by private banks. Solvay's social comptabilism, on the other hand, was of an extremely centralist character:

> In the place of a true economic anarchy of individuals acting within society for their own sake, in a separate way, distinct from one another, in all possible directions, it puts unity of action, concentration, supreme social organisation, and by consequence, simplification and economy. Society, taken as a whole, ... thus becomes a true organism that is brought to the utmost perfection, with the minimal amount of cogwheels, organs and specific movements, and that, as a result, is capable of performing the maximal amount of useful effects. It thereby saves for each individual the maximum of time, it provides

> him with the maximum of leisure, it gives him the full disposition of his productivist initiative and at the same time incites it, and finally it neatly and impeccably deals with all issues.
>
> (Solvay, 1900d; *NLD*, II, p. 278)

Solvay stressed that, in social comptabilism, all transactions would be legally guaranteed by the State. This would be the result of the fact that the State would make sure that no person received more comptabilist units than the value of his or her possessions: "under no circumstances would the account manager deliver a number of units which would exceed the present value of the pledge" (Solvay, 1900c; *NLD*, II, p. 271). Economic transactions would become completely separated from any form of exchange:

> The social account should be considered as a truly *authentic balance* kept by the State on behalf of each individual, *a copy of each individual's private balance*, in which only purely abstract units, represented by numbers and having no characteristics which might suggest a link with exchange, are recorded as entries and exits.
>
> (*ibid.*, pp. 271–272)

Compensated dollar and indirect convertibility

In contrast to Solvay, the unit of account in which bank accounts are kept in Wicksell's pure-credit economy (after monetary reform and assuming away outside currency) is not "abstract" or "separated" from the medium of exchange, in the sense that the nominal value of exchange media is not fixed in terms of the unit of account. There is no suggestion in Wicksell that the unit of account should be defined in terms of a commodity bundle, with a value independent of the amount of media of exchange. This is behind the crucial role of bank-rate policy in Wicksell's proposal to stabilize the price level. But Wicksell also discussed critically other plans designed to eliminate or diminish price-level fluctuations, which are closer to the general framework of Solvay's social comptabilism: Irving Fisher's (1913, Ch. xiii) famous "compensated dollar plan" and especially Benjamin Anderson's (1917) suggestion that it would be feasible, by means of "indirect convertibility", to use as the standard of value a commodity that is not itself either the medium of exchange or the medium of redemption of notes and deposits.

Fisher (1913) assumed a gold-standard economy where all gold coins have been replaced by gold certificates which can be redeemed upon demand from the government for a certain quantity of gold bullion, but with a variable seignorage, determined according to changes in the price level: if the price level increases by, say, 1 per cent, then the purchasing power of a dollar gold-certificate would be restored by increasing the "gold content" of a dollar by 1 per cent, which means to decrease the dollar price of a given quantity of gold. This way, Fisher claimed that any change in the gold price of the basket of commodities that defines the price index can be compensated by an appropriate change in the dollar price of gold, thereby keeping the dollar price of the basket constant (see Patinkin, 1993). Wicksell (1913, 1935 [1906], pp. 225–228) discussed Fisher's plan in detail. He pointed out that the plan assumes that the exchange value of the metallic gold in terms of goods is not affected by the seignorage, an assumption that is valid only for an individual country. But, in this case, the country's metallic gold would flow to other countries where it could be minted without seignorage, that is, changing the dollar price of gold actually meant changing the foreign-exchange rate. If all countries should adopt the same plan, the effect of the seignorage on the exchange value of metallic gold would constitute a hindrance to the planned increase of the purchasing power of gold. Wicksell further argued that a change of the mint price can only influence directly the production flow of new gold, which is a small fraction of the total stock of money, and that thereby the impact of Fisher's plan on the price level would be close to nil (1913, pp. 135–137 and 1935 [1906], pp. 226–227; see also Patinkin, 1993, pp. 7–9 and 10–11). Wicksell (1935 [1906], p. 228) noticed that Fisher's plan involved a separation between the medium of exchange and the unit of account, as "the very substance of (Fisher's) proposed reform is to raise something *else* to the position of a *measure of value*, and not gold as is now the case", and asked, "Why not, therefore, go the whole way, and choose something different by which the goal in view, a stable price level, may be secured with reasonable certainty?" His answer (1913, p. 138) was the replacement of gold as standard of value for banknotes, or, more generally, the unit in which bank accounts are kept, and its stabilization through bank-rate policy.[32]

Wicksell's (1919b) criticism of B. Anderson (1917) has attracted attention recently in connection with the suggestion of Greenfield and Yeager (1989, p. 410) that prices should be quoted in terms of bank-issued exchange media convertible into some medium of redemption (such as gold) "actually worth, at prevailing market prices, as many standard bundles as the Unit denominations of the banknotes and deposits being redeemed". This way, the medium of exchange would be "indirectly convertible" into the commodity bundle that defines the unit of account. As Wicksell pointed out, however, in his comments on a similar proposal by Anderson (1917, pp. 150–151), indirectly convertible systems suffer from a "paradox of indirect convertibility" that would prevent their practical implementation (see Trautwein, 1993, pp. 103–104; Dowd, 1995, pp. 76–78): if the price of the unit of account (the commodity bundle in Greenfield and Yeager, or 23.22 grains of gold in Anderson) should diverge from unity, then self-reinforcing movements in the price of the redemption medium (silver in Anderson's illustration) might destroy the indirectly convertible system. Anderson, as part of his argument against the quantity theory of money, imagined a "hypothetical case" in which the value of money would be entirely decided by the value of the commodity chosen as the standard of value, so that the "value of money would control the quantity of money", instead of the other way around. He assumed that the standard of value is defined as 23.22 grains of pure gold, but that no gold is coined and that the medium of exchange consists of paper money redeemable not in gold, but in silver at the market ratio of silver to gold. In this case, the amount of silver in which paper is redeemable is variable, but always just enough to procure 23.22 grains of gold. There would be no monetary demand for the standard of value, only non-monetary demand as a commodity. Anderson claimed that in this situation "the value of the paper money would be tied absolutely to the value of gold.... The quantity of gold [and silver as well] would be absolutely irrelevant as affecting its value." A higher value of money (lower price level) would reduce the transactional demand for paper money, which would be sent for redemption.

Wicksell (1919b, pp. 59–62) started his assessment of Anderson's thesis by assuming that the value of gold and silver are regulated by their respective production costs and that the market prices are one dollar per unit of weight of gold (23.22 grains) and five cents per unit of silver (one dollar for 20 units), which means that, according to Anderson's framework, the government buys and sells silver at a price of one (paper) dollar for 20 units of weight. If the cost of production should, say, double, then the immediate market price of a unit of gold would be two dollars (40 units of silver). In order to try to keep its notes at parity with gold, the government would now buy and sell silver at a price of one dollar for 40 units of silver. However, this would interrupt the production of silver, while the production of gold would continue as before, but, because of the higher costs, a unit of gold would fetch in the market two dollars, which means that its price in silver will now be 80 units of silver. The government will then have to increase the redemption price for its notes to 80 units of silver for one dollar, but then a unit of gold will fetch in the market 160 units of silver, and so forth, with the price of silver in the process falling in the limit toward zero because of the initial change in the relative price of gold. Wicksell concluded that indirectly convertible systems would feature the "seeming paradox" that a rise in the price of the standard of value leads to a collapse in the price of the medium of redemption. Accordingly, a "separation" of the unit of account and the medium of exchange does not provide a key to price-level stabilization.[33]

5.5 Concluding remarks

Initially, Solvay and his collaborators presented the case for social comptabilism as a constituent part of a more wide-ranging, and controversial, economic and social reform proposal. Later, they decided to advocate social comptabilism as a purely monetary-reform experiment. In both cases, however, the idea was not developed from a careful study of the determinants of the demand for money and its relationship with the aggregate demand for goods, which was precisely what caught the profession's attention in Wicksell's approach to pure credit. Furthermore, there is no reference by Solvay to the stability analysis of the price level, a key concept in Wicksell's neoclassical framework. Understandably, economists have treated Wicksell's carefully elaborated monetary theory much more respectfully than Solvay's rudimentary intuitions about the future of the monetary system.

Respect from fellow economists, however, is no guarantee for immediate practical success. Economic legislators did not carry out the experiment Wicksell described in 1917. Yet, since the abandonment of the gold standard, monetary systems have gradually become increasingly similar to his pure-credit economy (see, e.g., Hicks, 1989; Leijonhufvud, 1997; Woodford, 2003). In the same vein, Solvay did not succeed in carrying out the social comptabilism experiment in Belgium, despite his propaganda effort. Nevertheless, as our discussion of the New Monetary Economics has shown, his notion of an abstract unit of account is back on the research agenda of monetary economics.

Despite their different backgrounds, Solvay and Wicksell shared the view that experimentation is an important part of economics and social sciences in general. From that perspective, social sciences do not differ from natural sciences, but there is a crucial difference concerning the possibility of carrying out social experiments that could affect the working of the socio-economic system. This is especially true of economic legislation in general and of monetary reform in particular, as shown by their respective proposals to adopt a comptabilist or pure-credit system in order to stabilize the price level. Although their monetary experiments differ on the specification of the connection between the unit of account and the media of exchange, Solvay and Wicksell shared the same ground insofar as they stressed the interpretation of the workings of the credit system as the key to their suggested experiments of price-level stabilization.

Acknowledgements

We thank our discussant Flavio Comim and other participants of the Cachan conference, as well as Philippe Fontaine, Albert Jolink, Robert Leonard, Wilfried Parys and three anonymous referees for useful comments on previous drafts. We are also grateful to Didier Devriese of the archives of the Université Libre de Bruxelles, and to Daniel Lefebvre and Suzanne Lecocq of the Mundaneum in Mons, for their help. Mauro Boianovsky gratefully acknowledges research funding from CNPq (Brazilian Research Council).

Notes

1 With respect to Solvay's writings, the date given in the text corresponds to the year of the first publication. For publications included in Solvay (1929), *Notes, Lettres et Discours d'Ernest Solvay* [*NLD*], we refer to the volume number and page numbers of that edition; for the remaining ones, the page numbers refer either to Solvay (1900b), *Etudes Sociales. Notes sur le Productivisme et le Comptabilisme* [*NPC*], or to the original publication. See References for more detailed information. Unless otherwise stated, all translations from the French and Swedish are our own.

2 Solvay explained this in a secret *mémoire* which he deposited at the Académie des Sciences de Belgique; excerpts have been published by Lorentz and Herzen (1923) (*NLD*, I, pp. 273–283).

3 See Max Weber (1922 [1909], pp. 378–382). An echo of these statements can be found in Friedrich Hayek (1979 [1952], pp. 90–91, 171–172n), who reacted very critically to Solvay's energetics. On Solvay and the energetics movement, see also Warnotte (1946), Mirowski (1989, pp. 52–59, 266–270) and Erreygers (1998, pp. 253–254).

4 He returned to the same theme in a speech held a year later, declaring that his scientific action for almost 30 years had been dominated by "a great philosophical preoccupation, which consists of finding for the science of the universe a simple interpretation, by means of deduction, starting from perfectly established postulates like the one that governs universal gravitation" (Solvay, 1912; *NLD*, I, p. 261). Hence mathematics was his great example, and certainly not the experimental, inductive sciences, like chemistry, whose "abundance of hypotheses, complicated theories and limited ways of doing experiments" he abhorred (*ibid.*, pp. 261–262). His mathematical abilities seem to have been rather limited, however.

5 He did occasionally cease to cooperate with collaborators who did not go far enough in his direction; cf. Solvay (1895); *NLD*, I, p. 16.

6 For a more detailed analysis of the foundation, see Crombois (1994, pp. 23–33) and Erreygers (1998, pp. 228–229).

7 Two years later, he referred to his own contribution as "an exposition, in an exclusively theoretical form, of the conception which we have submitted to the examination of our collaborators, and to which their inductive investigations are related" (Solvay, 1896; *NLD*, II, pp. 230–231).

8 The *Annales* are our main source of information. Only for the years 1894 and 1895 did we find some internal notes and reports of the discussions. This material is located in the archives of Henri La Fontaine, Box HLF 121, conserved in the Mundaneum in Mons, Belgium. La Fontaine was the *administrateur* of the Institute in 1894–95.

9 Tassel (1920, pp. 45–46) had access to a draft of letter of March 1890 in which Solvay mentioned "*la taxe à la mort, le compte social*" as solutions to the social and economic questions of his time.

10 Together with an article and a bill written by Hector Denis, the article was reprinted in 1897 as a "propagandistic pamphlet" under the title *Le Comptabilisme Social*; the pamphlet was also published in English and German.

11 We will quote from the English translation of the article as it appeared in the pamphlet *Social Comptabilism*.

12 Solvay specified that the real value of a good, $E(t)$, could be seen as a function of $d(t)$, the "average desire to possess the good", $h(t)$, the "number of those who demand the good", and $o(t)$, the "supply of the good". He returned to these equations in Solvay (1899c; *NPC*, pp. 111–112n), where he tried to connect them to his energetics doctrine.

13 Solvay (1897b; *NLD*, II, p. 255) was nevertheless sceptical about the institution since it was not "entirely comptabilist", based as it was upon metallic money.

14 In La Fontaine's archives we found another undated draft entitled "Clauses fondamentales d'un avant-projet de Loi". It begins as follows: "Article 1. – A partir du 1 Janvier 1900 la monnaie sera supprimée. Article 2. – Le système monétaire sera remplacé par le système comptabiliste."

15 In their book on the history of economic thought, however, Gide and Rist (1915, p. 319) were much more critical of Solvay's ideas. Later Rist (1938, p. 260) even said that they contained "a lot of phantasmagoria".

16 A slightly different version of this letter, addressed to Emile Vinck, the Institute's secretary, was published by Jaffé (1965, vol. II, pp. 722–724).

17 Afterwards, the article was included in Léon Walras's *Etudes d'Economie Politique Appliquée: Théorie de la Production de la Richesse Sociale*; cf. Walras (1992 [1898], pp. 343–361).

18 Cf. Bourguin (1913, p. 85n) for a similar viewpoint.

19 Walras himself advocated the creation of a "Banque de virements à base de monnaie métallique" (1898, p. 219).

20 The occasion to write these letters was the proposal to renew the privileges of the Belgian National Bank. In the first letter, Solvay urged the members of Parliament to ask the Government to make a study on the transformation of the National Bank into a "Établissement Comptabiliste National" (1899a; *NPC*, p. 89). In the second, he indicated more precisely how one could gradually move towards social comptabilism (including designs of comptabilist booklets and accounts), with the clear message that Parliament and Government should without further delay decide "à tenter un essai du système comptabiliste" (Solvay, 1899b; *NPC*, p. 101). The third letter deals mainly with the issue of interest in a comptabilist regime; Solvay considered it to be his last contribution on social comptabilism and hoped that "les intéressés à compétence spéciale" would continue his work (Solvay, 1899c; *NPC*, p. 124).

21 Hutchison (1953, p. 240) has contrasted Wicksell's notion of "conscious control" in the monetary realm with Carl Menger's well-known hypothesis about the origins of money as a "spontaneous social phenomenon". Such a contrast, however, does not apply, as Wicksell did not dispute Menger's description of the origins of money as the most saleable commodity, and the latter did take part in the monetary reform debate in Austria in the late nineteenth century (see also Boianovsky, 1998, pp. 583–584). It should also be noted that, despite Wicksell's apparent restrictions to tariff policy, he made it clear that it could bring about, under certain circumstances, a higher utility for the community as a whole (see Wicksell, 1997 [1896], pp. 104–105).

22 This is the famous "square root formula" advanced by Edgeworth (1888) to explain banks' demand for reserves. It was used by Wicksell in his account of precautionary demand for money by individuals and banks alike. It is based on a stochastic model in which sampling from an infinite population generates a normal distribution (cf. Wicksell, 1898, appendix). If an individual holds a reserve r (proportional to the standard deviation of his excess of payments), the aggregate holding of one hundred independent individuals would have to be just $\sqrt{100} = 10$ times as great, and the aggregate reserve would be $10r$ (Wicksell, 1936 [1898], pp. 66–67).

23 Such a comparative-statics exercise (where there is a once-and-for-all change in the price level, followed by a return to its previous level) should be distinguished from Wicksell's dynamic cumulative process proper. In this case, a (say) increase of the "natural rate of interest" brings about excess demand for commodities and an ensuing continuous process of rising prices. "Business requires greater cash holdings, bank loans increase without corresponding deposits, bank

reserves, and often bullion reserves, *begin* to fall and the banks are compelled to raise their rates somewhat, though this does not prevent the continuous rise in prices, until the interest rates have reached the level of the normal rate" (Wicksell, 1935 [1906], pp. 206–207, italics added). The price level does not return to its original level when the rate of interest approaches the normal rate, which is precisely what gives the process its "cumulative" character.

24 Wicksell (1936 [1898], p. 118) pointed out that a pure credit system without a central bank would feature a deflationary tendency, for profit-maximizing banks would prefer to set interest rates at a level higher than the natural rate, as "banking activity would *expand relatively* to the level of prices".

25 See Laidler (1992, p. 197), who maintains that "free banking" is inconsistent with the economies of scale that result from the pooling of reserves, as this would prompt unregulated banks to merge into one institution or to centralize their reserve holdings with a central bank.

26 Wicksell's (1917, 1919a) notion of the pure-credit economy as a system with a central bank (that sets the basic rate on deposits) plus specialized intermediaries is remarkably close to Hicks's (1989, Ch. 12) "revision" of the pure-credit models of *Interest and Prices* and *Lectures*. (It should be noted, though, that Hicks completely ignored the fact that Wicksell's models applied most of the time to a gold-standard economy.) Hicks (p. 104) suggested that a "monocentric" pure-credit system would emerge naturally if there was just one central entity whose "promises to pay have superior quality" than those of any other entity. He did not explain, however, why any of the independent private banks in a competitive system should have a better "reputation" (or more confidence) than the others. Alternatively, assuming, as Hicks does, that this central entity is a non-private central bank, it remains to explain why such an institution would remunerate deposits, as it would be under no competitive pressure to do so. Cowen and Kroszner's (1994, pp. 144–147) description of Wicksell's pure credit as a system with an "abstract medium of account" *à la* Fama (1980) is unwarranted and inconsistent with Wicksell's suggestion on how to render the price level determinate through the central bank's interest-rate policy.

27 As Hoover (1988, pp. 102–103) pointed out, an important characteristic of financial assets of a developed financial system in a non-Walrasian economy is the "absence of direct connection between the claims represented by the asset and the underlying goods against which it is a claim", which opens up the possibility of default and reinforces the importance of money as a single good which is generally accepted as settling accounts.

28 Wicksell (1936 [1898], p. 68, n. 1; see also 1935 [1906], p. 87) referred to the Austrian Post Office Saving Bank as a "quite unique institution" formed by banks that are branches of one single monetary institution serving the whole country. See Cowen and Kroszner (1994, p. 144) for references to the "Giro system" used in continental Europe at the time.

29 The list of authors with similar ideas has even been extended to Major Douglas; cf. Baudin (1947, p. 623) and Warnotte (1946, Vol. I, pp. 323–327).

30 Denis (1901, p. 125) was well aware of both the similarities and the differences between the two approaches:

> One is struck by the similarity between the monetary conception of Mr Kitson and the comptabilist one of Mr. E. Solvay. By different paths, at the same time, two men greatly endowed with the gift of abstraction managed to conceive of a final form of money which would no longer be wealth, but the sign, the symbol of wealth, and which, losing forever its material character, would appear as an ideal money ... *a symbolical money*, in the words of James Steuart beginning in the 18th century.

31 Cf. the "psychological explanation" of Solvay's abstract unit of account by Aucuy (1908, pp. 335–336).

32 As pointed out by Patinkin (1993, pp. 16–17), Fisher (1920, pp. 129–131) introduced a major modification in his 1913 plan, that is, he added a "definitive-reserve system" in which changes in the price of gold also revalue the existing monetary stock of gold and, by that, bring about changes in the quantity of certified gold that can be issued. According to Fisher, this would increase the speed of the plan, but, as shown by Patinkin, that change marks the start of Fisher's movement away from the compensated dollar, until eventually he gave it up in the mid-1930s. In any event, despite similarities with the New Monetary Economics, Fisher's compensated dollar did not really "separate" the unit of account" from the redemption medium, since the dollar was legally defined as a certain amount of gold (see also Patinkin, 1996).

33 The paradox was independently rediscovered by Schnadt and Whittaker (1993). See also Dowd's (1995, pp. 78–81) attempt to establish conditions that could prevent the paradox and render indirect convertibility feasible.

References

Anderson, B. Jr. (1917), *The Value of Money*, New York: Macmillan.

Aucuy, M. (1908), *Les Systèmes Socialistes d'Echange*, Paris: Félix Alcan.

Baudin, L. (1947), *La Monnaie et la Formation des Prix* (2ième édition), Paris: Recueil Sirey.

Bilgram, H. (1895), "A standard after all", *Liberty*, June, vol. 15: 2–3.

Black, F. (1987 [1970]), "Banking and interest rate in a world without money", in: F. Black, *Business Cycles and Equilibrium*, Oxford: Basil Blackwell, 1–20.

Blaug, M. (1980), *The Methodology of Economics*, Cambridge: Cambridge University Press.

Boianovsky, M. (1995), "Wicksell's business cycle", *European Journal of the History of Economic Thought*, vol. 2(2): 375–411.

Boianovsky, M. (1998), "Real balances, the price level and the unit of account: from Wicksell to Patinkin and beyond", *American Journal of Economics and Sociology*, vol. 57(4): 579–612.

Bourguin, M. (1913), *Les Systèmes Socialistes et l'Évolution Économique*, Paris: Librairie Armand Colin.

Cohn, A.W. (1920), *Kann das Geld Abgeschafft Werden?*, Jena: Gustav Fischer.

Cowen, T. and R. Kroszner (1994), *Explorations in the New Monetary Economics*, Oxford: Blackwell.

Crombois, J.-F. (1994), *L'Univers de la Sociologie en Belgique de 1900 à 1940*, Bruxelles: Éditions de l'Université de Bruxelles.

De Bie, P. (1988), *Naissance et Premiers Développements de la Sociologie en Belgique*, Louvain-la-Neuve: Ciaco.

De Greef, G. (1899), *Le Crédit Commercial et la Banque Nationale de Belgique*, Bruxelles: O. Mayolez & J. Audiarte.

Dejongh, Ch. and E. Hanssens (1901), *Procès Verbal*, Bruxelles.

Denis, H. (1898), "La critique du comptabilisme par M. Walras et les formules de la valeur de la monnaie", *Annales de l'Institut des Sciences Sociales*, vol. 4(4): 275–289.

Denis, H. (1901), *Les Théories de la Valeur et les Conceptions du Système Monétaire. IVe Étude. A. Kitson* [Extrait des *Annales de l'Institut des Sciences Sociales*], Bruxelles: Institut des Sciences Sociales.

Dony-Hénault, O. (1942), "Ernest Solvay, pionnier des sciences expérimentales", *Académie Royale de Belgique. Bulletin de la Classe des Sciences*, 5e série, vol. 28(12): 927–967.

Dowd, K. (1995), "The mechanics of indirect convertibility", *Journal of Money, Credit and Banking*, vol. 27(1): 67–88.

Edgeworth, F.Y. (1888), "The mathematical theory of banking", *Journal of the Royal Statistical Society*, March, vol. 51: 113–126.

Elkhadem, H. and Th. Mayer (1997), "La soude, une histoire ancienne et moderne", in: A. Despy-Meyer and D. Devriese (eds), *Ernest Solvay et son Temps*, Bruxelles: Archives de l'Université Libre de Bruxelles, 137–147.

Erreygers, G. (1998), "The economic theories and social reform proposals of Ernest Solvay (1838–1922)", in: W.J. Samuels (ed.), *European Economists of the Early 20th Century, Volume 1. Studies of Neglected Thinkers of Belgium, France, The Netherlands and Scandinavia*, Cheltenham: Edward Elgar, 220–262.

Fama, E. (1980), "Banking in the theory of finance", *Journal of Monetary Economics*, vol. 6(1): 39–57.

Ferber, R. and W. Hirsch (1982), *Social Experiments and Economic Policy*, Cambridge: Cambridge University Press.

Fisher, I. (1913), *The Purchasing Power of Money* (revised edition), New York: Macmillan.

Fisher, I. (1920), *Stabilizing the Dollar*, New York: Macmillan.

Gide, Ch. (1897), "Lettre de M. le Professeur Charles Gide [Au sujet du comptabilisme]", *Annales de l'Institut des Sciences Sociales*, vol. 3(4): 220.

Gide, Ch. and Ch. Rist (1915), *A History of Economic Doctrines from the Time of the Physiocrats to the Present Day*, London: George G. Harrap & Co.

Greenfield, R. and L. Yeager (1983), "A laissez-faire approach to monetary stability", *Journal of Money, Credit and Banking*, vol. 15(3): 302–315.

Greenfield, R. and L. Yeager (1989), "Can monetary disequilibrium be eliminated?", *Cato Journal*, vol. 9(2): 405–421.

Hawtrey, R.G. (1934 [1919]), *Currency and Credit* (3rd edition), London: Longmans, Green.

Hayek, F.A. (1979 [1952]), *The Counter-Revolution of Science. Studies on the Abuse of Reason*, Indianapolis: Liberty Press.

Henriksson, R. (1991), "The facts on Wicksell on the facts: Wicksell and economic history", *Research in Economic History*, vol. 6 (supplement): 33–50.

Hernandez-Aramburo, L. (1996), "Financial innovation and the price level: Wicksell and the New Monetary Economics", in: D. Vaz and K. Velupillai (eds), *Inflation, Institutions and Information: Essays in Honour of Axel Leijonhufvud*, London: Macmillan, ch. 10.

Hicks, J. (1989), *A Market Theory of Money*, Oxford: Clarendon Press.

Hoover, K.D. (1988) *The New Classical Macroeconomics*, Oxford: Blackwell.

Hutchison, T.W. (1953), *A Review of Economic Doctrines: 1870–1929*, Oxford: Oxford University Press.

Ingram, J.K. (1897), "Lettre de M. John K. Ingram, Professeur à Dublin [Au sujet du comptabilisme]", *Annales de l'Institut des Sciences Sociales*, vol. 3(5): 311–312.

Jaffé, W. (ed.) (1965), *Correspondence of Léon Walras and Related Papers*, Amsterdam: North Holland.

Jevons, W.S. (1883), *Methods of Social Reform*, London: Macmillan.

Keynes, J.N. (1973 [1891]), *The Scope and Method of Political Economy*, Clifton: A. M. Kelley.

Kitson, A. (1895a), *A Scientific Solution to the Money Question*, Boston: Arena.

Kitson, A. (1895b), "Mr. Kitson's defence", *Liberty*, June, vol. 15: 6–8.

Laidler, D. (1991), *The Golden Age of the Quantity Theory*, New York: Philip Allan.

Laidler, D. (1992), "Free banking: theory", in: Peter Newman, Murray Milgate and John Eatwell (eds), *The New Palgrave Dictionary of Money and Finance*, vol. 2, London: Macmillan.

Langelütke, H. (1925), *Tauschbank und Schwundgeld als Wege zur Zinslosen Wirtschaft. Vergleichende Darstellung und Kritik der Zirkulationsreformen P.J. Proudhons und Silvio Gesells*, Jena: Gustav Fischer.

Leijonhufvud, A. (1997), "The Wicksellian heritage", *Economic Notes*, vol. 26(1): 1–10.

Lorentz, H.-A. and E. Herzen (1923), "Les rapports de l'énergie et de la masse, d'après Ernest Solvay", *Comptes Rendus des Séances de l'Académie des Sciences,* vol. 177; in: *NLD*, I, 273–283.

Loria, A. (1902), "Des méthodes proposées pour régulariser la valeur de la monnaie", *Revue d'Economie Politique*, vol. 16(2): 109–124.

Lucion, R. and A. Brichaux (1924), "Expériences entreprises par Ernest Solvay de 1877 à 1881 sur l'unité fondamentale de la matière et de l'énergie", *Bulletin de la Classe des Sciences de l'Académie de Belgique*; in: *NLD*, I, 285–294.

May, D. (1896), "L'Institut Solvay et le 'Comptabilisme'", *Revue Politique et Parlémentaire*, vol. 7(23): 385–397.

Mill, J.S. (1992 [1844]), *Essays on Some Unsettled Questions of Political Economy*, Bristol: Thoemmes Press.

Mirowski, Ph. (1989), *More Heat than Light. Economics as Social Physics: Physics as Nature's Economics*, Cambridge: Cambridge University Press.

Ohlin, B. (1934), "Knut Wicksell – father of the Swedish monetary experiment", *Economic Forum*, vol. 2 : 159–168.

Ostwald, W. (1909), *Energetische Grundlagen der Kulturwissenschaft*, Leipzig, Verlag von Dr. Werner Klinkhardt.

Otlet, P. (1898), "Observations à propos de la note de M. Solvay relative au comptabilisme", *Annales de l'Institut des Sciences Sociales*, vol. 4(4): 290–294.

Pareto, V. (1965 [1903]), *Les Systèmes Socialistes*, vol. II, in: G. Busino (ed.), *Vilfredo Pareto, Oeuvres Complètes*, Genève: Librairie Droz, vol. 5.

Patinkin, D. (1965), *Money, Interest and Prices* (2nd edition), New York: Harper and Row.

Patinkin, D. (1993), "Irving Fisher and his compensated dollar plan", *Federal Reserve Bank of Richmond Economic Quarterly*, vol. 79(3): 1–33.

Patinkin, D. (1996), "Indirect convertibility and Irving Fisher's compensated dollar", *Journal of Money, Credit and Banking*, vol. 28(1): 130–131.

Poudou, F. (1919), *Les Procédés Amétalliques de Paiement et le Chèque Postal*, Paris: Librairie d'Enseignement Technique.

Rist, Ch. (1938), *Histoire des Doctrines Relatives au Crédit et à la Monnaie depuis John Law jusqu'à nos Jours*, Paris: Recueil Sirey.

Roche-Agussol, M. (1903), *Essai sur le Clearing System*, Thèse pour le Doctorat ès-Sciences Economiques, Montpellier: Imprimerie G. Firmin, Montane et Sicardi.

Schnadt, N. and J. Whittaker (1993), "Inflation-proof currency? The feasibility of variable commodity standards", *Journal of Money, Credit and Banking*, vol. 25(2): 214–221.

Schumpeter, J. (1917–1918), "Das Sozialprodukt und die Rechenpfennige. Glossen und Beiträge zur Geldtheorie von heute", *Archiv für Sozialwissenschaft und Sozialpolitik*, vol. 44: 627–715.

Solvay, E. (1871), "Lettre d'un inconnu"; in: *NLD*, II, 9–10.

Solvay, E. (1894a), "Discours au Sénat. Séance du 24 Mai 1894", *Annales Parlementaires*, in: *NLD*, II, 62–69.

Solvay, E. (1894b), "Le programme de l'Institut des Sciences Sociales. Avant-propos", *Annales de l'Institut des Sciences Sociales*, vol. 1(1): 1–3.

Solvay, E. (1895), *Gravitique*; in: *NLD*, I, 9–113.

Solvay, E. (1896), "Principe et raison d'être du comptabilisme social", *Annales de l'Institut des Sciences Sociales*, vol. 2(5); in: *NLD*, II, 229–249.

Solvay, E. (1897a), "Social comptabilism. Its principle and ground of existence", in: *Social Comptabilism*, Bruxelles: Institut des Sciences Sociales, 1–17.

Solvay, E. (1897b), "Le comptabilisme social (note complémentaire)", *Annales de l'Institut des Sciences Sociales*, vol. 3(1); in: *NLD*, II, 251–256.

Solvay, E. (1898a), "Comptabilisme et fixité de l'unité de la valeur abstraite", *Annales de l'Institut des Sciences Sociales*, vol. 4(4); in: *NLD*, II, 257–267.

Solvay, E. (1898b), "Le productivisme social", *Annales de l'Institut des Sciences Sociales*, vol. 4(5); in: *NLD*, II, 207–227.

Solvay, E. (1899a), "La monnaie et le compte", *Annales de l'Institut des Sciences Sociales*, vol. 5(2); in: *NPC*, 83–91.

Solvay, E. (1899b), "La monnaie et le compte (note complémentaire)", *Annales de l'Institut des Sciences Sociales*, vol. 5(3); in: *NPC*, 93–101.

Solvay, E. (1899c), "La monnaie et le compte (seconde note complémentaire)", *Annales de l'Institut des Sciences Sociales*, vol. 5(4); in: *NPC*, 103–124.

Solvay, E. (1900a), "Discussion du projet de loi prorogeant la durée de la Banque Nationale", *Annales Parlementaires*; in: *NLD*, II, 112–123.

Solvay, E. (1900b), *Études Sociales. Notes sur le Productivisme et le Comptabilisme* [*NPC*], Bruxelles: Henri Lamertin.

Solvay, E. (1900c), "La notion de l'échange, la notion du compte social et la notion du droit social", *Annales de l'Institut des Sciences Sociales*, vol. 6(2); in: *NLD*, II, 269–273.

Solvay, E. (1900d), "La théorie des échanges et la notion du productivisme social", *Annales de l'Institut des Sciences Sociales*, vol. 6(3); in: *NLD*, II, 275–279.

Solvay, E. (1911a), "Allocutions relatives à la gravito-matérialitique prononcées à l'ouverture et à la clôture du 'Conseil de Physique' tenu à Bruxelles du 29 Octobre au 3 Novembre", in: *NLD*, I, 115–121.

Solvay, E. (1911b), *Sur l'Établissement des Principes Fondamentaux de la Gravito-Matérialitique*, Bruxelles: Imprimerie Bothy.

Solvay, E. (1912), "Contribution à l'étude de la constitution de la matière, de l'éther et de l'énergie", *Bulletin de la Société Chimique de Belgique*; in: *NLD*, I, 259–275.

Solvay, E. (1929), *Notes, Lettres et Discours d'Ernest Solvay* [*NLD*], Bruxelles: Lamertin.

Solvay, E. and R. Lucion (1877), "Remarques sur l'action d'acides anhydres stables sur des bases anhydres stables: explosion du composé", *Comptes Rendus de l'Académie des Sciences de Paris*, vol. 85: 1160–1168.

Stengers, I. (1997), "La pensée d'Ernest Solvay et la science de son temps", in: A.

Despy-Meyer and D. Devriese (eds), *Ernest Solvay et son Temps*, Bruxelles: Archives de l'Université Libre de Bruxelles, 149–165.

Sumner, S. (1990), "The forerunners of 'New Monetary Economics' proposals to stabilize the unit of account", *Journal of Money, Credit and Banking*, vol. 22(1): 109–118.

Sweeney, R. (1988), *Wealth Effects in Monetary Theory*, Oxford: Basil Blackwell.

Tassel, É. (1920), *Notes sur les Travaux Poursuivis par Ernest Solvay de 1857 à 1914*, Ixelles: Imprimerie G. Bothy.

Trautwein, H.-M. (1993), "Preisniveaustabilität durch indirekte Konvertibität?", in: H.-J. Stadermann and O. Steiger (eds), *Der Stand und die nächste Zukunft der Geldforschung*, Berlin: Duncker & Humblot.

Trautwein, H.-M. (1995), *Pure Credit Economies in Monetary Theory*, Working Paper no. 106, Department of Economics, University of Hohenheim.

Vanderrydt, H. (1898) "Note sur l'article de M. Walras concernant le comptabilisme social", *Annales de l'Institut des Sciences Sociales*, vol. 4(4): 271–274.

Vandervelde, É. (1895), "Le comptabilisme social. Deuxième mémoire", *Annales de l'Institut des Sciences Sociales*, vol. 1(5): 230–246.

von Mises, L. (1980 [1912]), *The Theory of Money and Credit*, Indianapolis: Liberty Press.

Wagner, A. (1862), *Die Geld- und Kredittheorie der Peelschen Bankakte*, Vienna: W. Braumuller.

Walras, L. (1897), "Lettre de M. le Professeur Walras [Au sujet du comptabilisme]", *Annales de l'Institut des Sciences Sociales*, vol. 3(4), 219–220.

Walras, L. (1898), "La Caisse d'Épargne Postale de Vienne et le comptabilisme social", *Revue d'Economie Politique*, vol. 12(3), 202–220; also in: Walras (1992 [1898]), 343–361.

Walras, L. (1992 [1898]), *Etudes d'Économie Politique Appliquée: Théorie de la Production de la Richesse Sociale*, in: A. and L. Walras, *Œuvres Économiques Complètes*, Paris: Economica, vol. X.

Warnotte, D. (1946), *Ernest Solvay et l'Institut de Sociologie. Contribution à l'Histoire de l'Énergétique Sociale*, Bruxelles: Ets. Emile Bruylant.

Weber, M. (1922 [1909]), "'Energetische' Kulturtheorien", in: *Gesammelte Aufsätze zur Wissenschaftslehre*, Tübingen, J.C.B Mohr (Paul Siebeck).

Wegelin, W. (1921), *Tauschsozialismus und Freigeld. Eine Dogmengeschichtlich-kritische Untersuchung zur Freigeldlehre*, München, Berlin & Leipzig: J. Schweitzer Verlag (Arthur Sellier).

Wicksell, K. (2001 [1889]), "Knut Wicksell's Bank rate of interest as the regulator of prices", edited and translated by Mauro Bioanovsky and Hans-Michael Trautwein, *History of Political Economy*, vol. 33(3): 509–516.

Wicksell, K. (1997 [1896]), "On the theory of tax incidence", in: Wicksell (1997), Vol. 1, 57–115.

Wicksell, K. (1898), *Geldzins und Guterpreise*, Jena: G. Fischer.

Wicksell, K. (1936 [1898]), *Interest and Prices: A Study of the Causes Regulating the Value of Money*, London: Macmillan.

Wicksell, K. (1934 [1901]), *Lectures on Political Economy*, vol. 1, London: Routledge and Sons.

Wicksell, K. (1902), *Guld och Sedlar*, Stockholm: Jacob Bagges Soner.

Wicksell, K. (1958 [1904]), "Ends and means in economics", in: E. Lindahl (ed.), *Knut Wicksell – Selected Papers on Economic Theory*, London: Allen and Unwin, 51–66.

Wicksell, K. (1935 [1906]), *Lectures on Political Economy*, vol. 2, London: Routledge and Sons.

Wicksell, K. (1998 [1907]), "Some additional remarks on the verification of the law of diminishing returns", in: B. Sandelin (ed.): *Swedish Economics*, vol. 1, London: Routledge, ch. 6.

Wicksell, K. (1913), "Penningvärdets reglerande", *Ekonomisk Tidskrift*, vol. 15: 134–142; also in: Wicksell (1997), vol. 2: 46–52.

Wicksell, K. (1914), "Review of Mises (1912)", *Zeitschrift für Volkswitschaft und Sozialpolitik*, vol. 23: 144–149; also in: Wicksell (1997), vol. 2: 220–224.

Wicksell, K. (1917), "Skandinviens penningväsen", *Statsøkonomisk Tidskrift*, vol. 31: 169–186.

Wicksell, K. (1919a), "Riksbanken och privatbankerna", *Ekonomisk Tidskrift*, vol. 21: 177–188.

Wicksell, K. (1919b), "Ett angrepp på kvantitetsteorien", *Ekonomisk Tidskrift*, vol. 21: 59–63.

Wicksell, K. (1997), *Knut Wicksell – Selected Essays in Economics*, ed. B. Sandelin, London: Routledge, 2 vols.

Woodford, M. (2003) *Interest and Prices – Foundations of a Theory of Monetary Policy*, Princeton: University Press.

Zaleski, L. (1897), "Lettre de M. Ladislas Zaleski, Professeur à l'Université [Au sujet du comptabilisme]", *Annales de l'Institut des Sciences Sociales*, vol. 3(5): 312–316.

6 The vanity of rigour in economics

Theoretical models and Galilean experiments

Nancy Cartwright

6.1 Introduction

My topic in this essay is the old and familiar one of the unrealism of assumptions in economic models. For a long time I have maintained that economics is unfairly criticized for the use of unrealistic assumptions (see Cartwright 1989, 1998). I can summarize my view by comparing an economic model to a certain kind of ideal experiment in physics: criticizing economic models for using unrealistic assumptions is like criticizing Galileo's rolling-ball experiments for using a plane honed to be as frictionless as possible. This defence of economic modelling has a bite, however. On the one hand, it makes clear why some kinds of unrealistic assumptions will do; but, on the other, it highlights how totally misleading other kinds can be – and these other kinds of assumptions are ones that may be hard to avoid given the nature of contemporary economic theory.

The theme for this volume is *experiments in economics*. My project is not to understand experiments but rather to use experiments to understand theorizing in economics; more specifically, to understand one particular mode of theorizing that is prominent in economics nowadays – theorizing by the construction of models for what Robert Lucas describes as 'analogue economies' (1981, 272). Lucas does not define exactly what an analogue economy is. What I have in mind is theorizing by the construction of models that depict specific kinds of economies and depict them in a certain way. We do not in this kind of theorizing simply lay down laws or principles of a specific form that are presumed to obtain in the economy, as we might in setting out a large-scale macroeconomic model whose parameters we aim to estimate. Rather we justify them from our description of the agents, or sectors, or other significant causal factors in the economy and our description of their significant actions and interactions. Economic principles are employed of course, of necessity, such as the demand for equilibrium of some kind, or the assumption that economic agents act to maximize what they take to be their self-interest. But the detailed form of any principles or equations used will be peculiar to the kind of economy described and the kinds of interactions that occur in it.

Analogue economies generally have only a small number of features, a small number of agents and a small number of options for what can happen, all represented by thin concepts. I call the concepts 'thin' because, although they are often homonymous with everyday economic concepts or occasionally with concepts from earlier economic theories, little of their behaviour from the real world is imported into the model. Seldom, for instance, do we make use of 'low-level empirical' relations established by induction. Instead, as we shall see, the behaviour of the features they represent is fixed by the structure of the model and its assumptions in conjunction with the few general principles that are allowed without controversy in this kind of theorizing.

Lucas is a good spokesman in favour of this kind of theorizing, and that is why I cite him. But the method is in no way peculiar to his point of view. Modelling by the construction of analogue economies is a widespread technique in economic theory nowadays; in particular, it is a technique that is shared across both sides of the divide between micro- and macroeconomics. It is the standard way in which game theory is employed; the same is true for rational expectations theory and also for other kinds of theorizing that rely primarily on the assumption that agents act to maximize their utility. As Lucas urges, the important point about analogue economies is that everything is known about them – i.e. their characteristics are entirely explicit (Lucas 1981, 7–8) – and within them the propositions we are interested in 'can be formulated rigorously and shown to be valid' (Lucas 1981, 67). With respect to real economies, generally there is a great variety of different opinions about what will happen, and the different opinions can all be plausible. But for these constructed economies, our views about what will happen are 'statements of verifiable fact' (Lucas 1981, 271).

The method of verification is deduction: we know what does happen in one of these economies because we know what must happen given our general principles and the characteristics of the economy. We are, however, faced with a trade-off: we can have totally verifiable results but only about economies that are not real. As Lucas says, 'Any model that is well enough articulated to give clear answers to the questions we put to it will necessarily be artificial, abstract, patently "unreal"' (Lucas 1981, 271).

How then do these analogue economies relate to the real economies that we are supposed to be theorizing about? Here is where experiment comes into play, ideal experiments, like Galileo's balls rolling down a smooth inclined plane. For a long time I have maintained that experiments like Galileo's are the clue to understanding how analogue economies can teach us about empirical reality. They show us why the unrealism of the model's assumptions need not be a problem. Indeed, to the contrary, the high degree of idealization involved is essential to the ability of the model to teach us about the real world, rather than being a problematic feature we had best eliminate. But I will return then to the feature of these models that is generally thought to be unproblematic – their use of deduction. For my overall suspicion is that the way deductivity is achieved in economic models may undermine the possibility I open up for them to teach us genuine truths about empirical reality. So in the end I may be taking back with one hand what I give with the other.

As I mentioned at the start, this essay is about a very familiar topic: the unrealism of assumptions in economic models. Section 6.2 will put this problem in a somewhat less familiar perspective by identifying it with the problem of external validity, or parallelism, in experiments. Section 6.3 explains why experiments matter: because many models aim to isolate a single process to study on its own, just as Galileo did with his studies of gravitational attraction. Using the language of John Stuart Mill (1836, 1843), models aim to establish *tendencies* to behave in certain ways, not to describe the overall behaviour that occurs. For this job, it is essential that models make highly unrealistic assumptions, for we need to see what happens in the very unusual case where only the single factor of interest affects the outcome. Section 6.4 raises the question of how we can draw interesting and rich deductive conclusions in economies given that we have so few principles to use as premises; Section 6.5 answers that often it seems we fill in by relying on the detailed structure of the model. But then it takes back the solace offered in Sections 6.2 and 6.3. For in that case the conclusions are tied to these structural assumptions, assumptions that go well beyond what is necessary for Galilean idealization; the results do not depend just on the process in question but are rather overconstrained. This means that Galilean inference to tendencies that hold outside the experimental set-up is jeopardized. So in the end the problems involved in using highly unrealistic assumptions can loom as large as ever.

6.2 External validity: a problem for models and experiments alike

Lucas speaks of the analogue economies of contemporary economic theorizing as stand-ins for experiment:

> One of the functions of theoretical economics is to provide fully articulated, artificial economic systems that can serve as laboratories in which policies that would be prohibitively expensive to experiment with in actual economics can be tested out at much lower cost.
>
> (1981, 271)

As we know from Mary Morgan, many of the originators of econometrics viewed their econometric models in a similar way, for they thought of situations in which the parameters of their structural models could be identified as situations in which by good luck nature is running an experiment for us (see Morgan 1990).

Francesco Guala too talks about the similarities between laboratory experiments in economics and the kinds of theoretical models I am discussing here (see Guala 1998). Guala has been studying how experiments work; I have been trying to understand how theoretical models work. We have both been struck by the structural similarities between the two. I am particularly interested in the fact that both laboratory experiments and theoretical models in economics are criticized for the artificiality of the conditions they set up. As Lucas says, the assumptions of our theoretical models in economics are typically 'artificial', 'abstract' and 'patently unreal'.

Thinking about this very same complaint with respect to the laboratory experiments we perform nowadays in economics provides us with a useful vocabulary to describe the problems arising from the unrealism of assumptions in theoretical models – and to see our way around them. When we design an experiment or a quasi-experiment in the social sciences, we aim simultaneously for both *internal validity* and for *external validity*. An experimental claim is internally valid when we can be sure that it has genuinely been established to hold in the experimental situation. External validity – or 'parallelism' as economists call it – is more ambitious. For that the experiment must be designed to assure us that the result should hold in some kinds of targeted situations or populations outside the experimental set-up.

It is a well-known methodological truism that in almost all cases there will be a trade-off between internal validity and external validity. The conditions that we need in order to increase the chances of internal validity are generally at odds with those that provide grounds for external validity. The usual complaint here is about the artificiality of the circumstances required to secure internal validity: if we want to take the lessons, literally interpreted (you should note the 'literally interpreted' – I shall return to it below), from inside the laboratory to outside, it seems that the experimental situation should be as similar as possible in relevant respects to the target situation. But for the former we need to set up very special circumstances so that we can be sure that nothing confounds the putative result, and these are generally nothing like the kinds of circumstances to which we want to apply our results.

This is exactly what we see in the case of economic models. Analogue economies are designed to ensure internal validity. In an analogue economy we know the result obtains because we can establish by deduction that it has to obtain. But to have this assurance we must provide an analogue economy with a simple and clear enough structure that ensures that deduction will be possible. In particular we need to make very special assumptions matched to the general principles we use: we must attribute to this economy characteristics that can be represented mathematically in just the right kind of form, a form that can be fed into the principles in order to get deductive consequences out. And this very special kind of dovetailing that can provide just what is needed for deduction is not likely to be provided by conditions that occur in the economy at large, as Lucas and all other theorists using these methods admit. In this kind of theorizing it looks as if we buy internal validity at the cost of external validity.

Nor is the problem confined to the 'thought experiments' we conduct with our constructed models. It also appears in the real experiments we conduct nowadays in economics; and it reveals a significant difference in concerns between economics and many other branches of social science. Experimental economists report astounding confirmation of a number of economic hypotheses they have been testing recently (cf. Plott 1991 and Smith 1991). These experimental economists are also very proud of their experimental designs, which they take to have minimized the chances of drawing mistaken conclusions. Yet, apparently, it is difficult for them to get their results published in social-science journals outside their own field, because, referees claim, they have virtually no guarantees of external validity (conversation, Charles Plott, California Institute of Technology, May 1997). So the results, it is felt, lack general interest or significance.

6.3 Tendencies and Galilean idealizations

Now I should like to argue that a great many of the unrealistic assumptions we find in models and experiments alike are not a problem. To the contrary, they are required to do the job; without them the experiment would be no experiment at all. For we do not need to assume that the aim of the kind of theorizing under discussion is to establish results in our analogue economies that will hold outside them when *literally interpreted*. Frequently what we are doing in this kind of economic theory is not trying to establish facts about what happens in the real economy but rather, following John Stuart Mill, facts about *stable tendencies*. Consider a stock example of mine – a model designed by my colleague Chris Pissarides to study the effects of skill loss on unemployment (see Pissarides 1992). What we want to learn from the analogue economy described by Pissarides is not whether there will be persistence in unemployment in the real economy but instead what skill loss will *contribute* to persistence – what skill loss *tends to* produce, not what is produced whenever skill loss occurs.

So what I maintain is that the analogue economies described in contemporary economic models look like experiments, where the *experimental* aspect matters. The models almost always concentrate on a single mechanism or causal process. For example, Pissarides' model studies the effect (if any) of skill loss during unemployment on the persistence of unemployment shocks via the disincentives arising from loss of skills in the labour pool for employers to create jobs in areas where skill affects productivity. The idea is to isolate this process; to study it in a setting where nothing else is going on that might affect the outcome as well. The model is constructed to assure us that whatever result we see is indeed due to the process under study.

Consider the skill-loss model. Loss or not of skill during unemployment is the only exogenous variable. Firms act to maximize profits and only to maximize profits. We can trace through the model to see that the only variation in profits will be due to the number of jobs that firms decide to create in the face of a labour pool containing unemployed workers and to the productivity of the workers hired. For this model we can derive rigorously that unemployment in one period is dependent on unemployment in the previous period if and only if skills are lost during unemployment. It looks as if this model allows us to see exactly what effects loss of skill has on unemployment persistence via the disincentive it creates for job creation.

What can we conclude? Can we conclude that we have learned a fact about skill loss *per se*, a fact we can expect to be generally true, true not just in this analogue economy but in other economies as well? Certainly not if we try to read the conclusion as one about the association between loss of skill and unemployment persistence with some kind of quantifier in front: *always*, or *for the most part*, or even *sometimes*, *if there is skill loss in sectors where skills matter to productivity, there will be unemployment persistence*. Clearly a good deal else could be going on to offset the effects of skill loss, even to swamp them entirely; indeed we might never see persistence in any case of skill loss, even though the model shows correctly that 'skill loss leads to unemployment persistence'.

This is why we turn to the notion of stable tendencies:[1] *in any situation skill loss tends to produce persistence in unemployment shocks*. What does this mean in terms of what actually happens? There does not seem to be any general rule in economic theory that answers, as vector addition does on Mill's account of the tendencies of different forces in classical mechanics. Nevertheless, if economic theory is to aspire to be an exact science, there had better be at least a case-by-case answer. And presumably this answer can in general be generated by the specific model that testifies to the tendency, in conjunction with any general economic theory we are in a position to assume (Cartwright 1989, 1998, 1999).[2] For the skill-loss tendency, I take it that we assume roughly that, in any situation where skills matter to productivity and the decision to create new jobs by a firm is in part determined by its expected profit, unemployment at one period will depend on previous levels of unemployment if workers are thought to lose skills during unemployment and not otherwise, even if this dependency on past levels plays only a small part in determining present levels.

Probably no-one thinks we have established even that, though, because economists, like other social scientists, are alert to the possibility of interaction, as Mill himself warned. In some situations some factors may distort the skill-loss mechanism so much that loss of skill behaves differently in those situations from the way it behaves in our analogue economy. Of course if we are going to avoid manoeuvres that are entirely *ad hoc* we shall have to ensure that 'interaction' is given real verifiable content whenever it is invoked. In principle this should be possible since the theoretical model is supposed to lay bare how the process operates in the first place – 'distortions' are judged relative to it.

We can see the general points more clearly by thinking again about the kind of laboratory experiment that aims to establish a tendency claim. Perhaps rather than thinking of economics experiments, which tend to be controversial, we should take an illustration from physics, let us say Galileo's famous experiments to establish the effect of the attraction of the earth on a falling body, one of which is illustrated in Figure 6.1.

Galileo's experiments aimed to establish what I have been calling a *tendency* claim. They were not designed to tell us how any particular falling body will move in the vicinity of the earth; nor to establish a regularity about how bodies of a certain kind will move. Rather, the experiments were designed to find out what contribution the motion due to the pull of the earth will make, with the assumption that that contribution is stable across all the different kinds of situations falling bodies will get into. How did Galileo find out what the stable contribution from the pull of the earth is? He eliminated (as far as possible) all other causes of motion on

Figure 6.1 Leaning tower (designed by Emily Cartwright).

the bodies in his experiment so that he could see how they move when only the earth affects them. That is the contribution that the earth's pull makes to their motion.

Let us call this kind of idealization, that eliminates all other possible causes to learn the effect of one operating on its own, *Galilean idealization*. My point is that the equivalent of Galilean idealization in a model is a good thing. It is just what allows us to carry the results we find in the experiment to situations outside – in the tendency sense. We need the idealizing assumptions to be able to do this. Otherwise we have no ground for thinking the behaviour we see in the experiment is characteristic of the earth's pull at all. Indeed, we know it will not be.

We can contrast these Galilean experiments with experiments that have a quite different aim and, correlatively, a quite different structure. Consider what happens when we build a prototype of a new device and experiment on it to ensure that it will work correctly when put to use. In this case we do not aim to learn an abstract tendency claim. Instead we want to find out what actual behaviours occur. So the experimental conditions should be very realistic to the conditions in the target situations and vary appropriately across them. And, without more said, we have no reason to expect the results in the experiment to obtain in any situations except those that resemble the conditions in the experiment.

Here we see another trade-off. If an experiment is very, very unrealistic in just the right way, its results can be applicable almost everywhere. But they will not be able to tell you *what happens* anywhere else since they only establish the *contribution* or *tendency* of the factor in question. Experiments that are very realistic can tell you what happens. But they are highly limited in their scope, for they can only tell you what happens in situations that look like the experimental set-up. And experiments in between are usually pretty uninformative on both matters. Of course we may be very lucky. It may be, for instance, that the cause or small set of causes that we isolate in our experiment (or in our model) is also the *dominant* cause in the real situations we want to know about. In that case our Galilean experiments (and the corresponding models) will not only give us tendencies but will be approximately descriptively accurate as well.

Back to models again. If the deductions have been carried out correctly and the general principles employed are true in the target situations, the results of the model will obtain in any real situations that fit the description that the model provides. And in general we have no reason to think they will obtain anywhere else. But if what the model describes satisfies the requirements to be a Galilean-style experiment, it can do more. It can tell us what happens in an experimental situation and thereby tell us about the tendency of the features in question. So Galilean idealization in a model is a good thing.

6.4 How deductivity can be secured and at what cost

The problems I worry about arise when not all of the unrealistic assumptions required for the derivations in a model are ones that characterize an ideal experiment. What I fear is that in general a good number of the false assumptions made with our theoretical models may not have the form of Galilean idealizations. Before I go into details about these kinds of extra-Galilean assumptions, I shall first lay the groundwork by explaining why we might expect to find them as features of our analogue economies. The need for these stronger constraints – the ones that go beyond Galilean idealization – comes, I believe, as a result of the nature of economic theory itself. To see how, let us look again at what kinds of theory are available in economics to aid in the construction of models and at what kinds of concepts they deploy.

The bulk of the concepts used in these models are concepts naming socio-economic quantities that are familiar to the layman, not only as the targeted results to be explained but also as the proposed explanatory factors, concepts like *persistence in unemployment* and *loss of skill during unemployment*, or *current price*, *tax*, *demand*, *consumption*, *labour*, *wages*, *capital*, *profit* and *money supply*, or *assessment of skills*, *private information* and *in-firm training*, or, to take an example from game-theoretic political economy, *power to redistribute*, *incentives for credible information transmission* and *political failure in the transmission of information*.

This is my first observation: most of the concepts employed in these models are highly concrete empirical concepts. My second observation is that the task is to establish useful relations among these via deduction. The problem comes with my third observation: the theory that is presumed is very meagre. There aren't many principles available to use in the deductions. We have only a handful of very general principles that we employ without controversy in economics, such as the principles of utility theory. Nor are there usually many concrete empirical principles imported into the models either. I take it that this is part of the strategy for the models. Almost any principle with real empirical content in economics is highly contentious and we try to construct models that use as few controversial assumptions as possible. But this makes difficulties for the scope of the theory. If the results are supposed just to 'fall out' by deduction from the principles, where there are not many principles, we will not get many results either. How can we, then, deduce results in our models when we have few general principles to call on?

To answer, let us consider what typical models for analogue economics look like. These models tend to be simple in one respect: they usually have only a few agents with few options and only a narrow range of both causes and effects is admitted. Yet there is another way in which they are complex, at least by comparison with physics models doing the same kind of thing: they have a lot of structure. The list of assumptions specifying exactly what the analogue economy is like is very long. Consider one of Lucas's own models, from his 1973 'Expectations and the Neutrality of Money' (1981, 66–89). I choose this example because it is a paper whose 'technically demanding form' is explicitly defended by Lucas (1981, 9). Section 2 is titled 'The Structure of the Economy' – i.e. the structure of the analogue economy that Lucas uses to study money illusion. What follows is section 2 in its entirety:

> In order to exhibit the phenomena described in the introduction, we shall utilize an abstract model economy, due in many of its essentials to Samuelson. Each period, N identical individuals are born, each of whom lives for two periods (the current one and the next). In each period, then, there is a constant population of $2N$: N of age 0 and N of age 1. During the first period of life, each person supplies, at his discretion, n units of labor which yield the same n units of output. Denote the output consumed by a member of the younger generation (its producer) by c^0, and that consumed by the old by c^1. Output cannot be stored but can be freely disposed of, so that the aggregate production-consumption possibilities for any period are completely described (in per capita terms) by:
>
> $$c^0 + c^1 \leq n, \qquad c^0, c^1, n \geq 0 \tag{1}$$
>
> Since n may vary, it is physically possible for this economy to experience fluctuations in real output.
>
> In addition to labor-output, there is one other good: fiat money, issued by a government which has no other function. This money enters the economy by means of a beginning-of-period transfer to the members of the older generation, in a quantity proportional to the pretransfer holdings of each. No inheritance is possible, so that unspent cash balances revert, at the death of the holder, to the monetary authority.
>
> Within this framework, the only exchange which can occur will involve a surrender of output by the young, in exchange for money held over from the preceding period, and altered by transfer, by the old. We shall assume that such exchange occurs in two physically separate markets. To keep matters as simple as possible, we assume that the older generation is allocated across these two markets so as to equate total monetary demand between them. The young are allocated stochastically, fraction $\theta/2$ going to one and $1-(\theta/2)$ to the other. Once the assignment of persons to markets is made, no switching or communication between markets is possible. Within each market, trading by auction occurs, with all trades transacted at a single, market clearing price.
>
> The pretransfer money supply, per member of the older generation,

is known to all agents. Denote this quantity by m. Posttransfer balances, denoted by m', are not generally known (until next period) except to the extent that they are 'revealed' to traders by the current period price level. Similarly, the allocation variable θ is unknown, except indirectly via price. The development through time of the nominal money supply is governed by

$$m' = mx, \tag{2}$$

where x is a random variable. Let x' denote next period's value of this transfer variable, and let θ' be next period's allocation variable. It is assumed that x and x' are independent, with the common, continuous density function f on $(0, \infty)$. Similarly, θ and θ' are independent, with the common, continuous symmetric density g on $(0, 2)$.

To summarize, the state of the economy in any period is entirely described by three variables m, x, and θ. The motion of the economy from state to state is independent of decisions made by individuals in the economy, and is given by (2) and the densities f and g of x and θ.

(Lucas 1981, 67–69)

But this is not an end to the facts set to obtain in Lucas's 'abstract model economy'. Section 3 continues, 'We shall assume that the members of the older generation prefer more consumption to less, . . .' and so on for another page; and more details are still to be added to the economy in section 4. There is nothing special here about Lucas though. Just write out carefully in a list the assumptions for almost any of your favourite models and you will see what I mean. For example the skill-loss model of Pissarides contains some 16 assumptions and that is just for the first of six increasingly complex economies that he describes.[3]

I believe there is good reason why economic models must give a lot of structure to the economies they describe: if you have just a few principles, you will need a lot of extra assumptions from somewhere else in order to derive new results that are not already transparent in the principles. In the models under discussion the richness of structure can fill in for the want of general principles presupposed. The general principles can be thought of in two categories, familiar to philosophers of science (cf. Hempel 1966): *internal principles* and *bridge principles*. Internal principles make claims about the relations of abstract or theoretical concepts to each other, like the axioms of utility theory. But the results we want to know about generally involve not abstract or theoretical concepts, but empirical ones. The bridge principles of a theory provide links between the two sets of concepts. (The usual example is the identification in an ideal gas of the theoretical concept *mean kinetic energy of the molecules* with the empirical concept *temperature*.)

The theory presupposed in our economics models tends to employ few principles of either category and often no bridge principles at all. This means that the additional assumptions put in via the description of the model must do two jobs. On the one hand they must provide sufficient constraints to serve as premises to increase the range of deductive consequences. On the other hand they must establish an interpretation of the terms that appear in the theoretical principles. They must tell us, for instance, what *utility* amounts to in terms of an employer's opening a job and of work versus leisure for the employee, or of entrepreneurs investing in a project and of managers defaulting on their contracts, or of fair treatment for one's fellow citizens and of the cost of demonstrating or contributing to the American Civil Liberties Union.

Sometimes the job left open by the want of bridge principles is done by an explicit assumption: *we will assume that the only source of utility is* ... Sometimes the abstract principles themselves are explicitly given a concrete form: *we will assume that firms act to maximize profits and labourers to maximize wages* ... Often the interpretation is implicit: perhaps there is nothing else in the model for agents to care about except power or profit or leisure and wages, and the very choice of these words indicates that the agents' utility should depend on them in certain characteristic ways.

My claim then is that it is no surprise that individual analogue economies come with such long lists of assumptions: the model-specific assumptions can provide a way to secure deductively validated results where universal principles are scarce. But these create their own problems. For the validity of the conclusions appears now to depend on a large number of very special interconnected assumptions. If so, the validation of the results will depend then on the detailed arrangement of the structure of the model and is not, *prima facie* at least, available otherwise. We opt for deductive verification of our claims in order to achieve clarity, rigour and certainty. But to get it we have tied the results to very special circumstances; the problem is how to validate them outside.

Consider for example the Lucas model from 'The Neutrality of Money' (1981, 70). We begin with the fairly vacuous claim:

> [T]he decision problem facing an age-0 person is:
>
> $$\max_{c,\, n,\, \lambda\geq 0} \left\{U(c, n) + \int V\left(\frac{x'\lambda}{p'}\right) dF(x', p'; m, p)\right\} \quad (9)$$
>
> subject to:
>
> $$p(n-c) - \lambda \geq 0 \quad (10)$$

where c is current consumption; n, current labour supply; λ, a known quantity of nominal balance acquired; p and p', price levels in the current and successor period; and *F*, an unspecified distribution function. Despite the fact that there is not much that is controversial yet, we can see that even at this stage the exact form of the equation depends on the details of the economy. This is even more obvious by the time we get to the condition for equilibrium in each separate market (equation (16), which is derived from (9) plus the more detailed assumptions about the analogue economy studied in the model (Lucas 1981, 72)):

$$h\left(\frac{mx}{\theta p}\right)\frac{1}{p} = \int V'\left(\frac{mxx'}{\theta p}\right)\frac{x'}{p'}dF(x', p'; m, p) \qquad (16)$$

Sections 6 and 7 of the Lucas paper are entitled, respectively, 'Positive Implications of the Theory' and 'Policy Considerations'. Yet the results he establishes are about *this* economy: they follow from equation (16), which is an equation specific in form to the economy that satisfies the lengthy description laid out in Lucas's sections 2, 3 and 4. How can they teach us more general lessons, lessons that will apply to other, different, economies?

The view that I have long defended is that such model results teach us about general tendencies (in my own vocabulary, 'capacities'), tendencies that are nakedly displayed in the analogue economies described in our economic models but that stand ready to operate in most economies. On this view the analogue economy that Lucas describes is like an experiment. We know that an experiment of the right kind, a Galilean experiment that isolates the tendency in question,[4] can teach us lessons that carry outside the experimental situation. If we are lucky, however, we will not need to carry out the experiment. We can find out what *would* happen were we to conduct it because we can find out by deduction what *must* happen. But for that to work, the analogue economy must be of just the right kind: were we to construct it in reality, it would meet the conditions of Galilean experiment. This whole strategy is threatened, however, if non-Galilean idealizations play a role in our deductions – which looks to be the case with Lucas's equation (16).

From the perspective of establishing tendencies, it becomes crucial then to look carefully into the deductions used in our economic models to see if all of the unrealistic assumptions required for the derivations are ones that characterize an ideal experiment. Let us look at another simple physics example for an analogous case.

In classical Newtonian mechanics massive bodies have an *inertial tendency*: a body will remain in motion unless acted on by a force. When it is acted on by a force the actual motion that occurs will be a combination of the inertial motion and that due to the force. So, what is the natural behaviour of a body when inertia acts on its own? Say we do some experiments to find out. We know that forces cause motions. So eliminate all forces and watch the bodies move. What will we see?

Imagine that our experimental mass has been confined for reasons of convenience to move on a particular surface, but that we have been very careful to plane the surface to eliminate almost all friction. Then what we will see will depend on the geometry of that surface. For example, if all our experiments are done on a sphere, we always get motion in great circles, as in Figure 6.2. But that is not the 'natural' motion in other geometries. Look for instance at Figure 6.3. There, motion on great circles is available, but it is not the motion that inertia will contribute. The results in our experiment are over-constrained. We thought that by eliminating all the factors we

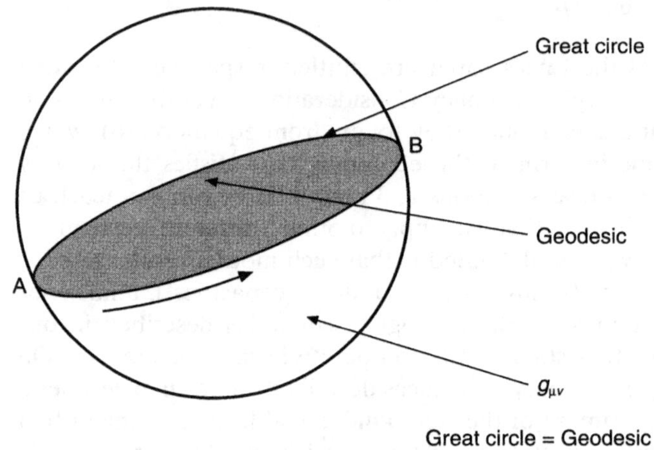

Figure 6.2 Geodesic on the simple sphere geometry (designed by Sang Wook Yi).

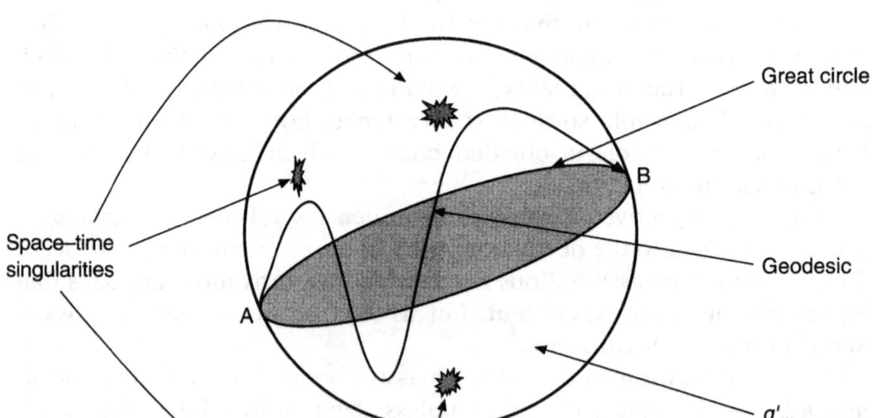

Figure 6.3 Geodesic on the sphere geometry with space–time singularities (designed by Sang Wook Yi).

think of as causes of motion – all the forces – we would see the results of inertia by itself. Instead what we see is a result of inertia-plus-geometry.

This can always happen in an experiment: we never know whether some features we have not thought about are influencing the result. But in a good many of our analogue economies we are not even this well off. In a real experiment we are after all in a position to assume with good justification that the fact that there are, for instance, only two markets or only two generations does not matter because the number of markets or of generations is not relevant to the conclusion: it has no *causal* bearing on the outcome, and what happens in the real experiment is just what is *caused* to happen. Analogue economies are different. What happens in them is exactly what is implied deductively. The problem is that we often know by looking at them that the specific derivations made in our models depend on details of the situation other than just the mechanism itself operating in accord with our general principles. So we know that in the corresponding experiment there are features other than the mechanism itself determining the outcome. That means that the experiment does not entitle us to draw a conclusion about the general tendency of the mechanism under study.

We now know what would happen – indeed, what must happen – in some very particular constrained real experimental situation in which the features of interest really occur. But we know it for exactly the wrong reason. We know that the results obtain because we know that they follow deductively given the formal relations of all the factors that figure in an essential way in the proof. But the whole point about an experiment designed to establish the tendency of a factor is that the background factors should not matter to what happens. We are supposed to be isolating the effects of the feature or process under investigation acting on its own, not effects that depend in a crucial way on the background.

So, were such a set-up to occur, it would turn out not to be a good experiment after all. It may have seemed to be a good design because our independent causal knowledge told us that in general none of the background factors should have any bearing on the effect. But by bad luck that would not be true of the particular arrangement of them we chose. The formal relations of the background and targeted feature together are enough to guarantee the result – and that is one of the things our design is meant to preclude. We would have to judge the result (even if by chance it should turn out to be correct) to be an artifact of the experiment.

6.5 Conclusion

Let us look at Lucas's own conclusion in his paper on the neutrality of money:

> This paper has been an attempt to resolve the paradox posed by Gurley, in his mild but accurate parody of Friedmanian monetary

> theory: "Money is a veil, but when the veil flutters, real output sputters." The resolution has been effected by postulating economic agents free of money illusion, so that the Ricardian hypothetical experiment of a fully announced, proportional monetary expansion will have no real consequences (that is, so that money *is* a veil). These rational agents are then placed in a setting in which the information conveyed to traders by market prices is inadequate to permit them to distinguish real from monetary disturbances. In this setting, monetary fluctuations lead to real output movements in the same direction.
>
> In order for this resolution to carry any conviction, it has been necessary to adopt a framework simple enough to permit a precise specification of the information available to each trader at each point in time, and to facilitate verification of the rationality of each trader's behavior. To obtain this simplicity, most of the interesting features of the observed business cycle have been abstracted from, with one notable exception: the Phillips curve emerges not as an unexplained empirical fact, but as a central feature of the solution to a general equilibrium system.
>
> (1981, 84)

I have argued that in a model like this the features 'abstracted from' fall into two categories: those that eliminate confounding factors and those that do not eliminate confounding factors but rather provide a simple enough structure to make a deductive study possible. The former I claim are just what we want when we aim to see for rational agents, what effects inadequate information about money disturbances has on the short-term Phillips curve, that is, when we want to establish the *tendency* it has independent of the effects anything else might have on a Phillips curve as well. But the assumptions of the latter kind remain problematic. They not only leave us with the question still unanswered, 'Can we think that what we see happen, literally happen, in this economy, is what the combination of rationality and limited information will *contribute* in other economies?' Worse, they give us reason to think we cannot. For inspection of the derivation suggests that the outcome that occurs in the analogue economy does depend on the particular structure the economy has.[5]

Does it? This is a question that is generally not sufficiently addressed. Frequently of course we do discuss how robust the results from a specific model are. But, not surprisingly, these discussions usually refer to assumptions in the first category, for these are the ones that are of concern to economic theory. Notice for instance that Lucas notes in the passage just cited that 'most of the *interesting* features of the observed business cycle have been abstracted from' (my italics). In the end we want to know what happens when other causes *are* at work, either because they may interfere with the one under study, or because we are starting down the road towards a model that will be more descriptively accurate when the results are read literally, i.e. more descriptively accurate about the real economies we want to study. But my central point is that we need robustness results about the second category of assumptions as well if our results are to be of use in the tendency sense.

I realize of course that economists do not use just models to find out about tendencies. The models are merely one strand in a net of methods used together for establishing, testing, expanding and revising economic hypotheses. Moreover, it is often the general lesson rather than the precise form of the conclusion that is taken seriously (even when the conclusion is understood in a tendency sense). Nevertheless, rigorously deriving a result in a model is supposed to provide *prima facie* evidence in favour of that result. My concern is about just this relation of evidence to hypothesis. To the extent that the derivation in a model makes essential use of non-Galilean 'idealizing' assumptions, then I do not see how the fact that the result can be derived in such a model can provide *any evidence at all* for the hypothesis.

If we aim to establish conclusions interpreted in a tendency sense, there is a good reason why the derivation of a conclusion in a model that makes Galilean idealizations, and no others, should count as evidence in favour of that conclusion: to the extent that the general principles employed in the derivation are true to the world, behaviour derived in the model will duplicate to behaviour that would obtain were a Galilean experiment to be performed. But when non-Galilean idealizations are made as well, this reason no longer has force. So we need another reason to show why this procedure has evidential force. And I do not know one that can be stated clearly and defended convincingly. Hence I think we should be concerned to ensure that non-Galilean idealizing assumptions do not play an essential role in our derivations.

What, then, does this tell us about the demand for rigorous derivations? I have here been discussing one of the central and highly prized ways that economics theory is done today: by the construction of models for simple analogue economies in which results about issues of interest can be derived rigorously, employing as general principles only ones whose use is relatively uncontroversial within the discipline. The achievement of rigour is costly, however. It takes considerable time. It requires special talents and special training and this closes the discipline to different kinds of thinkers who may provide different kinds of detailed understanding of how economies can and do work. And rigour is bought at the cost of employing general concepts lacking the kind of detailed content that allows them to be directly put to use in concrete situations. What are its compensating gains? Unless we find different answers from the one I offered here,[6] the gains will not include lessons about real economic phenomena, it seems, despite our frequent feeling of increased understanding of them. For we are not generally assured of any way to take results out of our models and into the world.

There has been some tendency to blame our failures on the attempt to make economics rigorous. I am inclined to go the other way. *If it is rigour that we want*, the problem with economic theorizing of this sort is that rigour gives out too soon. For the models themselves, though abstract and mathematized, are not *formal theories*. To see why I say this, consider again the structure of my argument in this essay. I have raised questions about the external validity of the results established in these kinds of models. My worries focus not on the unrealism of the assumptions but on the model-dependence of the results. The kind of model-dependence involved seems to undercut not only the claim that the results can be read literally, but also the hope that they can be read as facts about tendencies.

But I have to say 'seems' here because the models themselves are not presented in a way that allows this question to be taken up easily or answered rigorously. What exactly are the assumptions that are really necessary for the derivations to go through; and what is the range of circumstances across which these assumptions can be relaxed and qualitatively similar results still follow? We cannot generally answer that question given the way the models are presented. To answer it we need to formalize our models. Supposing then that my worries about the model-dependence of the results are valid. What should we conclude about the need for rigour in economic theory? It looks as if the natural conclusion is this: should economics stick to mathematizing rather than formalizing, it will not be easy to know whether the models it constructs can teach us general facts about concrete features of the economy or not; the trouble with this kind of theorizing is not that it is too rigorous, but rather that it is not rigorous enough.

Acknowledgements

Work on this project has been supported by the Measurement in Physics and Economics Project at the LSE and by the Leverhulme-funded project on the Historical School at the Centre for History and Economics, Cambridge. I am grateful for both the financial and the intellectual help from these two groups, as well as to Sang Wook Yi for helping with the last stages of argumentation and preparation.

Notes

1 I have myself defended the importance of tendencies throughout the social and natural sciences, wherever the analytic method is in play (see Cartwright 1989) and have specifically maintained, possibly incorrectly given the arguments here, that we can learn about them via our formal models (see Cartwright 1998). Daniel Hausman (Hausman 1992) in his arguments that economics is a separate but not an exact science also sees tendencies as standard in economics theory.

2 I have elsewhere (Cartwright 1999) described a variety of rules for combining tendencies besides vector addition, as well as explaining what we can do with tendency knowledge even when there are no general rules available for combining tendencies.

3 Economists, I think, get used to models with lots of assumptions. But I am often

talking to mixed groups, people who study economics and people who study physics; those whose background is in physics are often astounded at the richness of description provided in models in economics.

4 If such a tendency exists.

5 Notice that we still have this problem even if we are lucky enough to have selected a few causes to study that for most real situations will be the dominant causes. For we still need to see why the very behaviours that occur in the analogue economy when these causes are present are behaviours that reveal the tendency of this arrangement of causes and hence will approximate the behaviours that occur in the real economies.

6 There are of course a variety of other accounts of the use of models that do not demand either predictive accuracy or the correct isolation of a tendency. See for instance the studies found in Morgan and Morrison 1999.

References

Cartwright, Nancy 1989, *Nature's Capacities and their Measurement*, Oxford: Oxford University Press.

Cartwright, Nancy 1998, 'Capacities', in John B. Davis, D. Wade Hands and Uskali Mäki (eds) *The Handbook of Economic Methodology*, Cheltenham: Edward Elgar.

Cartwright, Nancy 1999, *The Dappled World: A Study of the Boundaries of Science*, Cambridge: Cambridge University Press.

Guala, Francesco 1998, 'Economic Experiments as Mediators', *Measurement in Physics and Economics Discussion Paper Series*, Centre for Philosophy of Natural and Social Science.

Hausman, Daniel 1992, *The Inexact and Separate Science of Economics*, Cambridge: Cambridge University Press.

Hempel, Carl G. 1966, *Philosophy of Natural Science*, Englewood Cliffs, NJ: Prentice-Hall.

Lucas, Robert E., Jr. 1981, *Studies in Business-Cycle Theory*, Cambridge, MA: The MIT Press.

Mill, John Stuart 1836 [1967], 'On the Definition of Political Economy and on the Method of Philosophical Investigation in that Science', reprinted in *Collected Works of John Stuart Mill*, vol. 4, Toronto: University of Toronto Press.

Mill, John Stuart 1843 [1973], 'On the Logic of Moral Sciences', a chapter from *A System of Logic*, reprinted in *Collected Works of John Stuart Mill*, vol. 7–8, Toronto: University of Toronto Press.

Morgan, Mary S. 1990, *The History of Econometric Ideas*, Cambridge: Cambridge University Press.

Morgan, Mary and Margaret Morrison (eds) (1999) *Models as Mediators: Perspectives on Natural and Social Science*, Cambridge: Cambridge University Press.

Pissarides, Chris 1992, 'Loss of Skill During Unemployment and the Persistence of Unemployment Shocks', *Quarterly Journal of Economics* 107: 1371–1391.

Plott, Charles R. 1991, 'Will Economics Become an Experimental Science?', *Southern Economic Journal* 57: 901–919.

Smith, Vernon L. 1991, *Papers in Experimental Economics*, Cambridge: Cambridge University Press.

Index

Abreu, Dilip 60
Allais, Maurice: development of thought 26; experiment 25, 31–3, 40; and French marginalist school 28–31; lunch with Savage 2, 26, 33, 35–6, 40; works (1949–1953) 31; (1952a) 30, 32; (1952b) 32; (1952c) 33; (1952d) 27, 33, 36, 37–8, 40; (1953b) 32, 36, 40; (1955) 33; (1974) 33; (1979) 25, 26, 31, 33, 36, 40; and Hagen (1979) 32
Allais Paradox: consequences 26; as counterexample 30; experimental refutation of a theory of rational behaviour 36–8; fading out of Savagian positive interpretation 34–6; historical significance 25; presentation 32, 36, 40; and the questionnaire 31–3, 40; role 2, 38, 40; steps 40
Allen, Thomas B. 6
American school 28, 33
analogue economies: critique of 3, 135–6, 139–40, 149, 151; internal validity 138–9; Lucas's work 135–6, 137–8, 144; typical models 143–4
Anderson, Benjamin 122, 123–4
Andrews, J. M. 14
Andrews, W. 54
Ann Arbor 14–15
Annales de l'Institut des Sciences Sociales 102–3
Arrow, Kenneth J. 33, 51–2, 54, 56–7, 58, 59
assumptions, unrealistic 135–7, 138
Aucuy, Marc 119
Austrian tradition 72–3
Axelrod, Robert 15

Bacon, Francis 110
Baumol, William J. 33
Becker, Gary S. 64
Bellamy, Edward 119
Bellman, Richard 16
Bernard, Jessie 14
Bernoulli, Daniel 26–7
Bilgram, Hugo 121
Binmore, Ken 63
Black, F. 120
Blaug, M. 110
Blinder, Alan S. 5
Boianovsky, Mauro 3, 113, 119
Boiteux, Marcel 29, 32
Bolton, G. E. 62
Boulding, Kenneth 14
Brichaux, A. 100
Bush, Robert R. 57

Caldwell, Bruce J. 85
Camerer, C. 32, 62
Carré, J.-J. 29
Cartwright, Nancy 3, 110, 135, 140
Chammah, A. M. 14
Chamberlin, Edward 6–8, 18, 19
CNRS 29, 32
Cohn, Arthur Wolfgang 119
Colman, Andrew 6, 10, 11, 19–20
Conseils de Physique 100–1
Coombs, Clyde 8, 19, 25, 57
counterexamples 30
Cowen, T. 120
Cowles Commission/Foundation 5, 8, 54, 57
Crombois, J.-F. 102

Darmois, Georges 29–30
Davis, D. D. 11, 62
de Bie, P. 102
de Finetti, Bruno 30, 33

De Greef, Guillaume 102, 120
Debreu, Gérard: career 29; on economic theory 50, 53; general equilibrium theory 52, 53; Santa Monica seminar 8, 57; Sonnenschein–Mantel–Debreu (SMD) theory 51, 58–60, 65; works: (1959) 51, 54; Arrow and (1954) 51, 56
decision theory 25, 31
deduction 136–7
deductive approach 72, 73, 79–80, 85–7, 87–8
deductivity 137, 143–9
Dejongh, Ch. 101
Denis, Hector 102, 105, 107, 108–9, 120
Diewert, W. E. 59
DiFedo, David D. 12
Dimand, Mary Ann 12, 13, 14
Dimand, Robert W. 2, 12, 13, 14, 18, 50
Dolbear, F. Trennery 16–17
Dony-Hénault, O. 100
Dowd, K. 123
Drazen, Allan 52–3
Drèze, J. 29

economic models *see* models
Edgeworth, Francis 113
Edison, Thomas 120
Edwards, Ward 25
Elkhadem, H. 99
empirical analysis: in deductive terms 85–7; role in economics 78–80
Engels, Friedrich 119
Erreygers, Guido 3
Estes, William 9, 11, 19, 57, 80
EUT *see* expected utility theory
evolutionary game theory 63–4
expected utility theory (EUT) 25–6; Allais' questionnaire 33; French attitude 30; interpretations of EUT by American authors before 1952 26–8; normative retreat 34–40; as positive theory 27–8, 34–6; as theory of rational behaviour 36–8; violation of 31
experiment(s): construction of 151; definition 1; performed 80–5, 87; Galilean 135, 136–7, 141–2, 147; realistic and unrealistic 142; Solvay on 99–102; thought 3, 72–8, 87, 116, 117; Wicksell on 110–12
experimentation 50–1; demise of general equilibrium theory 58–60; evolutionary game theory 63–4; general equilibrium theory 51–8; rational–choice bargaining theory 60–3
external validity 137–9

Fama, E. 120
Fellner, William 12, 16
Ferber, R. 111
Festinger, Leonard 57
Fishburn, P. C. 27
Fisher, Irving 122–3
Flood, Merrill M. 10, 11, 18, 80
foresight, perfect 75–8
Fouraker, Lawrence 11–14, 16, 19
French marginalist school 28–31
Friedman, James 14, 16–17, 18
Friedman, Milton: Allais questionnaire 33; on EUT 27, 28, 34; works: and Savage (1948) 28; and Savage (1952) 28, 34, 35; Wallis and (1942) 6, 56, 58
Frisch, Ragnar 35
Fuchida, Mitsuo 6

Galilean: experiments 135, 136–7, 141–2, 147; idealization 137, 142, 143, 151
Galileo 135, 136–7, 141
game theory: business and 81–2; creation 71–2, 82; in 1945–60 era 8–9, 18–19; evolutionary 63–4
games, experimental 5–6; in business and economics 16–17; Chamberlin 6–8; early, beyond North America 17–18; *Journal of Conflict Resolution* 15–16; Penn State 11–14; Rapoport at Ann Arbor 14–15; Santa Monica seminar 8–10
general equilibrium theory 51–8; demise of 2–3, 58–60; Hayek's view 72
Gesell, Silvio 119
Gide, Charles 106
Goldstein, D. A. 11
Greenfield, R. 120, 123
Grodal, B. 59
Guala, Francesco 138
Guilbaud, Georges 26, 28–30, 32
Güth, W. 62

Haavelmo, Trygve 54–5
Haeck, François 119
Hagen, O. 32
Hahn, F. 52, 58

Hanssens, E. 101
Harnett, Donald 13
Harsanyi, John C. 14
Hart, Oliver 59–60
Hawtrey, R. G. 115
Hayek, Friedrich A.: on competition 71; deductive approach 72, 73, 79–80, 85–7, 87–8; on equilibrium and foresight 75–7; on general equilibrium theory 72; thought experiments 3; works (1928) 74; (1937) 73, 75–6, 79; (1941) 72, 76; (1942) 85; (1946) 76; (1955) 86; (1964) 86; (1968) 87
Henriksson, R. 110
Hernandez-Aramburo, L. 114
Hicks, John 118, 125
Hildenbrand, Werner 59
Hildreth, Clifford 57
Hirsch, W. 111
Hoggatt, Austin C. 16, 81
Holt, C. A. 62
Hood, William 54
Hooper, John W. 17
Humphreys, L. G. 9, 11

Ingram, John K. 106
Innocenti, Alessandro 3, 9
Institut de Sociologie 109
Institut des Sciences Sociales 98, 101, 102, 109, 120

Jaffé, W. 109
Jallais, Sophie 2
Jevons, W. S. 111
Journal of Conflict Resolution 15–16
Journal of Economic Literature 50

Kagel, John H. 6, 50
Kalisch, G. K. 9, 18, 80
Karlin, Samuel 57
Katona, George 5
Kehoe, Timothy J. 59
Kelly, Jerry S. 56
Keynes, John Neville 110
Kitson, Arthur 120–1
Klein, Lawrence 5
Koopmans, Tjalling: on general equilibrium theory 53–4, 56, 58; influence 14; Santa Monica seminar 8, 57; work on econometric theory 5; works: (1957) 51, 53–4
Kreweras, Germain 29
Krishna, Vijay 60
Kroszner, R. 120

La Fontaine, Henri 102
Lachmann, Ludwig 73
Laidler, D. 113
Langelütke, Hans 119
Larsson, S. 31
Leijonhufvud, A. 125
Leonard, Robert J. 77, 82
Lesourne, Jacques 29
Levitan, Richard 16
Lindahl, Erik 118
Loria, Achille 119, 121
Louvain meeting (1952) 32
Lucas, Robert 135, 136, 137–9, 144–7, 149–50
Luce, R. Duncan 9, 12
Lucion, René 100

McClennen, E. F. 27
MacCrimmon, K. R. 30, 31
McCulloch, Warren 56
McKinsey, J. C. C. 10
macroeconomics 5, 52
Malinvaud, Edmond 29, 32, 33
Marschak, Jacob 8, 27, 33, 35, 54, 57
Mas-Colell, A. 59
Massé, Pierre 29–30
May, Dick 102
May, Kenneth O. 53, 56–7, 60, 65
Mayberry, John P. 17
Mayer, Hans 73
Mayer, Th. 99
Menger, Carl 77, 80
Michigan, University of 19, 57, 80
Midway, Battle of 6
Milgate, Murray 74
Mill, John Stuart 1, 110, 137, 139, 140
Milnor, John W. 9
Minas, J. Sayer 15
Mirowski, Philip 82
models, economic: concepts used in 143, 151; construction of 3, 135–6, 143, 151; unrealism of assumptions in 135–7
monetary reform 98–9; compensated dollar and indirect convertibility 122–4; experiments 110–12; influence of Solvay's and Wicksell's monetary ideas 118–19; Kitson connection 120–2; new monetary economics 120–4; pure credit economy 112–16; pure credit experiment 116–17
Morgan, Mary 54, 55, 137

Morgenstern, Oskar: collaboration with von Neumann 82; on competition 76; contributions to economics 71–2; development of thought 3; on empirical analysis 78–9, 87–8; on equilibrium 76–7, 78; on EUT 27–8, 34, 35, 40; on experiments 71, 81, 83–4; game theory 71–2, 81–2; on perfect foresight 74–5; response to Allais 33; Santa Monica seminar (1952) 8, 57; on thought experiments 72–3; works (1935) 73, 74–5, 77, 78–9; (1936) 83; (1950) 83; (1954) 81, 84; (1962) 82; (1972) 40; (1974) 40, 41; von Neumann and (1944) 5, 7, 19, 27–8, 35, 40, 81, 83
Morlat, Georges 29–30
Moss, Laurence S. 72, 86
Mosteller, Frederick 5, 25, 31, 57
Munier, B. R. 32
Muth, John F. 17
Myerson, Roger B. 83

Nash, John F. 8, 9, 10, 18, 57
neo-Bernoullian formulation 27, 33, 36–7, 38
Nering, E. D. 9
New Monetary Economics 120–4
Nogee, Philip 5, 25, 31
Nordhaus, William 1

Ochs J. 62
Ohlin, Bertil 117
Okumiya, Masatake 6
Orwant, Carol 6, 14, 50
Ostwald, Wilhelm 100
Otlet, Paul 102, 107
Owen, Robert 119

Pareto, Vilfredo 119
Paris Conference (1952) 25, 27, 28–31, 32, 33
Patinkin, Don 113, 118, 123
Pearce, David 60
Pennsylvania State University 11–14
perfect foresight 73–8
Perry, Motty 60
Phelps, Edmund 17
Pissarides, Chris 139
Plott, Charles R. 139
Popper, K. 86
Poudou, F. 119
Pradier, Pierre-Charles 2
principles: bridge 145–6; internal 145
prisoner's dilemma games 10, 14–15
Proudhon, Pierre-Joseph 119

Radner, Roy 57
Raiffa, Howard 8, 12, 57
RAND Corporation 2, 8–9, 10, 57, 80
Rapoport, Anatol 6, 14–15, 19–20, 50
rational behaviour, theory of 36–8
rational-choice bargaining theory 60–3
Recht, Justus 119
Rellstab, Urs. 8282
Ricciardi, F. M. 16, 18
Richardson, Lewis Fry 14
Riley, V. 6
Rist, Ch. 118
Rizvi, Abu Turab: works (1994a) 59, 61; (1994b) 52, 58, 59; (1997) 58, 59; (1998) 61, 63; (this volume) 2–3, 9, 33
Robbins, Lionel 53, 55, 56, 58
Roberts, John 59, 60
Roche-Agussol, M. 119
Roth, Alvin E. 6, 10, 50, 62
Roy, René 29
Royal Swedish Academy of Sciences 2
Rubinstein, A. 61, 63

Sakaguchi, Minoru 17, 18
Samuelson, Larry 62, 63, 64
Samuelson, Paul 1, 27, 33
Santa Monica seminar (1952) 8–11, 19, 57–8, 80
Sauermann, Heinz 17, 18
Savage, Leonard Jimmie: on counterexamples 30; independence axiom 28, 37–8; interpretation of EUT 26, 27, 34–6, 39–40; lunch with Allais 2, 26, 33, 35–6, 40; on normative status of theory 38–40; response to Allais 26, 33, 34–6; works (1954) 27, 30, 34–5, 38–9, 41; Friedman and (1948) 27, 28; Friedman and (1952) 27, 28, 40
Schelling, Thomas 9, 11, 16
Schotter, Andrew 71, 82
Schumpeter, Joseph 119
Scodel, Alvin 15
Selten, Reinhard 9, 17, 18
Shackle, G. L. S. 33
Shannon, Claude 14
Shapley, Lloyd 8, 57
Shubik, Martin: career 14, 16; on game theory 19; interview with 11–12, 17; on oligopoly theory 13–14, 16; Santa Monica seminar 8; on Siegel 11–12;

Shubik, Martin *continued*
works (1959) 12; (1962) 16; and Levitan (1980) 16
Siegel, Alberta 14
Siegel, Sidney 5, 10, 11–14, 16, 19, 80
Simon, Herbert 8, 10, 17, 57, 80
Simon, Leo 60
skill-loss model 139–40
Slovic, Paul 25, 26, 31, 41
Smith, Vernon: experimental games 7–8, 17; influences on 14; works (1962) 7, 17; (1965) 17; (1989) 72; (1991) 139; (1992) 7, 9, 10, 11, 12, 14, 17, 18, 57–8
social comptabilism: case for 124–5; final phase 109; initial proposal 102–3; mature proposal 103–5; Solvay's system 98; Walras's critique 106–9
social energetics 3, 100
Solow, Robert M. 14
Solvay, Ernest: on experiments 99–102; final phase of social comptabilism 109; influence of monetary ideas 118–24; initial social comptabilist proposal 98, 102–3; mature proposal 103–5; social energetics 3, 100; Walras's critique 106–9; works (1894a) 101, 103; (1894b) 102, 103; (1896) 104; (1897a) 104–5, 107; (1898a) 107–8; (1898b) 101; (1900a) 109; (1900c) 122; (1900d) 122; (1911a) 101; (1911b) 100; and Lucion (1877) 100
Sonnenschein, Hugo 57, 59, 60
Sonnenschein–Mantel–Debreu (SMD) theory 51, 58–60, 65
Stas, Jean Servais 99
Stengers, Isabelle 100
Stigler, George J. 14, 64
Stoker, Thomas M. 59
Sumner, S. 121
sure–thing principle 27, 41
Sweeney, R. 115

tendencies 137; general 147; stable 110, 139, 140
Thaler, R. H. 62
Thompson, Gerald L. 8
thought experiments: definition 72; in Hayek's and Morgenstern's work 3, 72–3, 87; in 1930s 73–8; Wicksell's 116, 117
Thrall, R. M.: at Paris conference (1952) 35; works: *et al.* (1954) 9, 11, 18, 19, 57, 80
Thurstone, L. L. 5, 56, 58, 65
Tietz, R. 62
time, role of 73–4
Tobin, James 17
Trautwein, H.-M. 118, 123
Tucker, A. W. 15, 17
Tukey, John W. 14
Tversky, A. 25, 31, 41

Vanderrydt, Henri 107
Vandervelde, Emile 102
Vaughn, Karen I. 79
Vickrey, William 17
Vidal, François 119
Ville, Jean 29
von Mises, Ludwig 73, 118
von Neumann, John: career 10–11; collaboration with Morgenstern 82; on EUT 27–8, 34, 35, 40; game theory 71–2, 82; Santa Monica seminar (1952) 8, 10, 57; works: and Morgenstern (1944) 5, 7, 19, 27–8, 35, 40, 81, 83

Wagner, Adolf 114
Wakker, P. P. 27
Wallis, W. Allen 6, 56, 58
Walras, Léon 98, 102, 106–9, 121
Warnotte, D. 102
Waxweiler, Émile 109
Weber, Max 100
Wegelin, Walter 119
Weintraub, E. Roy 52
Wicksell, Knut: on experiments 110–12; influence of monetary ideas 118–24; pure credit economy 3, 98–9, 112–16; pure credit experiment 116–17; works (1898) 98, 109, 111, 113, 114, 115, 116, 117; (1901) 112; (1902) 116; (1904) 110, 111, 112; (1906) 111, 113, 114, 115, 117, 118, 123; (1907) 112; (1913) 123; (1914) 115; (1917) 115, 116, 117; (1919a) 115, 116, 117; (1919b) 123, 124
Woodford, M. 117

Yeager, L. 120, 123
Young, J. 6

Zaleski, Ladeslas 106
Zappia, Carlo 3, 9

For Product Safety Concerns and Information please contact our EU representative GPSR@taylorandfrancis.com
Taylor & Francis Verlag GmbH, Kaufingerstraße 24, 80331 München, Germany

www.ingramcontent.com/pod-product-compliance
Lightning Source LLC
LaVergne TN
LVHW011133300926
849160LV00008B/637